THE SURVIVOR OF THE HOLOCAUST

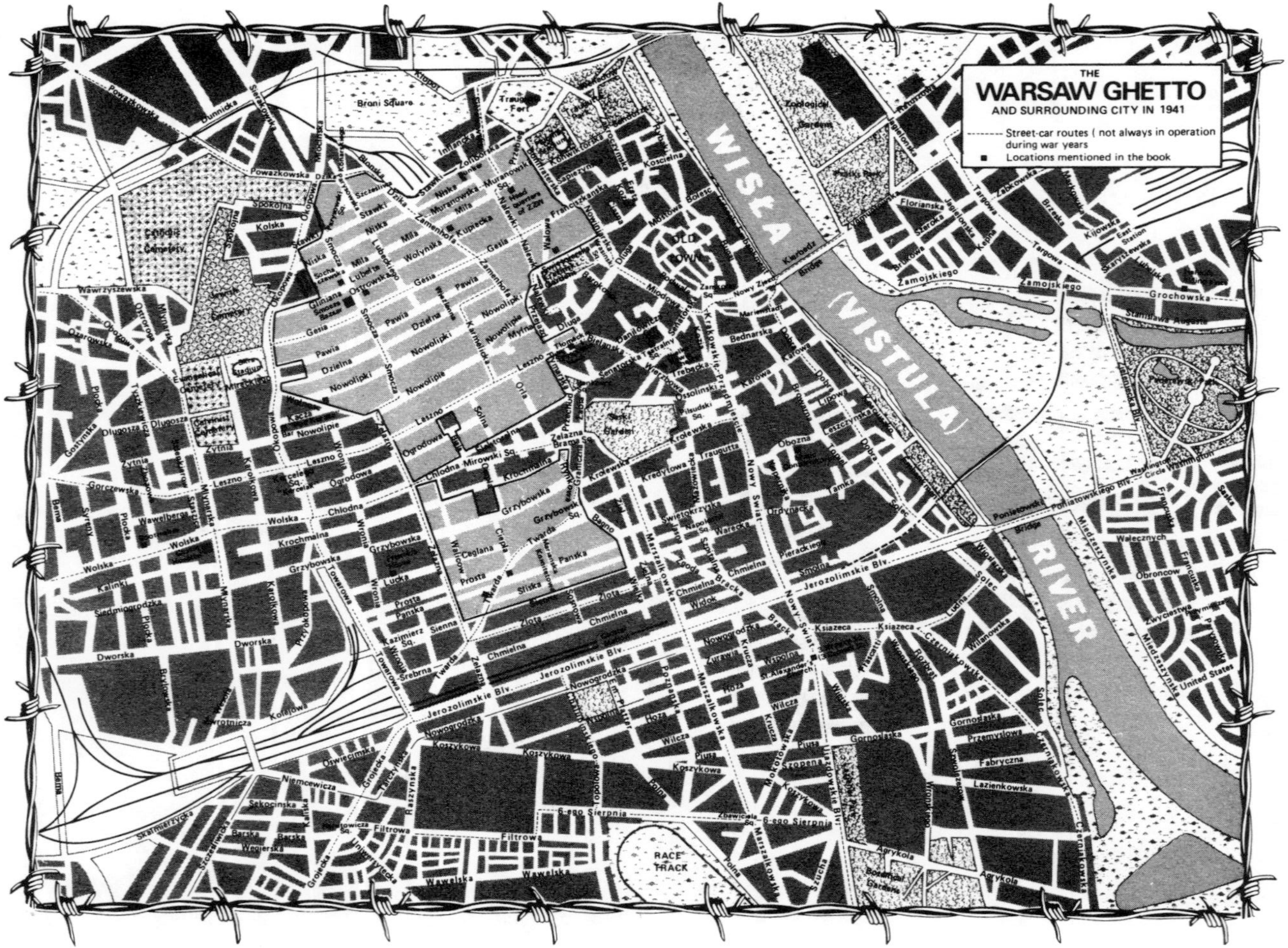
THE
WARSAW GHETTO
AND SURROUNDING CITY IN 1941
Street-car routes (not always in operation during war years
Locations mentioned in the book
WISŁA
(VISTULA)
RIVER
OLD TOWN
RACE TRACK
Broni Square

THE SURVIVOR OF THE HOLOCAUST

JACK EISNER

Kensington Books

KENSINGTON BOOKS are published by

Kensington Publishing Corp.
850 Third Avenue
New York, NY 10022

ISBN 1-57566-104-7

First Kensington Books Printing: December, 1995
First Kensington Trade Paperback Printing: November, 1996

Printed in the United States of America

10 9 8 7 6 5 4 3 2 1

"I do not think it would be wise to exterminate the adult Jewish men and women . . . leaving their children to grow into avengers against our sons or grandsons.

"The decsion had to be made to annihilate as well every Jewish child and to make this people disappear from the face of the earth.

"This is being accomplished."

—Excerpt from a speech by Heinrich Himmler, Reichsführer-SS, to Gauleiters, October 6, 1943—Germany

I dedicate this book to the memory of my childhood love, Halina, age nineteen; my sister, Hela, age fifteen; and my thirty young cousins:

Yosek	Age 13	Sara	Age 7
Rozka	13	Reizele	7
Gershon	12	Cesia	7
Hela	12	David	6
Reizl	12	Marek	6
Heniek	11	Mietek	6
Moniek	11	Srulek	6
Szymek	10	Duvele	6
Surele	10	Mietek	5
Sabcia	10	Davidek	5
Tosia	9	Motek	4
Haimek	9	Basia	4
Marylka	8	Salcia	3
Joziek	8	Genia	2
Szajek	8	Esterka	2

who were all murdered in cold blood at the hands of the Nazis.

ACKNOWLEDGMENTS

I wish to express my gratitude and appreciation to my editor, Irving A. Leitner, for his dedicated services in editing this book, and to Susan Einhorn and Paul Spiro for their contributions as assistant editors.

Additionally, I would like to acknowledge my dear daughter Shirley and my sons Arnold and Philip. The encouragement received was so very helpful to bring this work to conclusion.

This edition has been published thanks to the constant demand by the public. In particular, I am grateful to the many teachers and students who have taken the time to write to the publishers pleading for another printing.

And last but not least, I express my appreciation to Caroline Latham for her overall guidance.

PROLOGUE

If you saw me at a distance, you would think I was an ordinary person.

Even if you got closer, you still couldn't tell.

Maybe if you observed me very carefully, you might notice that I seem somehow alone, even in the middle of a crowd. You would be right.

But you would also be wrong. For I am never truly alone. Thousands of people are always with me.

My head is so crowded with ghosts I sometimes think it will burst.

My ears ring with cries from the voices of the dead.

My dreams flame with horror.

My memories are gray with ash.

I am a survivor.

I am about to tell you a story.

It is not the whole story—of the Warsaw ghetto, of gas chambers and crematoria, of the extermination of more than one million children, Jewish children. Leave that for the historians.

This is my story. The story of a boy who was thirteen when it all started, nineteen when, centuries later, it ended. Like thousands of other young people in the ghetto, I defied the German murderers. Unlike most of them, I survived.

It is also the story of my friends and family. People who are no longer here to tell it themselves. People who would have been completely forgotten if they didn't live in my memories. If I forget them, no one will ever know they lived and smiled and played and cried.

I promised them I would tell the story.

I am a survivor.

Sometimes I think about the way I must look to the eyes of the world. Do I seem lucky?

I know I seem persistent. I guess I am.

I must seem arrogant. Perhaps I am that, too.

When I decided to abandon my business and to dedicate my life and my resources to tell this story, people thought I was unbalanced, obsessed. It sounded grotesque. But eventually the verdict was: Refreshing.

This is the story of how I escaped from the Warsaw ghetto, concentration camps, execution squads, the gallows, and gas chambers.

I am the one in a thousand who survived. Why me? Was I better than the half million Jews in Warsaw who did not?

Why not Grandma, why not Halina, why not Hela, Lutek, Shmulek, Mala, Mrs. Grinberg? What about Shmeel, the shoemaker; Shmerl, the gravedigger; Artek, the fighter; Markowski, the teacher and policeman; Tosca, the choirboy; Rudy, the hero; Yankele Rotzo, the soccer player; and all the others?

I can still see them all.

They are in front of me now, talking to me.

Yankele, a boy of fourteen, lying in his own blood in the wheelbarrow, while I just made it across the ghetto wall.

Rudy, with a Molotov bottle in his hand, trying to blow us all up as we faced a squad of SS storm troopers.

Grandma Masha, concealing my presence under her big Victorian bed.

Papa, pacing the bunker while explaining the Germans' diabolical schemes with Spinoza's laws of the inevitable.

They are all living in me. They stay with me so they will not become part of the faceless, nameless dead.

Only I can mark their passing.

I am their gravestone, because I am a survivor.

* * *

I have visited Warsaw many times since the war.

Each time, I take a long walk, always alone.

The town is new, rebuilt, especially the sections where the Germans created and then destroyed a medieval ghetto.

Only the Jewish cemetery is still there, as it was when I was a young boy. It has thousands of monuments, gravestones, memorials to the dead, to Warsaw's once thriving community of Jews.

Now I can see the irony. It was in that cemetery that I first learned how to survive, with my gang of teenage smugglers. Everything's still there—the same tree marked with a "Z" that was our meeting place, the same wall.

Only I'm not the same.

Only I am.

I am a survivor.

Sometimes I feel like I am arranging my own funeral, my own gravestone and inscription. And when I visit the famous Ghetto Memorial in Warsaw, where the wreaths of many world leaders have lain, I often feel that I, too, belong there. I was there, suffering and fighting. I should attach myself to that place, become a permanent part of that mute agony.

The last visit, I stood there holding on to a huge bronze figure of a young boy throwing a grenade. Just as I did.

A little girl stood nearby, watching me curiously. She wondered about my stillness, thought maybe I was disrespectful. She picked up a flower and handed it to me. Instead, I asked her to put it on the figure of a mother holding a child.

"Pray for the thousands of children like you who were murdered here," I said. She closed her eyes and I held her hand. Other chldren came over and asked questions.

And I told them about the Jewish boys and girls who were starved, abandoned, even thrown over the wall.

"Yes," I said, "once there was a wall. Over there." I pointed to a spot a hundred meters away. They could not see it, but for me, it was still there.

And I was still there.

I am still there.

I will always be there.

CHAPTER 1

"No!" I shouted. "I won't go. I won't hide in a basement. The world is in flames, and you worry about the linens, the silver, the books. No, I'll fight this war my own way!"

As Mama screamed at me, I dashed through the street and into another courtyard. An instant later, an enormous blast rocked the area. Debris rained down on my head. A large wooden trash bin caught my eye. I ran to it, climbed inside, and slammed the lid shut.

Another blast.

Even the sealed bin filled with smoke and dust. Choking, I raised the lid and peered out. Flames were shooting from a nearby building. People lay dead and wounded. Across the yard, a group of soldiers fired their rifles at low-flying planes.

Another explosion.

I could see the dead soldiers lying on the street.

I leaped from the bin, grabbed a rifle, and climbed back in.

Ammunition.

Out again, I stripped the bullets from the dead soldiers.

Back in the bin.

Breathlessly, I studied the weapon. Then I loaded, aimed at the sky, and pulled the trigger. The kick of the butt almost tore my shoulder apart. I gasped. I reloaded, supported the rifle against the lip of the bin, and waited.

The planes came again, low and fast, one after another. I fired. I loaded and fired. Loaded and fired, as fast as I could.

Suddenly, there it was. Smoke trailed from one of the planes.

"I shot him!" I yelled. "I shot him!"

Dropping the rifle, I climbed out of the bin and raced to the street, pointing to the plane. "I shot him! I shot him!"

People stared at me and shook their heads. They thought I was mad.

The time was September 1939; the place was Warsaw.

Adolf Hitler was about to plunge the planet into chaos.

I was thirteen years old. I actually believed I had shot down that German plane.

"It's insanity," my father had said, just the previous week. "Madness. The whole world can't commit suicide. After all, the Germans are an intelligent, cultured people."

Mama frowned and shook her head. "I don't trust them. Murderers in white gloves."

Papa ignored her words. "There's no reason for panic. This whole mobilization business is absurd. The Poles are actually provoking the Germans."

"Mobilization? What mobilization?" Mama's eyes narrowed. "What are you talking about?"

"The notice came on Thursday. I'm to report in ten days to the Twenty-first Infantry Division in Praga."

Mama raised her hands in despair. "In ten days? What'll happen to the business?"

"What can I do?" Papa said. "I'm not the only one. Everyone'll have to go."

"But how can I take care of everything alone?" Mama turned to me. "You hear, Jacek? From now on, you'll come straight to the shop from school. No more soccer. And Grandma Masha you can visit only on *Shabbes.*"

"Zlatka, please. Please don't worry," Papa said. "I'll be back before you know it. This war simply can't happen. The papers have to make news. . . ."

My father was a dreamer, a philosopher, a gentle man. He believed in the goodness of humanity. His happiest hours were spent in discussions of politics and philosophy with his friends.

He was self-educated and spoke five languages fluently. His books cluttered our apartment. They were stacked behind the sofa, hidden under tables, piled atop cabinets. They were his most treasured possessions. In fact, they were his passion.

I had inherited my father's fair complexion, blond hair, and clear blue eyes. He taught me to play chess and to think logically. I loved and respected him, but sometimes I wished he were a more forceful man.

My mother's domineering, aggressive personality—like her dark eyes and her hair—was the complete opposite of Papa's. Her constant prodding was largely responsible for his accomplishments in business. Mama's life was centered mainly on her home and family—me and my sister, Hela, at twelve a year younger than I—and to these she devoted herself entirely. I wanted and needed her love and affection, but our mutual stubbornness kept us apart.

For consolation and understanding, I would go to my mother's mother, my Grandma Masha, who lived among Warsaw's Jewish poor, some distance away from my middle-class neighborhood. I would tell her the latest family gossip and help her with her chores at the wholesale coal business left to her by Grandpa Benjamin.

Grandma Masha worked hard and long, but she always found time for her seven children and all their problems. Her twenty grandchildren were her greatest joy, and I, the eldest, could do no wrong.

Each Sabbath she would immerse herself in her *Commentaries on the Bible* and in her *Book of Psalms,* seeking and finding solace and spiritual inspiration. Thus, she would regenerate her strength for the coming week.

Grandma Masha possessed a pure and absolute belief in God. To her, God was a continual presence with Whom she shared all her feelings, and she was certain that the Messiah was about to arrive and bring salvation to all.

I saw the collapse of Warsaw in my father's eyes.

In the early hours of September 1, Hitler's Wehrmacht stormed across Poland's borders. It was the birth of the Blitzkrieg. It was the death of freedom.

I watched the first scattered air raids from the courtyard of our apartment.

"The planes are ours," Papa insisted. "They're on maneuvers, preparing our defenses."

I watched the smoke rise in thick black columns over Warsaw. And I saw my father's faith in a civilized Germany falter.

On September 3, there was a glimmer of hope. Great Britain and France declared war on the Third Reich, but by then the Nazi Panzer divisions were well into Poland, and the Luftwaffe controlled the skies.

Polish resistance crumbled against the mechanized might of the German armies. Stukas dive-bombed. Artillery pounded. Soldiers and civilians died.

By the end of the first week of the invasion, German tanks were on the outskirts of Warsaw. German bombardments had leveled the power plants. The waterworks were demolished. Warsaw was encircled and under siege. On September 17, Stalin's armies attacked in the east, and Poland's fate was sealed.

Papa sat motionless by the radio, listening to the war reports. Hela screamed and clutched at Mama whenever bombs hit the buildings nearby. I tried to adjust to the loss of my future. As a soprano soloist at the prestigious Tlomackie Synagogue choir, I had been awarded a scholarship to the Warsaw Music Conservatory. But the day before I was to begin my studies, the conservatory was destroyed, and my dreams of a musical career lay in ruins.

Mama clamored around the apartment in her usual planned confusion. The air-raid sirens, combined with the dull thunder of distant explosions, hurried her already frantic pace. I marveled at her; she had candles ready when the lights went out and pots of water stored. We ate and slept in my uncle's basement, where my mother had decided to move us and all our possessions when the bombing began.

Warsaw's Jewish citizens were particularly fearful on the High Holy Days. On Yom Kippur, the Luftwaffe concentrated all day long on bombarding the predominantly Jewish areas. While the rest of the city remained blacked out, the Jewish neighborhoods blazed like giant torches in the night.

"*Yekes!*" Mama screamed. "Murderers! Murderers!"

Papa sat brooding by the silent radio. But I refused to wait, to panic, to hide in a basement. Already I knew instinctively that it was only by facing the terrible reality of our new situation that I could survive it.

* * *

On September 28, Warsaw surrendered. The Germans rounded up their prisoners, together with scores of battle-weary Polish soldiers who had shed their uniforms to seek safety in civilian clothes.

The German command was preparing for a victory parade. Rumors spread that Hitler himself would appear. The center of the city was blocked off while hundreds of civilians, mostly Jews, were forced to scrub the thoroughfares.

On the day of the parade, the population was ordered off the streets. Only Poles of German extraction, the *Volksdeutsche,* were permitted to view the spectacle, and they proudly donned swastika armbands.

The night before the German parade, I ran away from our apartment without telling my mother. I found a vacant attic high above Jerozolimskie Boulevard, overlooking the parade route and the large speakers' platform. Enormous flags, pennants, and swastika banners filled the streets.

The next morning, the Wehrmacht entered Warsaw with a conqueror's arrogance. Endless rows of tall, handsome soldiers marched proudly down the boulevard, their heels clicking against the pavement in precise cadence. Tanks, trucks, and heavy artillery rumbled by.

As a feeling of despair grew inside me, I knew that I was watching the army of the future.

A roar rose from the streets below.

"Sieg, Heil! Sieg, Heil! Sieg, Heil! Sieg, Heil!"

And there he was, Adolf Hitler, with his arm outstretched in the Nazi salute. The man who had promised to conquer the world. At that moment, it seemed nothing could stop him.

The parade continued, hour after hour. More stiff, mechanical, goose-stepping troops. More tanks. More guns. More transports.

Depressed and envious, I turned away from the spectacle. I remembered watching the Polish troops parading on Independence Day. They seemed pathetic in comparison. No wonder we lost so easily.

Why weren't the Poles as strong as the Germans? I wondered. And what about the Jews? Why didn't they have a land of their own? Couldn't Jews be brave fighters and defend themselves?

I knew that my Christian friends didn't believe in Jewish valor.

"Moshek is a trader," they mocked, "but never a soldier. Cowards can't be soldiers."

But I also knew, in my heart, that they were wrong.

When I returned home, the bombings and fires were over. But nothing was the same. There was no school to attend. There was no money and practically no food.

Several of my aunts and their little children had moved in with my family for safety. Some of my uncles had escaped to the Russian zone. My father had stopped going to work because it was too risky; German patrols were seizing able-bodied men for forced labor. So he immersed himself in his books and as a father, husband, and family leader, completely ceased to exist.

For the first time in my life, I knew what it was like to be hungry. I turned to my sister. "Hela," I said, "you're coming with me tomorrow. We're taking a little trip."

She looked at me, baffled. "Where are we going?"

I smiled. "You'll see. You'll find out tomorrow. Early, Hela. We leave at six."

Hela and I had never gotten along well before. I thought she was immature and silly, always acting like Mama's little puppet. She thought I was a troublemaker who would never study hard enough to bring home a report card as good as hers. But now our shared problems were bringing us closer together.

The next morning, Hela was up in time to wake me. We dressed hurriedly and drank our tea, knowing it would have to last us for the rest of the day.

"Okay, so where are we going? Are you going to tell me now? I'm so excited," my sister said.

"We're going out to the country to find some food to bring back home. Damn it, we are not going to be hungry all the time."

"But Jacek, how will we ever get out of here? The gendarmes patrol all the streets on their motorcycles, and there's a soldier on almost every corner. It's too dangerous. They'll catch us, punish us. You know Jews aren't allowed to leave Warsaw."

"Don't worry so much. I know how we can do it. But you have to listen to what I tell you and do everything I say. Okay, ugly face?"

Hela agreed, even though I could tell she was scared. "But please, Jacek, be careful."

"Now, the first thing to remember is that we're not Jews," I told her. "You hear me? At least not for today. Get that Star of David *shmate* off your arm and let's go."

She looked at me in shock. "That's crazy, Jacku. If they catch us without it, they'll kill us."

Just a few days earlier, the Germans had decreed that all Jews had to wear a white armband with the blue Star of David. Any Jew caught without it faced the death penalty.

I snapped at her, "Hela, the only way we can get out of here is to pose as Christians. So are you coming with me or not?"

She quickly removed her armband, and we were on our way.

As soon as we were outside, we began to learn what it was like to be a Jew in Warsaw under German occupation. On the street ahead of us was an old Jewish man with a cane and a long black coat. He was approaching a group of German soldiers. Obeying another new Nazi decree, the old man removed his hat as a gesture of respect, then stepped off the sidewalk into the gutter. But the Germans didn't feel the old man had done enough.

"Eil dich, du Sauhund!"

They shoved the old man, threw his hat away, and with glee in their faces, forced him to kneel.

The old man remained calm, lifted his eyes to the sky, and recited *Shma Israel,* the prayer for deliverance.

Then one of the soldiers took his big air force knife out of its sheath and began to hack at the old man's beard. The man squirmed in pain and the German kicked him. A group of young hooligans who had gathered to watch the spectacle cracked jokes and laughed. No passerby made a move to help.

Hela covered her face with her hands. She wanted to walk over and help the old man, but I held her back.

"Remember," I whispered, "if they find out we're Jewish, they'll kill us. We're not wearing armbands. We're Christians. We have to stay out of trouble if we want to get back home alive." I pulled her away.

On our way out of town, we saw a bakery that was offering bread at the official high prices. But I couldn't pass it up. We hadn't eaten bread for days.

Several hundred people crushed each other as they all tried to push through the bakery door. German soldiers suddenly appeared.

Someone screamed and pointed at a middle-aged woman. *"Jude,* Jew!" The gendarmes grabbed her.

"No, no *Jude!* No armband!" she pleaded. She raised her bare right arm. Others pointed at her. "Yes, *Jude!"*

A gendarme grabbed her hair and kicked her into the gutter. And then a Jew hunt began. With the help of some young "Jew experts," the gendarmes made their way through the crowd. "You! *Zyd, Jude—raus!"* Any hesitation invited a rain of rifle butts and whips.

I pulled Hela closer to me and hissed, "Let's get out of here. Fast!"

Hela was visibly shaken. "I think I want to go home. Take me home, Jacku."

"No, Hela. It'll be all right, I promise you. Let's just get out of here." I grabbed her hand and held it tightly.

After the things we had just seen, I knew the situation for Jews in Warsaw was worse than I expected or imagined. But I was not turning back.

After hours of walking, we finally reached the farm village of Grojec. Not a shop was open, and there was no sign of food. We approached a solitary peasant.

"Praised be Jesus Christ! We have no food," he shrugged helplessly. "Money, yes. But bread, chickens, eggs"—

We wandered on and found a large potato field that had long since been harvested. We spotted some tiny leftovers scattered about, which we dropped into our sacks. Here and there, we found a large, full-grown potato that had been overlooked.

Hours passed. Our fingers and hands were sore and scratched, but still we searched. At last, our sacks began to fill. The sun was setting.

"Jacku, let's go. It's getting dark. We won't make it back before curfew."

"We'll make it, Hela. Let's just look a while longer. Try that patch over there. Dig a little deeper."

Hela began to cry. Her fingers were oozing blood.

I clawed the earth frantically. "Here, Hela. Look. I've got three more big ones. We'll go in just one more minute."

"Jacku, please!"

"Okay. Okay. Don't cry. We've got plenty of time."

We shouldered our sacks and started on the long trek home. We walked briskly at first but soon slowed under the weight we were carrying.

Back in Warsaw, we made our way to the trolley line that was still running through the city. Darkness fell. A trio of young thugs began to trail us. They prodded our sacks and discovered we had food. With obvious envy, they offered to trade with us. We refused.

"Jude!" one of the trio screamed. *"Jude!"* Jew had become the word to denounce anyone, Jewish or not.

Feeling more secure in the dark, I decided to fight it out. I swiftly drew my pocket knife. "Come here, you bastards, and I'll cut your throats! I swear by Jesus and Holy Mary. Just try me!"

The young hoodlums looked at one another in silence. A trolley was passing by. I grabbed the sacks and my sister and I jumped on.

We were back in our apartment just in time for the 9 P.M. curfew. Mama asked no questions. Her twelve-year-old daughter and thirteen-year-old son were safe, and they had brought food for the family.

I looked at Hela. Her fingers were no longer bleeding, but her nails were broken and caked with blood and dirt. In less than a day, she had changed a great deal.

And in less than a day, I had discovered I would grow up very fast.

I was a Jewish boy in Warsaw in November 1939. If I wanted to survive, I had no other choice.

CHAPTER 2

I raced up the stairs. Immersed in his prayer book, Reb Shulem sat in the hallway, greeting all his friends and neighbors with his customary *"Gut Yom Tov"* and *"Gmar Chsima Tovah"* (Happy Holidays). He carried his tall body well despite his age, and with his long gray beard and heavy white eyebrows he resembled an ancient patriarch of Israel. Wrapped in a long white prayer shawl yellowed from the devotion of years, he spread an aura of holiness among the worshipers gathered in his apartment.

Reb Shulem was called the Rothschild of Grandma Masha's neighborhood. His lumberyard was well known among the poor people and the underworld elite of Ostrowska Street. He was respected and envied by all.

Reb Shulem turned away and put on his white robe, preparing to lead the worshipers in the *Musaf* service. I entered the apartment to search for my Grandma Masha.

I found her seated in an old wooden chair, her heavy prayer books cradled in her lap. I kissed her on both cheeks, and she pulled me down next to her, happy to share her seat with her favorite grandchild.

"I know I'm late, *Bobe,*" I explained, "but I couldn't help it. They were beating up Jews and breaking into shops on Solna Street. Even on our holiest day, these murderers don't leave us in peace. You remember last year on Yom Kippur how they bombed all day long? Even in the basement, we couldn't pray."

It was October 1940. In the year the Germans had occupied Warsaw, they had closed all synagogues and banned religious observances. So Reb Shulem had offered his apartment for the High Holiday services, despite the risk and the obvious dangers involved for himself and all those attending. In Reb Shulem's eyes, it would be a sin to send any Jew away from the service. So Marysia, his Christian maid, stood watching for Germans at the entrance to the building. Despite the German decree forbidding it, she continued to work loyally for the family that had employed her for more than twenty years.

Grandma Masha pulled my head close and superstitiously spat three times to each side. She thanked God for His watch over me. She dried her damp cheeks with a handkerchief as she begged God for mercy on her children and grandchildren, the sons who had disappeared to the Russian zone, the sons-in-law captured and sent to forced labor, and the others who had fallen ill. Out of the whole large clan, I was the only one able to serve as a provider for the family.

As Reb Shulem began the *Unsane Tokeff,* the holiest and most haunting of Yom Kippur prayers, Grandma Masha stood up and raised her tear-filled eyes to the ceiling. Each prayer rose like a direct and urgent appeal to God.

"Mi yichyeh, u'mi yomus . . . u'mi bacherev, u'mi baesh? Who shall live and who shall perish, who by the sword and who by fire, oh, Lord?"

She kissed me on the forehead with trembling lips. I saw in her face, and in her eyes, a fierce inner courage, an infinite, bottomless faith that was both serene and expectant.

"Goteniu!" she burst out, as she covered my head with a protective hand. "Let these young innocent ones grow. Let them survive!" Her eyes widened, and her voice shook.

"Oh, God, I ask nothing for myself! Just give my Izaakl the strength to survive, to continue caring and providing for the others."

She pulled me closer. I embraced her thin waist and stared into her wrinkled face. Her eyeglasses, held by an old piece of worn-out rope, were resting on the tip of her nose. A tear dropped onto my face. I did not feel it; I only saw it fall. I became part of my Grandma Masha's presence, which was way up in the heavens in front of a saintly jury, presided over by God.

Her appeal increased in fervor.

"Reboyne Shel Oilom, Ruler of the Universe, I ask mercy for our children; please punish me, not our offspring. I am your servant." She put her hand on my head and closed her eyes.

Boldly, I pulled her arm and exclaimed, "Grandma, *Bobe,* I don't want you to die, and I don't want to die. I want to live."

A sobbing woman in front of us, wiping her cheeks with a big white handkerchief, turned around and stared. I snapped out of my trance and looked around the tension-filled room. Emotionally drained, my grandma collapsed into my arms as I helped her back into her seat.

I stood there confused, the tears burning my eyes, a choking sensation in my throat.

Reb Shulem's voice, filled with anger and bitterness, drifted from across the hall and blended with the loud sobbing of the women.

I felt suffocated. I didn't know what to do. The walls closed in on me. Some inner force pushed me out into the hallway, down the stairs, and into the courtyard.

I caught my breath and choked back my tears. I, the big-shot provider, could not cry! I rubbed my eyes with clenched fists.

Earlier that holiday morning, the streets had been quiet, almost deserted. Now people rushed back and forth and shouted to each other, their voices tense and loud. In the distance, groups of pedestrians gathered in front of posters.

It must be a new German decree, a new *Bekanntmachung,* I thought. The people running and arguing told me it was serious.

I ran down Smocza Street to Mila. There, too, dozens of people were discussing the notice.

"It's a relocation," I heard one man say. "It restricts Jews to certain streets only."

"You idiots!" snapped an angry young man. "It's a ghetto. A medieval ghetto!"

The word "ghetto" froze people in their tracks. I pushed my way through the crowd to read the notice for myself. I read it in German. I read it in Polish. I couldn't believe it in any language.

"What's a ghetto?" a kid next to me asked.

"A real ghetto," I said out loud. "Right out of my father's history books. The first one in modern times."

It was no accident that the decree was issued on the Day of Atonement, our holiest day.

Mama panicked when she heard the news. "I knew it. I had a feeling that something bad would happen during the holidays. The *yekes* have done it again."

Papa talked to himself and paced the hallway of the apartment. "They cannot do it; this is not the middle ages." Pointing to a passage from Dubnov's *History of the Jews,* he said, "Here, you see, ghettos once existed in Germany. Italy also had them many centuries ago."

Twelve months had passed since the Germans had occupied Warsaw. Twelve months that had destroyed any hope of a quick end to our despair and terror. Twelve fear-filled, painful months during which dozens of decrees had been passed against Jews.

Jews must be identified with armbands and stars.

Jews must tip their hats before Germans and walk off the sidewalks.

Jews are excluded from schools.

Jews cannot pray or assemble.

Jews must subsist on less than half the food rations allowed Christians.

Jews must surrender sewing machines, pianos, fur coats, gold, jewelry, and all wholesale inventories.

Jewish males will be dragged from their homes for forced labor.

Jews cannot, should not, must not . . . A chain of decrees designed to destroy the will to exist, to breathe, to fight back.

And now, when our morale was lower than ever and our hope was waning, a medieval decree.

A ghetto in the middle of Warsaw.

CHAPTER 3

"We've been expecting you," Franek greeted me with outstretched hands. "With all the bad news, and now the wall, we were sure you'd come." He walked to the window. "You can see it from here, Jacek. From up here on the fifth floor, it's all visible." He pointed down to Zelazna Street. "They're splitting the street in two, one side for the ghetto, the other for non-Jews. You see?"

I looked, then swiftly turned away in disgust. "I can't believe it. It's a prison. They're building a prison for Jews."

It was six weeks later, and I was in Aryan Warsaw, at the home of my father's close Christian friend, Franek Malczewski.

Franek looked down again. "Even our neighbor, Piotr, and his Catholic-born children had to move into the ghetto because his grandfather was a convert from Judaism. What a disgrace! One day, I tell you, my dear Jacku—one day we'll fight these barbarian krauts, these *schwabs*. We'll fight them street by street, house by house. Jews and Christians together!"

Mrs. Malczewska joined us at the window. "Oh, wounded Christ, Holy Mother Czestochowska. It's unbelievable," she sighed.

We were talking about the nine-foot-high brick wall, topped with barbed wire and broken glass, that now surrounded the ghetto district. The Germans had forced hundreds of Jews, at gunpoint, to erect it practically overnight.

In their ghetto decree, the Germans had designated about fifty blocks in the northern sections of Warsaw as the "Jewish *Wohnungsbezirk.*" All non-Jews in the area—and there were thousands—were ordered to move out and trade apartments with Jews who lived in other parts of the city. Thirty days were allowed for the exchange.

I had watched the streets fill with carts, horse-drawn wagons, bicycles, and baby carriages. All were overloaded with household goods, personal belongings, furniture, clothing, bedding, dishes, pots, books, and anything else that could be transported.

More than 400,000 Jews were jammed into an area meant to house only 100,000 people. Available apartments vanished overnight. Thousands of Jewish families moved into stores, attics, or basements. Others rented one or two rooms from those with larger apartments. Fortunately, our apartment on Twarda Street and Grandma Masha's place on Ostrowska Street both fell within the ghetto confines, so we didn't have to move.

By November 15, 1940, the ghetto had been fenced off with barbed wire. Any Jews caught outside the Jewish district after the deadline faced death. Any non-Jew caught aiding or hiding Jews faced severe punishment.

The flow of food into the ghetto slowed to a trickle. Prices soared, 500 percent and higher. There was electricity for only two hours a night. Books, newspapers, and journals disappeared. Clothing stores were completely emptied. And with winter coming, coal and wood for heating were available only at a huge premium.

Then official posts were erected for the entry and exit of individuals with special permits. Germans stood guard at one-hundred-foot intervals with machine guns and dogs.

Then the wall.

Yet even the wall did not deter those who would risk their lives to venture outside. Of course, I was one.

I studied the trolleys that passed through the ghetto. They carried Aryan passengers, German guards, and Polish police. The trip through the ghetto was nonstop and swift, except for the few seconds when the trolleys slowed to turn a corner. At such moments, it was possible to leap on or off.

Soon I was jumping the trolleys and riding them in and out of the ghetto. It was risky and dangerous, but I would not be chained, confined, imprisoned.

So here I was, standing in Aryan Warsaw, peering down at this monstrous wall, still not able to accept the fact that my family and friends were imprisoned just beyond it.

Franek and his family made preparations to help me stay on the Aryan side indefinitely. They also wanted Hela to come.

"We'll take care of them," Franek told my parents in a coded telephone conversation. "We'll hide them in our cottage in Milanowek, away from Warsaw. It's safer there. There aren't so many Germans around. Here, on Lucka Street, we live in a big building, and the janitor has big eyes. He watches everybody. Besides, the house is full of anti-Semites."

I felt secure in Franek's apartment. I was treated like a member of the family. The Malczewskis slept on the living room sofa so that I could share the bedroom with their children, Ala, a girl several years younger than I, and Bolek, a boy of nine.

"Aryan Warsaw has become a hunting ground for Jews," Franek warned. "So you must learn the Catholic prayers by heart. And when you speak to people, throw in phrases like 'Oh, Jesus,' and 'Holy Mother Czestochowska.' The streets are full of hoodlums and blackmailers, *szmalcowniki,* who hunt down Jews and deliver them to the Gestapo.

"Learn all about the church, Jacku. Shout back at the bastards. Don't give them an opening. Make them believe you're one of them."

Then he lowered his voice. "But beware of one thing. Never—no matter what—never let them pull your pants down. Polish Catholics aren't circumcised. If it comes to that, run for your life."

I rehearsed daily. I went to Saint Alexander's church on Three Crosses Square with Ala and recited the Latin prayers. She showed me how to behave and respond during the various rituals.

One church practice, however, struck me as embarrassing and illogical: *spowiedz.* To confess to another human being all of one's most intimate thoughts and sins seemed to me unreasonable and unfair. I had trouble inventing sincere-sounding lies.

But I learned.

"We're all destined to perish in this ghetto prison," Mama yelled into the phone. "And you, our only hope, have settled into safety."

Safety! How could she call me safe when I felt in constant danger of being discovered and denounced? Still, I was relieved by Mama's call. My existence outside the ghetto was meaningless. It didn't suit my restless nature, and my conscience bothered me.

Weeks had passed since the ghetto was closed, and I was certain that my family had exhausted the food supply I'd left behind. Besides, I was homesick.

"Here, take this scarf, it's freezing outside," Mrs. Malczewska said as she tucked it in my shirt the next morning, preparing me for the return trip to the ghetto. "And these earmuffs, too."

She cooked the most lavish breakfast and was hovering over me as though I were her own child. I embraced and kissed her. Ala had tears in her eyes when we said goodbye.

Franek and I walked briskly to the Kiercelak Market. I couldn't pass up this opportunity to bring food back into the ghetto with me. The prices there were a bargain compared to those in the ghetto. My career as a smuggler was about to begin.

I bought some flour, kasha, salami, and a few kilos of sugar. I stuffed the food into long stockings, lowered them into my pants, and secured them around my waist. Franek watched me in amazement.

"Jacku," he said with a smile, "you're a real professional. The Nazi beasts will have a tough time getting rid of you."

Then I was ready to board the trolley. Franek stood and watched until it disappeared down the street. I knew I was fortunate to have at least one trustworthy friend in the hostile Aryan world.

Though I was trembling inside, I showed no outward fear as the trolley made its way through midtown Warsaw and stopped in front of the ghetto wall.

German gendarmes with submachine guns guarded the special exit-entry gate. Several Polish policemen stood before a wooden guardhouse a short distance away. Two Jewish policemen were stationed just inside the gate.

A gendarme and a Polish policeman boarded the two-car trolley, the gendarme in front and the Polish "blue" in the rear. The gendarme signaled to the conductor, and the trolley started on its fifteen-minute, nonstop journey through the ghetto.

I moved to the rear car and edged slowly toward the "blue." Most of the passengers riveted their attention on the ghetto, but some of them noticed me as I moved closer to the trolley steps. The Polish blue turned his head, fixed his eyes on me, and murmured, "Do you have a tip, a *stuve?*"

I nodded and stuffed a hundred-zloty bill in his leather belt.

"Jump when I push you," he whispered.

Several passengers began to laugh. "What? Moshek pays to get *into* the ghetto?" said one.

"Of course," replied another. "The monkey must go back to the zoo."

I ignored them. Taking my cue from the policeman, I leaped from the moving car, mingled immediately with the street crowd, then disappeared into a nearby house.

After a while, I emerged. Within minutes, I stood in front of my apartment. My sudden appearance excited everyone, except Mama. *"Oy wei iz mir,"* she started. "We'll all starve. God and the Germans have united to wipe us out."

But when I removed from my pants the stockings filled with food, Mama smiled, "I told you, my Izaakl will save us all."

Hela hugged me. "I missed you," she whispered. "Don't go away anymore."

"Hela, you'll be my partner from now on. I'm going into business. I'm going to smuggle food into the ghetto."

"How?"

"I have a plan."

I told her about the Polish policeman on the trolley. "I can bribe him. If all goes well, I'll make two or three trips a week."

Hela listened in awe. "It's just like a movie. Good guys and bad guys. Cowboys and Indians . . ."

"Yes," I smiled. "And I'm going to be the cowboy."

And so for the next month, I was in and out of the ghetto several times a week. I rode the trolleys recklessly, and my smuggling business thrived. Hela would wait for me at a prearranged time and place. When I spotted her, I would toss her a pack of supplies, jump from the moving trolley, and disappear into the ghetto.

One day I miscalculated. Unable to control the forward momentum of my jump, I ran into a number of pedestrians. The commotion alerted the German gendarme. He halted the trolley, drew his gun, and fired into the already startled crowd. People screamed and ran in all directions. Some were shot and fell to the ground, bleeding.

I unhooked my knapsack and bolted for the nearest house. I reached the attic and frantically felt my body, face, and head for blood. Unnerved, I removed the stuffed stockings from under my pants and around my waist. There was a hole in one of the stockings, and inside, a hot bullet.

How lucky Hela wasn't feeling well today, I thought. They'd have killed her with that spray of bullets. And how close I had come to death myself.

I left the food in the attic and hurried down to the nearest coffee house. I had to calm down before I went home.

"Tea and vodka," I ordered.

The waiter stared at my youthful face, but finally he served me. As he walked away, I heard him say to another patron, "Our new breed. The kid smuggler."

The kid smuggler.

One of thousands who jumped trolleys, climbed walls, tried anything to bring tons of much-needed food into the ghetto.

The stakes were high. Not a day passed without some youngsters being shot or disappearing forever into Gestapo headquarters.

Shaken and frightened, I ordered another drink and sat quietly while my heartbeat returned to normal. I knew I would have to find a better route.

Ironically, it was death that showed me the way.

CHAPTER 4

"I found him hanging in the closet," my friend Sevek sobbed. "His eyes were open, and he was staring at me like he was saying he was sorry he couldn't help me. I'm scared, Jacku." He grabbed me.

"A suicide!" Mama exclaimed. "The poor proud man." Mama clasped her hands, spat three times on the floor, and sighed. "Oh, God, protect our house from such shame."

I pulled the sobbing boy into the bedroom and locked the door behind me.

Sevek's father, a veteran officer of the Polish army, had lost an eye and sustained serious leg injuries during clashes with the Russian Bolsheviks in 1920. Since that time, he had survived on government grants and veteran's aid. When the Germans took over, they canceled his pensions and confiscated his small tobacco business. His feeling of helplessness within ghetto walls had made his life totally unbearable.

Sevek stayed at our house for two days. He was ashamed to face people. His father's suicide had cast a stigma on the family, since self-imposed death was alien to Jews. Overcrowding at the cemetery delayed the funeral. The ghetto had been in existence only a few months, but already thousands had died from hunger, disease, and suicide.

On the day of the funeral, Sevek didn't eat or speak. He was alone and lost, so I stuck close by him during the ceremony.

The procession walked along Gesia Street and up to the ghetto wall. The cemetery gates were in front of us. I was watching closely. The gate was guarded by German gendarmes with rifles and dogs. There were also some Pinkert men, Jews in black uniforms, who administered and performed the burials.

Christians were not permitted in the cemetery grounds, which were a no-man's-land. Jews could enter only with a funeral procession. They were counted and escorted during the burial. The guards made sure the same number of people returned to the ghetto. But no one inspected the casket or the funeral wagon.

"What a place to smuggle food," I thought. "From the cemetery, it would be an easy jump over the wall into Aryan Warsaw and freedom." But seeing the German patrol on motorcycles with mounted machine guns on the sidecars, I realized it wouldn't be quite so simple.

"But they're just passing by, and I know the place well, I can hide," I reasoned to myself.

"Do you think it's a sacrilege?" I asked my Grandma Masha later.

"No, my dear. To stay alive, God permits anything. Even on Yom Kippur, you don't have to fast if you're ill. But if they catch you, it won't be far to your own grave." She stroked my hair and sighed, "So many of us depend on you."

That night I couldn't sleep. I turned and twisted, dreaming about food.

Smuggling food, sackloads of food, entire wagons with sacks, a chain of children with sacks, an entire gang smuggling food. My gang, my own gang. Kids with guts. Kids who could spit in your face and tell you, "Up yours, bastard. Fuck off, you prick!"

By morning, I had decided to abandon my solo operation and recruit a gang. This would be bigger, much bigger, than a few stockings filled with kasha.

I boasted to Hela, "Wait till you hear my new plan. You won't believe it."

She lit up. "What, Jacku? Tell me this minute. What is it?"

"You'll just have to wait and see, Hayele. But now, follow me."

By that evening, I had rounded up the three boys I thought would fit best. Sevek, who had once been fragile and spoiled, jumped for joy when I explained my plan. "The bastards won't get me, Jacku," he said with bravado. "Papa's dead, and Mom's starving with swollen legs. I'm not gonna fold my hands or beg on the streets."

Lutek, my prewar choir chum, needed no pushing or prodding either. He was already climbing the wall and smuggling on his own.

"Jacku, you couldn't have asked me at a better time. Dad just kicked me out of his stinking basement apartment." Lutek angrily explained, "They're nuts. They think they're still in the ten-room apartment on Marszalkowska Street. 'We shall perish in dignity,' they say. 'We shall not have a smuggler for a son.' " Lutek stood up, waving his hands in desperation. "Not me, Jacku. I won't starve and get swollen. I want to eat, I want to survive!"

And then there was Yankele Rotzo, my soccer pal from Grandma Masha's Ostrowska Street neighborhood.

Yankele came to the meeting barefoot as usual, pulling on his pants and spitting. He didn't want to waste a minute. "What are we waiting for? Let's go tonight. I'm at home in that cemetery. I've been climbing those trees for chestnuts ever since I was seven." Yankele spat again and hitched up his sagging pants.

"And look, you guys, you *yatn!*" Yankele shouted at Lutek and Sevek. "Remember. This is no picnic! You rich kids better stay alert or you'll get your ass burned." Hela and I amused ourselves watching Yankele lecture. But suddenly he got serious and turned to me.

"Hey, Jacku, swear on your mother, the first apple we find on the Aryan side, I get. An apple, a whole, sweet, juicy apple in my mouth."

"Yes, Yankele. I swear, if we find one, it's yours."

So that was the gang. Sevek, Yankele, Lutek, and me. We were all the same age—just fourteen.

Before starting in earnest, I wanted to make a few trial runs. So we joined a couple of funeral processions and followed the mourners in and out of the cemetery, making believe we were grieving. I also succeeded in making a deal with Shmerl, the rumor-mongering cemetery worker. For a share of the loot, he agreed to count us in and out with any funeral.

"I've got a wife and three kids to feed. But," he warned, "if the gendarmes catch us, you know what'll happen."

I picked a Tuesday for our first run. We met in Yankele's one-room flat on Ostrowska 13. I pulled several switchblades out of my shirt. I flipped the button of one, curled my right hand forward, and a shiny blade snapped out.

The gang jumped back, staring in serious silence. "Here, *yatn*, look at that beautiful blade. It's like a rainbow, long and sharp. It can save your life." I couldn't contain my excitement. "I brought them into the ghetto just last week. They're stolen from Okecie, from the airport. They cost a fortune on the black market."

Yankele edged closer. "Jacku, that's a Luftwaffe switchblade. I heard people talk about it. The Haim Benkart gang, they have them."

The boys relaxed a bit as I explained how to handle one. "Sevek, Yankele, and Lutek, you each get one, and remember, use it without mercy. Close your eyes and use it. You hear me!" I shouted and added, "When you can't bribe your way out, don't hesitate. Cut that son of a bitch's belly open."

Everybody nodded. I could see that Sevek was far from ready for such action but didn't say anything. "Time will take care of Sevek," I thought.

With the switchblades and money in our boots, we ran out of the house.

We joined a procession on Gesia Street, some distance from the cemetery gate. I turned my cap sideways, threw my scarf over my shoulder, and squeezed close to a sobbing woman. She held her arms outstretched as she walked, as though trying to reach the casket on the horse-drawn wagon in front of her. Her long black shawl kept falling over her face. A young girl clung to her in fear. An older man in a long black coat and filthy boots tried to support both of them.

I felt anxious and awkward but determined to go through with the plan. I knew that funerals were full of violent emotions. I had known this to be true since I was nine, when my Grandfather Benjamin died. Dying, screaming, fear, and suffering were all the same to me.

Right behind me, Yankele fit easily into the scene. He looked as innocent and disheveled as any mourner. He had even lost a shoe along the way. Sevek simply trembled with fear. I pushed his beret down over his eyes to obstruct his vision. Dragging his feet, he held onto my scarf and followed blindly. I couldn't see Lutek, but I knew he was out there somewhere.

As we passed the gendarmes at the cemetery gate, my pulse quickened. I wasn't good at crying, so I shook my head in convulsive prayer. I pounded my chest with one hand and pulled Sevek along with the other. Two helmeted Germans with rifles slung over their shoulders looked us over. I kept on praying, shaking my head, and pounding my chest.

Suddenly, Shmerl appeared. "Hey, you, *mamzor,* don't overdo it," he whispered. "Get going!"

Shmerl counted the mourners and reported to the German. "Twenty-nine, Herr *Feldwebel.*"

We wound along the narrow paths through the old stones by the cemetery lanes. Lutek joined us, and I whispered to the gang, "*Yatn,* here's the *ohel,* the mausoleum of the Radzyminer Rabbi. Follow me." We straightened up and looked at each other. We were proud of our acting, and we wanted to laugh. But the stones, the graves, the wailing, the Germans, and the risks ahead kept us very quiet.

When no one was in sight, we climbed the cemetery wall into the former Skra soccer field and separately made our way as fast as we could through Aryan Warsaw to the Kiercelak Market. Without armbands, we passed as Polish Christians, shopkeepers' helpers purchasing supplies. Using the money I had saved from my solo smuggling operation, we shopped successfully all afternoon, despite the fact that the market was swarming with *szmalcowniki,* Jew hunters.

There was enough so we would each have several thousand zlotys' profit plus some food to take home.

Loaded with salami, sugar, and barley, we met back at the cemetery that evening. Night had fallen, and the silence of death was all around us. So quiet we hardly breathed, we helped each other over the wall. Old gravestones and monuments jutted out everywhere. Bushes and trees loomed in the darkness, assuming strange shapes and dimensions. A cold wind made eerie sounds as it swept through the underbrush. None of us had ever been in a cemetery after dark. We were each grateful for the presence of the others.

Slowly and without a sound, we found our way back to the *ohel,* the mausoleum. There, we devoured two loaves of bread with salami. We crouched close to one another inside the mausoleum and tried in vain to sleep.

"Sevek, why aren't you sleeping?" I whispered. I could see his eyes, wide open, staring at the round ceiling.

"I'm thinking," he said.

"He's scared," Lutek whispered from the other side. "We're all scared. We're lying here inside a grave."

"Yeah, it's spooky. My dad's buried here someplace." Sevek moved closer to me and hid his face under my arm.

"Hey, guys," I argued, "dead people can't hurt us. We're not kids anymore. It's the Germans we should be worrying about."

"Yeah, Jacek and me, we're old-timers in this place. Hey, *yatn!*" Yankele changed his tone. "Ssh, listen." He moved his ear close to the stone he was lying on.

"The Radzyminer Rabbi is saying something. Wait a minute. . . . Yeah, I hear him. He's warning us not to forget to pray in the morning." Yankele burst out laughing, and everyone joined in.

Sometime later, during that first long night's vigil, we all fell asleep.

In the morning, we awoke stiff and frozen. It was sunny and peaceful. We rubbed our aching muscles and ate some more food. Soon the day's first funeral arrived. It was a long procession, with at least fifty people.

"Here comes Shmerl," I whispered, "just as we planned. And not a gendarme in sight."

"What's the deal?" Shmerl asked, as the mourners gathered around the grave.

"Four sacks and the four of us."

"Good. Get the sacks in the wagon with the coffin, and join the crowd."

We loaded the food quickly and moved toward the mourners.

Then Shmerl inched close to me. "One thousand zlotys, Jacek."

"That's twice the price we agreed on," I protested.

"That's the price. I had to pay off the *yeke* gendarme. Otherwise, it would never have worked."

"Here's five hundred. You'll get the rest when we're out."

"Hevra, friends," Shmerl snapped back, smirking, "we must have confidence in each other, or we'll all end up in a grave."

CHAPTER 5

"The cemetery is full," I said to my Grandma Masha as I watched a cart move slowly down the street with its gruesome load of corpses, "so they have mass graves now."

Grandma Masha stared up at the ceiling. She was now bedridden for good. She had been hit by a rickshaw in the street and suffered several fractures. Because of her age, the doctors didn't offer much hope.

"There isn't enough room for the living," she said, "not to mention the dead. Sometimes it's hard to tell who's alive and who's not."

By May 1941, the ghetto had become a separate world. It was governed by a ruthless German command force which issued orders and regulations to the embattled *Judenrat,* the ghetto's self-administered Jewish council.

Under the *Judenrat,* community kitchens were organized, and free soup and bread were dispensed daily to thousands of starving people. A special medical unit was formed to treat the sick, but doctors and dentists were soon helpless because of the lack of medicine and supplies. A network of improvised, underground educational centers was organized, since Jewish children were forbidden to attend school.

Thousands of Jewish refugees from Holland, Germany, and Austria began to arrive. The ghetto population rose to over 500,000, more than five times its original size. Each day the streets and squares were filled with people looking for food.

Then, in June, the Germans invaded the Soviet Union, and life in the ghetto took an immediate turn for the worse. The Germans cut food rations further and increased their demand for human labor. Every day they rounded up professionals, intellectuals, and civic leaders, and shot them in front of their apartments.

Before long, the walled-in city became a seething hell of depressed and diseased people. Hunger was rampant, and thousands lay in the streets, starving, swollen, and dying.

The dead were lifted off the streets each morning, together with the sick and the starving who lay unconscious, unmoving but alive. They were gathered like rubbish, thrown aboard hand-drawn wagons, and carted off for burial.

This is what I was watching from my grandma's window.

"They almost quarantined me, Grandma."

She raised a startled hand to her mouth. "Typhoid?"

I nodded. "The gendarmes and blues took everyone from a whole block."

Grandma Masha replied, "I heard that they put you through showers and cover you with disinfecting powder." She shuddered. "They made your Aunt Perl and the children stand outside in the snow all night while they sprayed the apartment. Then they stole everything they could."

She leaned back on her pillow. "Where will it all end?"

As things worsened, my prestige as a smuggler rose, along with the risks. My gang had operated for many months with only minor incidents. As we gained experience, our loads increased, as did the prices for food and the payoffs to the Pinkert guards at the cemetery. The Germans were patrolling more strictly, and Shmerl demanded triple the amount of the original payoff.

Each time I saw a Jewish policeman, I felt an ugly rage inside me. I could understand the Germans' evil design in setting up Jewish police in the ghetto, pitting Jew against Jew. But I couldn't come to terms with it.

"What do you want? How much this time?" I muttered angrily as one of them backed me up against the wall.

"Up his ass, Jacek!" Yankele cried. "That's all he gets today. The fuckin' parasite!"

"Hey, Jacek, big shot, I protect you, don't I?" Markowski dug his long black club into my ribs. "Just this morning, I coulda had you down at the station. And who knows? Maybe to the Pawiak prison. Nobody returns from the Pawiak. But did I do that? Of course not. I knew you'd be smart."

"Panie Markowski, there's a limit, damn it!" I complained.

Markowski grinned. "I have a wife and kids and a lousy mother-in-law, too. We also want to eat, you know."

Pan Markowski had been Hela's history teacher before the war. Not so long ago we used to respect him. Now as I looked into his eyes, I recognized evil. So I paid off.

Our smuggling route had become much longer. After the Skra football field was made part of the Jewish cemetery, I picked the next adjoining crossing point. The wall there was high, maybe twelve feet, but in some spots, tall trees spread their branches above and over the wall.

We were pacing along the wall, examining all the places we could climb across into the Evangelical Cemetery.

"Hey, *yatn,* look here, it's perfect!" I shouted. I jumped onto a stone and up the tree, higher onto a branch, and there I was, sitting comfortably, practically on top of the wall. Yankele climbed up.

"I can see the whole place. The stones all have crosses."

Within seconds the gang was up there, admiring the setup.

"It'll be easy to throw down our sacks," said Lutek.

"Hey, look at those stone monuments attached directly to the wall. It'll be simple to climb down."

Yankele pulled out his switchblade. "I'll mark this tree with a 'Z' for my dad's name, Zalmen." Yankele's father had disappeared right after the fall of Warsaw. No one knew if he was still alive.

That tree became our rendezvous spot, our *meta.*

One day we entered the cemetery with the funeral procession of a rich person; by now, only people with money could afford funerals. Sevek, Yankele, Lutek, and I snuck away from the crowd of mourners and went quietly to the *ohel.*

I was dividing up our shopping money when suddenly I heard a noise. We all heard it at the same time. At first, it was distant. Then it grew louder, until it turned into an unmistakable roar.

"Motorcycles! Germans on patrol!" Sevek turned pale. I looked out and saw mourners screaming, running, hiding behind trees, squatting behind tombstones.

"That's strange, that's the third patrol this week," Lutek said with suspicion.

"Come on, *yatn,* scram. Over the wall!" I ordered. "If they catch us here, it's all over."

Yankele spun around. "Fuck 'em, let's join the mourners."

"It's too late," Lutek stammered. "They're after us."

I grabbed Sevek's hand. "Let's go. Follow me!"

We ran through a thicket of bushes, down a narrow path to the west wall and across to our "Z" tree. Lutek, fast as a cat, jumped on a stone and was on the tree.

"Quick, Sevek, move your ass." I bent down; Sevek stepped on my back and scaled the bare wall.

I motioned to Yankele. "Get going. Don't just stand there."

"Don't push me around. You first, anyway!"

"Shmuck, you, who do you think you are? Move it!"

The motorcycles roared to a stop. Two gendarmes crashed through the shrubs. I jumped from the stone onto the tree, reaching the wall with my left hand. Bullets bounced around me as I pulled myself on top of the wall.

I saw Yankele standing on the stone. Suddenly he jumped back down. He must have figured he wouldn't make it over the wall. So he started running.

"Halt, *verfluchte Hunde,* cursed dogs!" More shots.

I pulled myself over the wall and landed in Lutek's and Sevek's arms.

"Yankele, you brave idiot," I muttered.

"He'll make it, he'll hide, you'll see, he knows that place well," Lutek whispered.

We looked at each other in horror. Minutes passed. We didn't budge. We didn't speak. We only listened to the sound of more gunfire.

Did the Germans get you, Yankele?
Did they blow your head off?
Or did you climb a tree and outsmart those yeke bastard sons of bitches?

On the soccer field you could outrun us all.

I was jolted out of my thoughts by the pale faces of Lutek and Sevek.

"Let's get the hell out of here," I commanded, in a voice as ugly as my feelings.

CHAPTER 6

As soon as we crossed into Aryan Warsaw, we went to see Maciek, a Christian friend who owned the Pod Kaczka bar. Maciek was an old-timer whose prewar patrons had included many notorious characters from the Jewish underworld. He liked me and my gang.

"You'd better go back by another route," Maciek said. "It sounds like the Germans are on to you. Someone must have snitched."

I listened quietly, feeling heartsick about Yankele.

"Why don't you go back across the roof on Wolnosc Street? Stas, the super there, is an old friend of mine. You can trust him."

Maciek's sixteen-year-old daughter, Jadzia, was especially nice to me. We often flirted. "Oh, wounded Christ God, may He defend you all." Jadzia had brought us food and vodka and was standing very close to me.

I forced a smile as she stroked my hair.

"Papa Maciek," I said, "tell us more about this roof."

Maciek closed the drapes in the back room where we were sitting and told Jadzia to attend to the customers out front. Then he moved his chair close to mine.

"Well, Jacku, Stas's house is right on the border, one of the very few Aryan houses directly attached to a ghetto house. So, clever old Stas has been taking advantage of his setup and making some good money by letting Jews out across his roof. His daughter and son-in-law live on the fifth floor, right below the attic. At night, the Jews cross the roof, then climb into the attic and meet in his apartment. The *Zydki,* the Jews, stay over till morning; then they walk out into the city. And Stas has made himself an easy thousand zlotys.

"I swear on the Holy Mother, that's the truth. Why, only last week I saw two Jewish girls come across. Beautiful as roses. I spoke to them. They're somewhere out there right now.

"So, what do you think?" He patted my cheek with a fatherly hand. "You know, Jacku, I get along better with Jews than with my own kind. I wouldn't mislead you."

I turned from him to Sevek and Lutek, who had been silently picking at their food. "I know what you're thinking. It's a goddamn mess. But we can't help Yankele now."

"Do you think they killed him?" Sevek asked.

"I don't know. Don't think about it. We'll find out when we get back. Now, let's do what we came for."

Lutek rose from the table. "Okay, okay, don't get nervous, let's just get on with it."

"That's the way," I said. "Go to the market and buy all you can. We'll meet back here in an hour."

Sevek checked his shopping list. Lutek checked his cash.

"Shove off, damn it." I almost pushed them out the door.

I turned to old Maciek. "Can I talk with Stas?"

Maciek nodded. "Wait here. I'll just tell Jadzia where we're going."

We left through the back door. Within minutes, we stood in the backyard of Wolnosc Street 14, two blocks away. I looked up at the roofs in the already darkening afternoon light. The house on Wolnosc Street had five floors; the one behind it in the ghetto had only three.

"Stop worrying. Let's go talk to Stas." Maciek pushed me forward. We entered the hallway.

"Wait here." A few moments later Maciek returned, smiling. "Didn't I tell you? Stas is one of us. He's always ready for a deal."

Inside the apartment, Stas's smile and drooping Pilsudski mustache put me at ease. He was dipping sugar squares into vodka and twirling his mustache with his thick fingers.

"Yes, young man, I've helped many of your Jewish friends. Christ Almighty, it's criminal what these German Huns are doing."

I wanted to know everything right away—how many Jews were using the route, how often, how safe it was, how much it would cost. In the few months our gang had been smuggling through the cemetery, we'd made enough money to afford more payoffs.

"Take it easy, kid, what's your big hurry?" Stas said. "As soon as it gets completely dark, I'll take you up to the roof and explain everything. Here, have some tea and cookies."

I declined and nervously paced the apartment.

"He's upset," Maciek said, explaining my anxiety to the old Pole. "The German beasts may have killed his pal today."

Stas looked out the window. Night had fallen, quiet and black. He unlocked the door and motioned for us to follow. We climbed the stairs to the fifth floor. Stas knocked three times. His son-in-law, a husky young man named Antek, answered. Stas's daughter, Kasia, stood several steps behind, with a baby in her arms.

Without a word, Antek carried a ladder into the hallway and opened the attic hatch. While the others waited below, Antek and I climbed to the roof. We crawled to the edge and looked down.

"There, you see?" Antek pointed. "You slide down the drainpipe, and you land on that roof. That's Nowolipki Street in the ghetto."

My eyes picked out the roof hatch on the building below.

"It looks good, great," I whispered. "I'll get my gang, and we'll be back in an hour or two."

We returned to Stas's apartment. Maciek was beaming. "Stachu, you old rascal, just treat these young *Zydki* well. They're smart and gutsy, and you can make money with them."

Stas nodded, twisted his mustache, and turned to me. "It's a thousand zlotys a head, and three hundred for each sack."

"It's a deal," I said.

We shook hands. Maciek stepped closer. "You see, my son, old Maciek knows how to put a deal together. Let's drink to it." He slapped me on the back with his big hand. I grabbed a glass from a nearby table where Mrs. Staskova had set out vodka and platters of *zakaski*.

"To health and to good business," Stas toasted.

"To Yankele, to Yankele," I said.

"Yeah," Maciek yelled, clutching a tea glass brimming with vodka.

"To our clever *Zydki* and to Poland, to our country." We all gulped our vodka and shouted, "To Poland!"

"To Poland," I repeated, "and to their deaths, the fuckin' *yekes!*" I got angrier. "To those German bitches! May they convulse in agony, those whores, before they ever give birth to another bastard.

"Whores, parasites, fuckin' beasts," I roared on and drank some more.

Old Maciek finally pulled me away from the vodka bottle. He slapped me on the back again and turned to Stas. "Stachu, you treat these kids well, don't you forget that!"

We shook hands again. Maciek and I walked briskly to the Pod Kaczka bar. I thrust a five-hundred-zloty bill into his pocket.

"I wouldn't have asked for it, Jacku," Maciek said. "But you're a customer. So I'll consider it a generous tip."

As we came off the cold street, Jadzia told us that Lutek and Sevek were back. "They're out in front, having some hot soup."

I noticed three heavy sacks of food in the corner. Jadzia smiled at me, and I wanted to grab her. I felt her bare arm and pulled her closer, close enough to be warmed by her breath.

But then I moved away. Yankele was still on my mind. I tried to imagine him escaping that deadly rain of bullets. But in my heart I knew there could be no miracle.

Maciek and the gang entered the back room just as Jadzia was helping me close the sacks with rope. We were ready to go, and Jadzia offered to lead the way.

"It's only a short walk, but you never know. The gendarmes and *szmalcowniki* are all over the place."

Maciek agreed. "It might be a good idea, boys. Go, and may Christ pave the way."

We walked as swiftly as we could. We met no one, despite our fears, and in a few minutes we were safely inside Stas's apartment. While Stas's wife prepared tea and doughnuts, I stepped into the hallway to say goodbye to Jadzia.

The door closed, and she was in my arms. Our lips met in a moist, passionate kiss. She darted her tongue inside my mouth. Her whole body writhed against me. But I pulled away.

"Jadzia, it's the wrong time and the wrong place. Tonight my thoughts are in the ghetto."

I kissed her gently and slipped a bundle of zlotys between her breasts.

"This is for your dad. For supplies. I'll be back in a few days. I like this new route. And I like you."

"God Christ be with you," she murmured and disappeared into the dark.

Back in the apartment, I gave Stas the money we'd agreed on. "A deal is not a deal until it's paid for," I said.

"I always knew that *Zydki* make the best partners." He turned to his wife. "Look at them, Mama Stas. So young, and already such clever businessmen."

We drank our tea and ate the doughnuts Mama Stas placed before us, but none of us was comfortable. Lutek was restless and fidgety; Sevek kept eyeing the numerous Catholic icons and crucifixes in the room; and I was obsessed with thoughts of Yankele. Outside, snow had started to fall.

"It's time to go," I heard Stas say. "Once you cross over to the ghetto, stay overnight in the attic there. My house will be open to you when you return."

Upstairs, he continued his instructions.

"Come back at midnight. You can sleep in Antek's kitchen."

Antek nodded but said nothing. He had none of his father-in-law's warmth, and I didn't entirely trust him. He opened the attic and motioned for us to follow him up the ladder.

Moments later, we were standing precariously at the edge of the roof of Stas's house. I pointed to the drainpipe. "Sevek, you first—and watch yourself. It's slippery with snow. I'll be right behind you."

Sevek grasped the pipe tightly with his gloved hands, then stepped out into space. The pipe creaked and swayed under the strain.

"Will it hold?" I whispered. "That's a death trap, damn it."

Antek shrugged. "Papa Stas promised to fix it. Maybe next week, if he can find the parts."

This wasn't the time to worry. I took hold of the pipe and closed my eyes. I could feel the pipe moving sideways as I swung down. My heart almost stopped when I landed on the roof of the ghetto house below. My hands were bleeding.

I waved to Lutek, and he lowered the supplies on a rope. He followed, and Antek disappeared. We dropped down the hatch into the attic.

"We can't stay here, you guys; it'll be safer in the basement." We dragged ourselves down the steps with our sacks of food.

In the cold, damp basement we had to huddle against each other for warmth. We were exhausted and freezing, but we were still alive.

And you, Yankele?

CHAPTER 7

"Lutek, Sevek, come on, let's go."

They knew where.

Early in the morning, as soon as curfew was lifted, we ran to the cemetery gate.

"Wait here." I pointed to Zalmen's coffee shop at the corner.

Within minutes, I was surrounded by half a dozen Pinkert guards.

"Hey, Jacek! How'd you get back from the other world? Don't you like heaven? We heard you were all gunned down yesterday."

"Shut up!" I shouted as I grabbed one of them. "Damn you, where's Shmerl?"

"He's around here, near the gate. But your buddy Yankele ain't," another remarked.

"You're liars, all of you!"

Shmerl appeared. "It's true, Jacek."

A shudder went through me.

Shmerl led me aside. "Yankele didn't have a chance, but I'm glad at least you got away. What about the others?"

"They're okay," I snapped. "Just tell me what happened."

"Very simple," Shmerl replied. "It was murder. I was right there. I saw it all. The *yekes* didn't get him at first. They were shooting all over the place, remember? But Yankele was smart. He dropped to the ground and rolled into some bushes. The Germans kept firing, and Yankele slipped behind some stones and started running. He was zigzagging through the trees and graves like a deer. You should have seen him. Then he stopped and climbed a tree. All the way up. He'd lost the bastards. But only for a few minutes. Then they were back with dogs.

"I was praying for him," Shmerl continued. "But the dogs smelled him out. They were howling and barking, trying to leap up the tree. So the Germans spotted him. *'Jude, komm herunter! Laus! Schnell!'* they shouted. Yankele ignored them. He climbed out along a branch and jumped to the next tree. He was swinging like a monkey. Then they opened fire. They pumped bullets into the tree, and Yankele fell. He tried to grab the branches on the way down, but he missed. When he hit the ground, the dogs were all over him. The bastards fired some more shots and left him for dead.

"I ran over. He was still conscious. I tried to stop the bleeding with my shirt, but he was too far gone. I tried to tell him he'd be all right, but he knew he was finished. 'Shmerl,' his voice trembled, 'tell Jacek I'm not scared. My pop woulda killed 'em!' Then he died. I swear I did all I could."

"Yankele's dead, isn't he?" Sevek said quietly as I sat down beside him in Zalmen's café. When I didn't respond, Lutek put a comforting arm around my shoulders.

We sat for a long time staring at each other in silence. I didn't know how we were going to tell Yankele's mother. I kept delaying. I finally gulped down a glass of vodka and stood up.

"Let's do it now and get it over with. My aunt Edzia knows Yankele's mother well. We'll get her to help us."

The snow was high in front of Ostrowska 13. No one had cleared the walks. The small, street-level, one-room flat had been converted from a store into a bedroom, kitchen, and living room, all in one. The toilet was in the backyard.

Yankele's mother, older and grayer than her years, stood on thick swollen legs. She was gaunt from starvation.

"Sick as I am, I'm lucky," she greeted us warmly. "I'm lucky to have a son like Yankele. A breadwinner. But with so many mouths to feed, there still isn't enough. The Germans have already destroyed my family. My husband's gone, and my children are out of school. What'll become of them?"

Suddenly she stopped talking and looked suspiciously at Aunt

Edzia, Lutek, Sevek, and me. "What brought you here? What is it? Where's my Yankele? Something's wrong. Something's happened."

"Brace yourself, be courageous." Edzia took her into her arms. "They've killed him. They've murdered Yankele."

With a shriek, Yankele's mother collapsed. When she regained consciousness, her hysterical screams drew a crowd of neighbors into the apartment. They all accused me with hostile eyes.

"The end of a burglar is at the gallows. The end of a smuggler is by a bullet," someone said. The tension became unbearable. I felt so guilty.

Mama had heard the news, and she sobbed uncontrollably when I got home. She smothered me with hugs and kisses.

"No more smuggling, Izaakl. We won't eat. We'll starve. We'll find another way to survive. You mustn't give your young life to these murderers. We stayed up all last night waiting for you to come back."

The next morning, the Pinkert guards opened the cemetery gates and counted the mourners attending Yankele's funeral.

Shmerl took me into the morgue, and together we carried out the plain wooden casket. Shmerl had arranged for a grave by the west wall, near the tree marked "Z" where we had crossed so many times.

As we prepared to lower the casket, Yankele's mother completely surrendered to her hysteria. She pounded her fists against the casket and spoke to her dead son.

"Yankele! *Mein teirer* Yankele, listen to Mama. I know you're going to heaven. You deserve it. Nobody deserves it more. And when you're there, Yankele, please do something for your poor sisters. See they should survive. They should grow up in beauty and find good matches, *latishe* husbands. And maybe there's still a cure for my swollen legs and kidneys. Help us! Help us! I've always depended on you, Yankele. I still do."

We finally had to pull her away.

I tossed the first shovel of earth on the grave and said goodbye to Yankele, the friend of my childhood. Goodbye to my childhood itself.

CHAPTER 8

As I looked around the sorrowful crowd leaving Yankele's grave, I was astonished to see Haim Benkart among the mourners. Before the war, his exploits as a gangster had been legends on Ostrowska Street. Once the Germans came, he set up a smuggling ring that brought many supplies into the ghetto. He had always considered me and my gang a nuisance and a hindrance; he thought our activities might bring increased Gestapo attention and thus endanger his own cemetery operation.

Only a week before, he had tried to scare me into stopping.

"Hey, *yatn,* sons of bitches, you're endangering us all. For every sack you bring through, we bring in ten. If you get caught, the cemetery will be lost to all of us." He grabbed my lapels, pulled me close to his scarred, ugly face. "Stay out! You understand?"

Half a dozen tough bodyguards had surrounded me, but I forced myself to stand calmly and look him in the eye. "You want to get rid of us? Then take us in as partners. We want to eat, too."

He had shoved me to the ground. "Wise guy! I give you ten days to get out, and this time I mean it!"

Today he was standing next to me. "Too bad about Yankele. He was a good kid," he whispered. "But you're tough and smart. You've got what it takes. You can join us! We'll make you a full partner. Only you—not the other *yatn.* They're still kids. Just you alone. Take it or leave it."

I felt blood rush to my face. The great Haim Benkart, the king of smugglers who was thirty, twice my age, was offering me a full partnership.

Concealing my excitement, I looked directly into his eyes but said nothing. The offer was tantalizing. It meant graduating into the big time. But then I'd be just a member of someone else's gang. If I remained a solo operator, I couldn't hope to make it really big, but at least I'd be my own boss. And I wouldn't have to abandon my friends.

I decided on independence.

To keep my own gang together, I had to find a kid to take Yankele's place.

Taking Hela with me, I searched for a tough kid, Aryan-looking so he could pass on the other side.

The first try—Salek Radomski, a friend from the choir. No, Salek would not risk his life daily; he made a living singing at parties in the homes of the ghetto's nouveau riche.

The next stop—Shymekl Hochberg—a great friend from Grandma Masha's neighborhood. No luck; killed by a German bullet climbing the wall for food.

Another idea—Jakub Katz, a school pal. Gone; caught on the Aryan side and tortured at the Pawiak prison. At fourteen, he had become a memory.

"Hela, that's the last stop," I said.

"Oh, Jacku, everything is so sad," Hela lamented. "Let's go home. I'd rather read and listen to Papa's lectures on history and literature."

"I know he's angry at me for not spending enough time with his books," I admitted. "He's right, you know. His books, his lectures, that's our high school."

"So let's go home, I'm so tired," Hela interrupted.

"No. Damn it, one more visit. I have got to find a kid to replace Yankele.

"Listen, I know who!" I suddenly turned around. "Let's go back to Swietojerska Street. He would fit, yes, he has guts and nerve."

"But who, who is it?" Hela ran after me, as I picked up speed and paced the sidewalk, zigzagging to avoid the late evening crowds.

"Motek Grinberg, don't you remember, my classmate, my chess competitor? Motek, the kid with the patent-leather shoes and a sister

Mala, tall and beautiful.'' I talked and walked briskly, holding Hela's hand.

We asked the neighbors about the Grinberg family.

"Oh, the Grinbergs, down in that basement,'' a neighbor replied. "Their big second-floor apartment is now occupied by two *Judenrat* families,'' another neighbor interrupted.

We stood in front of a damp-smelling entrance, and I knocked at the door. An old woman stuck her head out.

"What do you want from us? Please go away.''

"But Mrs. Grinberg, it's me, Jacek,'' I stammered in embarrassment. I wasn't sure if it was really Mrs. Grinberg; she looked so old and gray and dazed.

She opened the door a bit wider and stared at me in silence.

"Where is Motek? I want to talk to him.''

"Oh, Jacek! And that one, that's your sister Hela—am I right? It must be. Please come in, come in.'' She led us inside. "I'm so sorry I did not recognize you. It's all so confused, all so fuzzy.''

I was stunned at what I saw. The once affluent Grinberg family was now living in a cold, foul-smelling basement. No furniture, no chairs, only a broken bench. Clothing that looked more like rags was hanging on nails from the walls. And instead of the lively and elegant Mrs. Grinberg I remembered, in front of me stood a depressed and sloppy woman who looked twice her age.

"It's so nice of you to come,'' she managed to say. "Sit on that bench. It's all we have left. We had to sell the furniture for food and heat.'' Her voice was still very delicate and refined.

"And Motek, is he around?'' I persisted.

"Motek? I thought you knew, I thought you came to pay respects.'' She sighed deeply, desperately.

"Motek is gone. From typhoid. Only last week!'' She began to sob. "He's lying somewhere in a mass grave. Oh, God, not even a grave to put a flower on or a stone to tell his name.'' She sat down next to me and wiped away the tears that streamed down her wrinkled face.

"Where are Shmulek and Mala?'' Hela asked.

"Shmulek's in bed.'' Mrs. Grinberg pointed to a curtained area. "It's the warmest place here. He is still so weak from typhoid! And Mala. Mala's the only bright spot in my life. Mala's with a girl friend on the Aryan side. She refused to stay here and die slowly, so she crossed over the wall with her friend. I couldn't stop her. And why should I? With all the disease and hunger here, how could I say no? For a few weeks, I heard nothing from her. I thought she was dead, caught by the Gestapo. Then I got this letter."

She handed me a thin piece of paper. "Here, read this. You know, somebody smuggled it to me."

There were only a few scrawled lines, apparently written in haste:

Dear Mama,

I'm safe and well in Praga. We're working for a Christian family doing housework. But I don't know how long we can stay here. They know we're Jewish, and they're afraid to keep us because of Gestapo raids in the neighborhood. As soon as we save some money, we'll leave. I'll keep in touch. Halina sends her love. I love you all.

Mala

"Who's Halina?"

"Mala's friend. You should remember her, Jacek. A tall girl with blond braids. They were with us in Swider every summer."

I thought my heart would stop beating. I couldn't believe my ears. Halina! A girl my age with large blue eyes and long blond hair. Our families had vacationed in Swider, a summer resort near Warsaw, for years. But the summer before the war, when she and I were both thirteen, Halina suddenly seemed different. She was no longer just another tall skinny girl. Her breasts were fuller, her lips more inviting, her walk provocative. I spent less time playing soccer with the boys and more time with Halina.

We used to swim to the old wooden bridge and hide. It was there that I kissed her for the first time, touched her breasts, felt her tremble. It was there that we planned to meet each other every Saturday on the Leszno Street *deptak,* the promenade meeting place. It was there that we shared our fears about the future, about the possibility of war. It was there that I heard her say, "I love you, Jacku."

When that summer ended, the bombings began. We never met at the *deptak.* And when I finally was able to go to her house, all I found was a bombed-out building. Neighbors said her family had escaped to the provinces before the bombing. I couldn't find out anything more about her.

Now, after all this time, the sound of her name was still overwhelming. Would she remember me? Would she be as beautiful as ever? How would we feel when we saw each other again?

It felt so good to think about the days before the war. It felt like another lifetime.

And all that mattered at that moment was seeing Halina. I had to find her as soon as possible.

I copied Mala's address from the letter and returned it to her mother.

"Maybe I'll be able to help them, get them some money," I said. "Meanwhile, here's something for you." I stuffed some bills into the pocket of her housedress.

"Where'd you get all this money?"

"We have to fight back, Mrs. Grinberg. We are learning to fight back and survive!"

Abruptly, I got up from my seat and walked to the curtain that divided the room. With no explanations or apologies, I pulled it aside and walked over to the big double bed.

"Shmulek, is that you under those *shmates?*" I pulled the stinking blanket off him. "Come on. Get over here and talk to me."

Slowly he pushed his emaciated body down the bed, like an old man. His face was pathetic, his skin drawn and yellow.

"Listen, you're fourteen, only one year younger than Motek," I said. "There's no reason why you can't join us. Whatever I can do, you can do. But first, you have to get out of this stinking grave of a basement. You can stay with my friend, Sevek. He's your age, and you'll like him. There's food in his house, and you'll recover fast."

Shmulek looked astonished. "I want to go back to bed," he stammered. "I'm still sick."

I grabbed his long unkempt hair and looked him straight in the eyes. "It's time you got well. And I won't take no for an answer."

Shmulek's resistance was weakening.

"Look, Shmulek, in here, the Germans have you beat. With us, you can fight back."

"Do you really want me?" he asked.

"Yes. So what do you say?"

A smile spread on Shmulek's face. He looked at his mother, at Hela, and then at me.

I placed my open palm in front of him. "Put it here, pal. You're now my partner. Get dressed."

I felt good when I left Swietojerska Street that night. I had a new member in my gang and Halina's address in my pocket.

CHAPTER 9

The next morning I told the gang, "Tonight at midnight I'll cross over to Stas for a trial run of the new route, the new *melina.* We've got to plan this thing carefully. I should be back in a day or two, so be patient."

Even though I often used Shmerl's hidden telephone line to the Aryan side, I still made the arrangements with Jadzia in code.

"Young Kowalski has recovered and is ready to go."

"Will Monday be all right to take him out of the hospital?"

"Monday is fine. But please prepare plenty of food for him."

"Okay. Thanks for calling."

My gang, including my sister Hela, accompanied me before curfew to the Nowolipki Street basement.

I waited there till midnight. Then, up on the roof, I watched for Antek's arrival, but all I could see was a dark blue sky with millions of stars. I crept to the drainpipe and examined it. It shook when I touched it. It was filthy, too, and had a few holes in it.

But we could tighten it, I thought. And then we could seal the holes with plaster or rubber patches. An exciting plan began to form in my mind. We would connect this pipe with another one that reached into the roof opening of the ghetto house. It would be a true pipeline! Anything we poured into the top of the pipe from the Aryan roof would go straight down to the ghetto attic.

So what if the pipes weren't clean? Dirty food is better than none at all. We would pour big quantities of grain—wheat, rice, kasha—into the ghetto. And then it hit me. Milk! With this setup, we could bring in milk, which was unavailable in the ghetto at any price. I could pour in hundreds of gallons, thousands of gallons, of milk for the kids.

I was in a world of my own imagining, feeling jubilant and victorious. Poland and France were in defeat, Russia was on her knees, my father and the *Judenrat* were beaten. But not me.

Suddenly I heard a soft whistle from above. It was Antek. I signaled, and he lowered a rope. I pulled myself up. Soon I was in his kitchen, in Aryan Warsaw.

I felt in my pocket for the small piece of paper with Halina's address. The sun couldn't rise fast enough for me to go to her.

I woke up early the next morning and rushed downstairs to Stas's apartment. Jadzia was already there, waiting for me. Together we walked over to the Pod Kaczka.

The bar was closed on Mondays, and old Maciek was away visiting his grandchildren. Jadzia looked radiant that morning, and she knew it. In her almost transparent housedress, she was provocative and irresistible.

I ate my breakfast, trying hard to control my desire to seize her as she hovered over me.

"By the way, Jadzia, did your father buy those supplies for me?"

"Of course, Jacku. Come with me and see for yourself."

She led me to the basement and pointed to several sacks of flour, beans, and sugar standing against the wall. "That's all for you, Jacku—and so am I." She unbuttoned her robe and confronted me, stark naked.

My resistance crumbled as she rubbed her body against mine. She felt so warm and soft, all breasts and lips. So there on that old sofa, we shared our pleasure as she slowly undressed me. She explored my body with her tongue, brushed my penis with butterfly kisses. I consumed her until she lay still in my arms.

"What a pity you're Jewish, Jacku. But maybe you're not really. Most Jews are dark, but your eyes and hair are just like mine."

I smiled and pointed to my penis. "That's true. But look, I am a Jew, because *all* Jews are circumcised."

We both laughed, and she kissed me again and again.

"Jadzia, I have to go now. I have to find someone in Praga. Tell your father I'll be back tonight. Tell him something's up. Something big."

Jadzia asked no questions. She led me gently to the back door. "Be careful, Jacku. Praga's very far. There'll be Gestapo and *szmalcowniki* everywhere. Please be careful. And hurry back."

By mid-afternoon, I was standing at the front door of a comfortable villa at Grochowska Street in Praga. I rang the bell. A young woman with a scarf on her head peeked out the window. I smiled and signaled for her to open the door. She opened it only partially.

"Mala, it's me, Jacek, Jacek Eisner."

She closed the door in my face, then looked at me again through the window.

I scribbled a few words of greeting from her mother and slipped the paper under the door. A moment later, I heard the chain fall from the latch.

She motioned for me to follow her to the basement, where she bolted the door behind us. Then she turned and looked me up and down.

"You're Jacek, Motek's classmate? I hardly recognized you. You've grown so tall. And in those clothes, you look so *goyish,* like a real Christian. I was afraid to let you in."

"You've got to be careful," I said. "I took some chances coming here myself. Your mother said you're here with a girl friend."

"Halina. She should be back soon."

I had really found her!

"Jacek, you wouldn't believe how lonely we are here. It's so good to see you. How is my family? Tell me everything."

"They're cold and hungry, but they're fine. They were sick for a while with typhoid. It's been moving through the ghetto."

"But now they're all right?" Mala asked.

"All except Motek." I reached out for her hand.

"What do you mean?"

"Mala, Motek is dead."

For a moment she just stood there, staring at me.

"Those goddamn Germans," she cried. "This goddamn war! When will it end? Why did you have to bring me this news?"

Mala moved to the other side of the room.

"I let myself have dreams," she said. "I let myself have silly hopes that this misery was going to be over soon. And now you come along and ruin it all for me. Poor Motek. Oh, what's the use! We're all doomed, I know it."

I went over to her.

"Now look, Mala. If anyone can survive in your family, it's you. You look gentile, and it'll be easier for you because you're a girl; you aren't circumcised. But you need will power and strength. I came to help you, but you've got to help yourself first."

I took out a packet of money. "I understand from your mother that you have to get out of here. This will help you find another hide-out."

There was a soft knock at the window.

"It's Halina." Mala ran upstairs to the door.

Halina entered the basement room and stopped abruptly. She caught her breath in disbelief. It was obvious she recognized me.

I stood transfixed. She was the same Halina I had known, but two years older, more mature, and strikingly beautiful. Her blond hair hung loosely below her shoulders. Her skin seemed translucent.

Our eyes met.

"Jacku! Is it you?" she said at last. "Is it really you? I thought I'd never see you again."

"You know each other?"

"He's the one I told you about, Mala. The boy I loved in Swider."

I took her in my arms and kissed her. Then I stepped back and looked at her again. "Halina, I can't believe it."

My eyes wandered up and down in delight. She was practically my height, and she had become a beautiful woman, but her smile was still innocent, and the way her eyelids opened only half way made her look slightly embarrassed.

"I came looking for you after the bombing. Your neighbors told me you'd gone. They didn't know where."

Mala discreetly disappeared, leaving us alone.

"Jacku, so much has happened. It's been so horrible . . ."

"Don't talk, Halina. Don't say anything. Just let me hold you."

In the dimly lit basement, her warmth and closeness exhilarated me. Her touch and her fragrance sent shivers through my body.

"Oh, Jacku," she continued, "everything we ever knew and loved is gone."

"I know, Halina. It's all madness. But tell me, how are your parents?"

"I don't know. We went to Wyszkow because my father thought we'd be safer there. Then, one day, the Germans came and made a selection, and we were separated. I got sent back to Warsaw. I don't know what happened to them. I never saw them again."

"You mean you were in the ghetto, and you didn't contact me?"

"I tried to find you. I looked for you. But I heard you were on the Aryan side."

"Yes, I was with a Christian friend of my father's."

"Anyway, the ghetto was so horrible," she went on, the story pouring out of her. "I stayed with a cousin until the Germans took him away for forced labor. I had nowhere to go. I was hungry and lonely. One day, I met Mala, and she took me home with her. But Jacku, you wouldn't believe how they were living. Everyone was sick and starving. It was awful. So Mala and I decided to leave, no matter what. We had no money, but we just went. We figured we'd find a job on the Aryan side with a Christian family.

"And we did. We were lucky. Mrs. Laskowska took us both in, and we've been here ever since. We work in the house and the garden. On Sundays we go to church, or sometimes we shop in the market. It hasn't been too bad. They know we're Jewish, and they've accepted it. But it's getting riskier every day. The Germans just caught some Jews hiding with Christian friends and dragged them all away to Auschwitz."

Halina continued without a pause. "Mrs. Laskowska has already given us two deadlines to leave, but when we start crying and begging, she always feels sorry for us and lets us stay. Since seven this morning, I've been looking for a job in some of the villages. But everywhere I go, they always ask for a *Kennkarte,* you know, an identification pass. I guess it's hopeless."

"It's not hopeless," I said. "I can help you. That's why I'm here. Listen, from now on, things are going to be different. You'll find another hideout in another suburb. And make sure Mrs. Laskowska doesn't know where you've gone. The Germans might question her."

Mala returned. "Mrs. Laskowska will be back any minute. I think you'd better go now, Jacek."

Halina and I clung together for a final moment. I pulled her face close to mine.

"Jacku, when will I see you again? How? Oh, my God! It's like a dream."

"It's like a dream for me, too, Halina. I can't believe you really exist and that I've found you again."

I gave her the coded addresses of Franek and Maciek. "You can trust these people. They'll know how to reach me. The money I gave Mala should last for awhile, but I'll bring more next time I see you. I promise, it'll be very soon."

I kissed them both, then walked to the door.

"And Mala," I said, "don't worry about your family. Shmulek has joined my gang. We're going to make it. Screw the Germans. We're going to survive."

CHAPTER 10

"Listen, you big hero," Maciek yelled. "We're loaded with sacks of food, and you vanish. You pick the best day we had to get the stuff out of here, and you cruise all over Warsaw. What's wrong with you?"

"Don't scream at me, old man. Just take it easy, okay? I'm back, right? And I've got it all worked out."

I outlined my scheme.

"Up their ass, Papa Maciek," I concluded. "We can even pour milk through that pipe. Milk! How do you like that!"

Maciek slapped me on the back. "Christ! The kid has done it again! Jadzia, bring the vodka. And quick. We're going to see Stas. Wait till he hears this one."

He poured me a glass of vodka. "Now, what about the sacks in the basement?"

"I'll take some with me tonight. But Stas has to fix the pipe, and I want him to get a rope ladder up to the roof."

We toasted to success, and Jadzia whispered in my ear, "May God protect you, you horny devil."

In a few minutes, I had explained my plan to Stas.

"Excellent," Stas said. "In fact, I had the same idea, but there was no one on the other side I could trust."

He promised that the repairs would be finished in a few days. "But remember, the deal is still three hundred a sack. No matter how many you deliver, no price reduction."

* * *

By the weekend, everything was set. We had found a small flat near the attic. It would be our base in the ghetto. We had to find other quarters for the elderly Viennese refugee couple we displaced, but the handsome sum of money they received more than compensated them for their inconvenience.

Friday evening, as prearranged, I received a coded telephone call from Jadzia. Hela, the gang, and I all prepared ourselves for Monday.

"We need twenty thousand zlotys and plenty of sacks and rope," I instructed them. "And remember, you guys, if it comes down to it, you use your Luftwaffe switchblades. Lutek, you're in charge while I'm gone."

Sunday night, Sevek and I crossed over the roof. With old Maciek's help, we spent all day Monday preparing more than ten sacks of supplies.

After nightfall, we carried the fifty-kilo sacks to Antek's attic. Promptly at midnight, we hauled them up to the roof and over to the drainpipe. I strained in the dark to see whether it actually extended into the opening of the ghetto attic, some thirty feet below. I couldn't tell, but Stas had assured me it was okay.

Sevek and I opened the first sack and began to pour. We started with kasha so we could track the sound. I looked for a sign from below. Nothing for a minute, then the roof hatch opened. A shadow emerged and waved. The kasha had been received.

We emptied sack after sack into the pipe. We finished at about three in the morning and fell asleep in Antek's kitchen. On Tuesday, we went shopping for new supplies. All day I worried about Lutek and Shmulek: whether they had proceeded as arranged; whether they had gotten the sacks safely to the hideout; whether they had disposed of the food.

Mendel Bonk, my contact man with the Smocza Bazaar black market dealers, was of great help. For a small cut, he auctioned the food off to the highest bidder. Soon I found out that the dealers divided each haul among themselves. They would transport the food on camouflaged rickshaws to different neighborhoods in the ghetto, where it would be sold from stands and shops.

On the second night, the process went much faster. We were more efficient and less anxious. We paid Maciek, Stas, and Antek for their services and were ready to leave. After the last sack was emptied, we descended into the ghetto house. Hela, Lutek, and Shmulek greeted us with great excitement. We were all jubilant; we could not suppress our feelings of accomplishment.

As the days went by, the smuggling process became virtually routine. My major concern was security. I figured we needed as much protection as we could get, so I followed Maciek's advice and put the local Polish blues on the payroll.

Soon we celebrated the first delivery of fresh milk to the ghetto. More than twenty huge glass jars. The jars used to hold the preserves my Grandma Masha made from the summer's fruits; now they held milk for the starving babies and children of the ghetto. We donated all of the first day's milk to the infirmary.

Our enterprise thrived. At least three days a week, Sevek and I posed as Christian kids from Praga and wandered around Aryan Warsaw, shopping, packing, bribing.

Occasionally some of the *szmalcowniki* would stop me. I was scared, but cash would usually get rid of them. Sometimes, though, if the street were quiet, I'd lure them into a backyard, draw my switchblade, and scare the hell out of their anti-Semitic souls.

We had really become big-time smugglers.

CHAPTER 11

"Jacku, you're risking your life every time you come to see me," Halina said. "And I'm going crazy here waiting. All I do is worry about you. I can't think about anything else. Let me come to the ghetto with you. Please. It's got to make more sense than this."

Instead of answering, I kissed her. The love we had once felt for each other had been rekindled. But now it was much deeper. Our kisses were consuming, our embraces desperate. Our passion was intensified by the constant danger we were in and by the long intervals between our visits. We both measured time by our need for each other. Our days apart seemed endless.

Nevertheless, I didn't want to bring Halina back to the ghetto. I had a different plan. I remembered that my father's friend Franek had offered to hide Hela and me in his summer cottage in Milanowek. If I could move Mala and Halina there, just twenty-five miles from Warsaw, that would be the safest solution. Later, Hela and I could join them.

So I contacted Franek. He was pleased he could help and promised to have the basement of his cottage ready for us in ten days.

Everything seemed so simple and well arranged. But I wasn't happy. Deep inside, I felt uneasy about abandoning the ghetto. I felt like a coward, running for my own safety, deserting my parents, my Grandma Masha, my cousins, and my gang.

My mother made me feel even worse. "If we're hungry, we're hungry together," she cried. "If we're sick, we're sick together. How can you talk of leaving? At least, here we know what it's like. What do you know about Milanowek?"

Each explanation I attempted brought forth a fresh gush of tears. Mama was inconsolable. I struggled to convince myself that my plans would work, that I could manage to live on the Aryan side and still not have to abandon my family. My torment was genuine, but events had taken on their own momentum.

The hideout was ready. On a Thursday evening, Halina and Mala secretly took a train to Milanowek. It was arranged that Hela would join them on Saturday.

"There's only one thing I still must do," I told Hela. "I've got to get a new pair of boots on Wolska Street. Just one more smuggling mission and these boots, and then, goodbye smuggling, goodbye gang. Papa can have the ones I'm wearing. They're still in good condition."

"He's taking away my only daughter, my Hayele, and all he thinks about is boots," Mama wailed.

"Thank you, Jacek," Papa mixed in. "But what would I do with fancy boots? *Es past nisht.* For you it's all right. You're a fighter, a rebel. But not for me. I belong to a different generation.

"I know what you think of us," Papa went on. "You think we are defeatists. This enemy is out to destroy us, and you want to fight them with your bare hands, to die a hero. But Jews aren't raised to be heroes. First we have to survive. You say the Nazis are different. I agree. But all of Europe has collapsed before this Austrian house painter, so what can *we* do?"

He placed his hands on my shoulders. "My son, you do what you feel you must do. But don't expect me or my generation to change. We are the product of two thousand years of exile." He looked at me with a mixture of pride and resignation.

Meanwhile, Hela tried to console Mama. "We'll come back, we'll visit you, maybe once a month. We'll be back, Mama, you'll see."

The atmosphere in the Kiercelak Market the next morning troubled me. There were rumors of Gestapo traps, and we saw Jew hunters all around. By noon, I had decided to leave the market.

"Huj wam w dupe, up your ass, you sons of bitches!" I snapped at

two of my regular suppliers. "You're out of your minds with these prices. I swear by Christ, Holy Mother Czestochowska, I'll buy nothing, absolutely nothing!"

One of them replied, "But, Jacku, wounded Christ, believe us. With everybody talking about a raid, there's hardly anything available. There are probably some Gestapo agents here right now. The dealers just aren't delivering today. Why don't you wait a few days?"

I turned to Sevek, who had just bought a bottle of vodka and a couple of salamis. "This market stinks. Let's get out of here, and go pick up the boots."

We took a trolley to Wolska Street, to Kowalczyk, the old master cobbler. No signs advertised his shop. Kowalczyk specialized in officers' boots, and he obtained all his leather on the black market. A customer had to be personally recommended before he would accept, or even negotiate, an order.

Maciek had recommended me, and my boots were ready. Kowalczyk held them up, one at a time. He spat on the leather and buffed the boots with his sleeves until they glowed. Tools, nails, wood pins, and pieces of leather lay scattered about on low worktables. Not a machine was in sight.

"All handmade," Kowalczyk beamed. "And did you know, you son of a bitch big shot, it takes me and my helper a whole week, twelve hours a day, to finish one pair?"

I loved them. There was a pair for me and one for Lutek.

"How about me?" Sevek complained. "When do I get mine?"

Kowalczyk promised to have Sevek's boots in a month. "Patience, young man. It takes time." He dropped the boots in an old sack. I paid him, and we left.

Then, on our way to the trolley, it happened. Two young thugs sprang at us with knives.

"*Zydy parchy!* You Jewish parasites, keep your mouths shut and do as you're told!"

"Hey! Jesus Christ, you scared the shit outta me!" I figured they were the kind of blackmailers I'd dealt with before. "What do you want? C'mon, let's talk this over."

I felt the knife against my jacket. One of them said, "I told you to shut your fuckin' mouth! Now walk down the block near the wall and turn right at the corner. Move!"

Frightened, we followed orders. At the corner, we turned and were immediately confronted by a Polish policeman, who shoved us into an alley.

The blue ordered us to empty our pockets and unload everything. I knew then that we'd been followed all the way from the Kiercelak Market, maybe even from Maciek's place.

I tried desperately to negotiate a deal as I turned over my money. No such luck. The thugs beat us, and the policeman cursed us. "You monkeys belong in the ghetto," he said, "not here, eating our bread."

"Holy Ghost, Jesus Christ!" I cried out. "What do you guys want? I told you, you're making a mistake. We're just as Catholic as you. Why don't we talk business?" They laughed at me.

"Let's strip these fuckin' worms and inspect their Jewish pricks," one of the thugs said.

My blood was boiling. In a flash, I drew my switchblade and grabbed the startled blue. Using him as a shield, I held the blade to his throat.

"You bastards! Now you've gone too far! Sevek, get the money and boots."

I dragged the policeman deeper into the alley.

"Hand it over, or this anti-Semitic son of a bitch'll have his cabbage head on the floor! Quick! I mean business!"

The thugs stood motionless, the loot and knives still in their hands. I turned to the blue.

"You! Talk if you want to live!"

I loosened my grip on his throat.

"Do what he says, boys. This kid has got the nerve to do it. *Rodacy.* Christ will bless you for saving me."

The thugs gave Sevek the money.

"You're pretty clever *Zydki,*" the blue stuttered. "Let's compromise. You keep the money. We keep the boots. And you go free. How about it, *Zydki?* A deal?"

"I should cut your fuckin' throat. Christ knows, you deserve it. But it's a deal—if you do what I say."

The entire incident had taken just a few minutes. Suddenly, a German patrol passed near the alley. As the gendarmes looked in, I pushed the policeman with all my strength. He reeled into his accomplices. Screaming, they fell against the Germans.

I grabbed Sevek's arm and pulled him deeper into the alley.

"Jude! Jude! Jude!"

Shots shattered the quiet.

We raced across the yard. Sevek lagged behind. I waved him on, and he picked up speed.

Into a building.

Up to the roof.

Now there were footsteps, Polish and German voices.

We were at the roof's edge, and Sevek froze.

"What do we do now?" he asked.

I peered down. "We've got to jump. We can make the roof below."

Sevek drew back. "It's two stories. We'll be killed."

"It's the only way."

"I can't, Jacku. I can't."

"Yes, you can. You have to." I seized and shook him. "I'll go first. You follow me. You hear?"

Sevek was trembling. "Whatever you say, Jacku. But here, take the money."

I pushed the bundles down my shirt and leaped. I fell forward and cried out in pain. My right palm and thumb were mashed and bleeding. I heard shots. The Germans had opened fire. Sevek jumped and sprawled beside me. He couldn't stand up. His right leg was bleeding.

"Go, Jacku! Go! My leg's busted. Go!"

"No, dammit. If you stay here, you're lost. They'll be up there on the roof any minute. Move," I screamed and grabbed Sevek's arm. On my hands and knees, I crawled backwards down the steep roof, pulling Sevek along.

"Here, Sevek, we'll slide down, you'll make it, you have to try . . ."

A hail of bullets ripped the roof apart. Sevek screamed. More bullets, more shouts in German, more blood, more smoke. I saw a bloody mess roll down the roof.

"Sevek!" I cried. "Sevek, Sevek!" I slid down the drainpipe. My hands were bleeding, my clothes were torn, my heart was crying, "Sevek!"

I landed on the street, and so did Sevek. His small, round face smashed against the pavement. Bloody clothing and twisted bones bounced. Then a fountain of blood.

I raised my bleeding hands to cover my face and hurled my body against the wall.

"Sevek, Sevek . . ." I screamed hysterically.

I heard noises, people shouting, running, pushing past me. I panicked. My instincts took over. I moved along the walls on the sidewalk across the street. I saw a streetcar. I ran. I jumped on it at full speed. I curled up in a corner of the platform and pretended to be drunk.

The sounds of machine gun fire, the sounds of Sevek's last scream echoed in my ears. I wiped the blood off my hands, and I sobbed.

I felt someone's boots battering my ribs. It was the conductor. I heard him say, "Hey, you drunk, *alembik,* you bum, get off at the next stop." The conductor kicked me down the steps.

I walked, then ran till I found a bar, where I ordered a double vodka, then disappeared into the toilet to clean up. Another vodka gave me the courage to venture out again. I paid the bartender and walked down Okopowa Street.

My mind went blank for a moment. I forgot what I was doing, where I was going. I saw Sevek's bullet-riddled body lying on the pavement. I saw his smashed face. I kept walking. I was in a daze. I couldn't stop shaking.

In the distance, I could make out Maciek's place. All I wanted was to go to Jadzia's bedroom, lock myself in with a bottle, and sleep.

But a shadowy figure stopped me. It was old Stas. He tugged at my sleeve and motioned me to follow.

"Not now, Stas. Get out of my way. I'm heading for Maciek's."

"For the love of Christ, Jacku, don't say a word. Just listen and follow me. You're in great danger, and so am I. We all are. Someone's spilled the setup.

"They carted off old Maciek this morning. They beat the hell outta him and put Jadzia under house arrest. Gestapo agents are in the bar right now, waiting for you to show up. They confiscated all the food, maybe ten sacks or more."

I was stunned. "Stas, don't play games with me. Tell me the truth, or I warn you . . ."

"It's all true, I swear on the Holy Ghost. God's my witness. I know you're not a squealer. But under Gestapo torture, who knows? You might give us all away."

"Fuckin' *mosrim,* squealers, bastards. Just wait till I lay my hands on them." At that moment I could have killed.

We reached the Evangelical Cemetery and headed for a dark corner.

"Jacku, we've taken down the pipe," Stas went on. "These German sons-of-bitches are really out to get us this time. Antek and I are going to my brother's in Powazki until this quiets down. I beg you, Jacku, please. No monkey business. Don't use the Wolnosc Street *meline*. Don't involve us any further."

We left the cemetery in opposite directions.

In complete despair, I headed for the center of the city, to the crowds, where I could sit safely at a café and think. I went to Gogolewski's on Jerozolimskie Boulevard and ordered tea. I sat in a corner and pretended to read a newspaper. A thousand thoughts went through my mind. Maciek and Jadzia were in trouble. But what about Lutek and Shmulek? If it really was a frame-up, the Gestapo would go to the attic and catch them.

I left the café and hurried to the nearby post office. I mailed a coded letter to Halina, warning her not to leave the house until she heard from me again.

There were only a few hours left before curfew. The trolley was the fastest way back to the ghetto. I took a deep breath and jumped on the last car.

At the ghetto gate, as usual, a Polish blue and a German gendarme got on board, and the streetcar proceeded into the walled-in zone. I looked the blue right in the eyes and waited for a response. He stood proud and stiff, showing no reaction.

Leszno Street and then Karmelicka disappeared behind us. I pretended to enjoy the ride through the "zoo." Suddenly I heard the blue whisper, "Are you Jewish?"

His voice was reassuring, so I handed him a bribe and jumped. Then I turned the corner quickly onto Dzielna Street, entered the Nowolipki Street courtyard, and looked up at the roofs around me. Nothing unusual.

I ran up the stairs to the attic apartment. Everything was neatly prepared for the delivery. The boys had lined the room with more than twenty jars. I removed them, then covered anything that might betray us.

Lutek and Shmulek arrived just as I was about to leave. I motioned to them not to talk, but to get out quickly with all the stuff. They obliged. They knew something was wrong. No one uttered a word. We loaded up and disappeared. I told them about the frameup, about the whole goddamn mess.

"What about Sevek?" they kept asking.

I kept avoiding the question. And then suddenly it spilled out of me.

"Sevek is on Mlynarska Street. His brain is smashed. His face and his body are torn apart. Sevek is dead."

CHAPTER 12

Mama threw herself at me the moment I entered our apartment and hugged me again and again.

"Something must have happened. Izaakl, *derbarm zich,* have mercy on yourself and all of us. I know something must have happened. But you are alive and well. Thank God for that!"

When she finally released me, I saw the distress in her eyes. "Oh, Izaakl, I am so worried about your sister. Come see." She led me into the bedroom where Hela was stretched out. Her cheeks were flushed and her eyes glazed. "She came down with chills and pains in her legs late this morning. Only half an hour ago, the thermometer showed almost a hundred and five degrees."

I knew my sister was very ill, probably with typhoid. I told Mama to prepare a bed in the basement.

"If the fever isn't down by morning, Hayele, we'll have to hide you below the shop on Twarda Twenty-nine," I told her. "Otherwise, we'll all have to go through the disinfection."

Hela nodded and asked me to sit with her awhile, to tell her what had gone wrong. I forced myself to stay awake and quietly and gently recounted to my sister and mother the day's sad story. Hela tried to listen but soon fell asleep.

Mother helped me spread out a blanket and pillow on the balcony. "Oh, *Goteniu,* keep watch over my children," she wailed. "As long as my Izaakl is well, we will not starve!"

It didn't take long before I, too, fell into a deep sleep.

Both Mama and Papa had come down with typhoid during the epidemic of 1918, so they were immune. But Hela and I were not. Mama was afraid I would get it, too. Since I'd gone through every childhood disease, she considered me especially susceptible, quite the opposite of Hela, who had never spent a day in bed.

Mama's instinct proved correct. I never got to meet my friends the next morning. Nor could I worry about Sevek's funeral. I woke up with all the symptoms: headache, fever, pains. We moved Hela into the basement, and by noon I was lying beside her in another bunk.

The disease took its toll. Hela and I lay semiconscious with high temperatures, oblivious to everything. There were no medicines available and no known cure. No one called a doctor, because he couldn't help. In fact, he might even betray our hideout. Our illness had to be kept a secret from everyone to avoid the dreaded disinfecting ordeal.

Mama attended us day and night, wiping our sweat, putting cold towels on our heads, giving us small sips of water, keeping out all visitors. She hardly slept. When she did, she was fully dressed, sitting on a nearby bench.

Occasionally Papa came down. When I opened my eyes, I could see him near Mama, reading. Straining to keep alert and to concentrate my thoughts, I asked, "Papa, what are you reading about? Have you found any precedent in history for what is happening to us now?"

Papa didn't answer me. He couldn't bear to explain his shattered world.

At times, I was conscious of what was happening around me, but often I would slip into a long dream. I traveled distances in time, across continents into wishful, imaginary worlds.

I dreamed of being a general in an illusionary Jewish state. I dreamed of visiting Warsaw, the ghetto streets, walking down Ostrowska and Smocza, being mobbed in greeting by the little Jewish kids of the neighborhood.

But the children turned into dancing skeletons. I tried to touch them but could not. I saw them laugh and shout, but I could not hear them. I yelled at them, "Look at me. I am strong and powerful. I am a Jewish general with an army. Do not be afraid, you are not being hunted any longer!"

But they ignored me. They continued dancing and jumping and laughing at me. Their sarcastic laughter echoed in my ears.

That dream persisted throughout my illness.

On the tenth night, I was almost unconscious, lying in a sea of sweat. Then, early the next morning when things looked bleakest, my fever suddenly broke. Mama put a trembling hand to my forehead.

"Izaakl, you're cold. And your eyes are clear. It's a miracle. God's will. *Kanane hore.*" She spat three times to ward off the evil eye.

I asked for water, food, then more water. I raised my head and looked over to Hela. "How is she?"

Hela was asleep, breathing heavily. She still had a high fever. I felt as if I'd just emerged from a dark tunnel into a bright blooming garden. My crisis was over.

Within a few days, I was back on my feet. My appetite returned, and I regained most of the weight I'd lost.

Mama was puzzled. She had expected Hela to recover first. She now focused her full energies on her daughter, who was still struggling in that dark, morbid basement.

Hela's condition worsened. She went down to less than eighty pounds. She was unconscious most of the time. After her third week in bed, we reluctantly called in Dr. Grynszpan, an old family friend. He diagnosed her condition as critical. Complications had developed, and she was suffering from uremia, a kidney disease.

Mama was beside herself, watching helplessly as her only daughter lay close to death.

Dr. Grynszpan and I searched the black market in vain for the necessary drugs to help Hela. "If only I had the proper medication, I might be able to do something," he said.

"Doctor, tell me what you need. Write a prescription."

I had no idea where I could find that medicine, but I was determined to save my sister.

"I doubt if there's any of this medicine in the ghetto," the doctor said as he wrote the prescription. "You'll have to try the Aryan side. But hurry. Your sister must have these shots within twenty-four hours. Her life is in your hands."

I stuffed some bills and a few gold coins into my boots.

Mama was there, listening to our conversation.

"Izaakl, I am scared for you," Mama said. "Maybe you should not go?"

She sounded perplexed and undecided. Her face revealed her conflict. She was afraid of losing her son while trying to save her daughter, risking the safety of one child for the chance of saving the other.

"I'll be back, Mama. I'll be back. Don't worry." I kissed her and ran down the steps.

I knew I had to make the trip across the wall if Hela was to have any chance at all. And I longed for Halina. A trip out of the ghetto would give me the opportunity to visit her for at least a few hours.

I walked in the direction of the cemetery. The years of smuggling had conditioned me automatically to choose the safest routes. Riding the trolley out of the ghetto was more dangerous than riding it back in, so I chose the old cemetery route. There were no more funerals now, only mass burials.

I found Shmerl and told him about Hela. I asked for his help and pushed a thousand zlotys into his hand. He refused the money and told me to wait at Zalmen's coffee shop across the street. His rejection of the money and his sympathy surprised me.

I'd grown cynical and distrustful of people. I had already witnessed man's cruelest and most inhuman behavior. I was fond of animals and would often play with stray dogs or cats. I'd take them home, feed them, pet them. They never harmed me. But I'd learned not to trust people.

I waited restlessly at the coffee shop. I thought about Hela. And about Halina. No one around me knew much about my relationship with her. My feelings of love and need were very private.

Shmerl returned at last. "What luck," he whispered. "We've got the right *yeke* on guard. Fritz is the best around here, and he owes me a favor." He put his arm around me. "You're a lucky son of a bitch, and I happen to like you. I know you made out good at that Wolnosc Street *meline.* Don't think we don't know about it here."

He noted my surprise.

"My dear Jacku, when you're involved with Haim Benkart, you know everything that goes on. I was sorry to hear about your misfortune. There are squealers all over the place, *mosrim* ready to sell you to the Gestapo for a loaf of bread."

He handed me a black Pinkert cap and armband, and we walked through the cemetery gate.

"Shmerl, you're a great partner and a hell of a guy. When Hela's better, you'll be our guest on *Shabbes.*"

I returned the cap and armband, then disappeared into the maze of stones, graves, and trees. I couldn't wait until sundown, so I took off over the wall and into the Evangelical Cemetery.

I headed for Lucka Street and Franek's place. I hadn't been there for weeks. Both Ala and her mother greeted me warmly. Franek asked me countless questions about conditions in the ghetto.

"But *Panie* Malczewski," I finally interrupted, "I'm here on an emergency." I explained my mission and asked him to help.

Franek made some phone calls.

"Jacku, what you need isn't available. Even on this side, the Germans allow us only a bare minimum. It's true they're killing your people by the thousands, but we're only one step above you. They're savages."

I pleaded with him. "*Panie* Malczewski, you've been our only hope outside the ghetto. Hela's dying, and I'll do anything to save her."

I slapped a stack of bills on the table. "And I have some Russian piggys, solid gold coins."

Franek explained that only the German hospitals had the drugs. "I've already contacted the right people, but I won't have an answer before morning."

"That'll be too late," I insisted.

"For Christ's sake, Jacku, you know I'll do everything I can. I'll make a few more calls now and offer the piggys. They'll help. But you have no choice. You must wait till morning."

"It's almost six," I said. "Since I have to stay overnight, maybe I can catch the last train before curfew to Milanowek."

Ala offered to accompany me.

"You're a more convincing Catholic in my company." She smiled, and I embraced her. The little girl had turned into a young lady, and I liked her. We promised to return early the next morning.

As the train approached Milanowek, my thoughts focused on Halina. When the train stopped, we grabbed a local *droshka* for the ten-minute ride to the cottage. The driver knew Ala, who introduced me as her cousin. But he knew nothing of Halina and Mala. They emerged from hiding for fresh air only at night and visited the market to get food only once a week.

Quietly, I unlocked the door with my key. I'd just started to whistle our prearranged signal when someone grabbed me from behind with a scream of joy. Halina and I came together in a tight embrace.

Soon we were all talking and stayed up well past midnight.

I told them everything that had happened since our last meeting.

About Sevek's murder on the rooftop.

About the collapse of the smuggling *meline.*

About my own narrow escape. About how Stas's warning had saved me from the Gestapo torture chambers.

About my illness and recovery.

And finally, about Hela who was on her deathbed at that moment.

The girls sat in silence, weeping.

I saw the innocence and purity in Halina's eyes. I didn't dare mention my deep longing for her. I quickly said goodnight and withdrew to the upstairs bedroom.

The bed had a thick soft mattress and a huge down pillow and was very comfortable. But with my thoughts full of Halina, I couldn't sleep. I opened the window and stared at the star-filled sky. A light northeast breeze cooled the warm summer night air in the attic.

Suddenly the door opened. Barefoot and silent, Halina walked in. She was wearing a short gown suspended by thin straps over her smooth, alabaster shoulders. Her hair, which reached almost to her waist, shone in the soft moonlight. A shiver of excitement went through me as I turned. I held my arms out to her. We stood together, silently clasping hands, while we looked deeply into each other's eyes.

Tears glistened on her cheeks. I kissed them gently, then her eyes, her nose, her lips, her neck. We moved slowly from the window toward the bed. I gently pushed the straps from her shoulders and felt the gown fall to my feet. I pressed my chest against her bare breasts. I bent and kissed them, licking her firm nipples and moving my hands slowly over her body.

I pulled her down to me on the bed. She gasped and moaned. I entered her slowly, gently. I felt her liquid warmth, her tightness. She didn't move. It was too much, too fast. I pulled her close and sank my lips into her mouth. She reacted slowly at first, then threw her arms around me. I felt her desire to consume me.

"Jacku, my love. My first and only love."

She moved up and down, slowly, then quickened her pace. I joined her, both of us wild with passion. Unchained, uncontrolled, until finally we climaxed together, screaming our joy, breathless and free.

Hot, exhausted, sweaty, we turned and looked at each other. We said nothing, but our eyes, our faces, our hands, spoke volumes.

We made love throughout the night. Desperate and passionate, we knew that this might be our last time together.

Halina's face was wet with tears. Her body trembled. "Jacku, if you die, I don't want to live. I want to die with you."

I felt the same way, uncertain of our future, but I calmed her, comforted her, reassured her. Exhausted and wrapped tightly in each other's arms, we finally fell asleep at daybreak.

Ala's gentle knocking woke me. "Papa's expecting us. We must leave soon."

I got out of bed and stood motionless. Halina opened her eyes. "Where are you going? Come back."

We embraced once more.

"Jacku, tell me, what'll happen to us? What are we going to do?"

I held her and stared out the window. I wanted to stay in peace and safety with Halina. But the devil out there was waiting to battle me. I was terrified of Hela's mortal danger. I didn't know what I should do. If I sought my own safety, Hela would die. If I died, Hela would also die.

Anger and frustration were rising inside me.

"Oh, God! Why was I born? Why in hell did I arrive in the twentieth century, and why was I born a Jew? Damn it, who needs a Jewish race or religion altogether?"

Halina was stunned at my bitterness and tried to calm me, but I wouldn't let her. I had to go on screaming.

"There's nothing but pain and blood in our past. The so-called forefathers that we learned about in school were nothing but slaves. They knew that I, the Jewish kid, could do nothing but suffer and struggle. I hate them all. I hate them."

Finally Halina managed to grab my head and press her face to mine. She sobbed with me. She touched my face and kissed me. In her own way, she brought me back to reality. She knew that words couldn't do it, so she caressed me and hugged me.

"The German 'master race,' the whole goddamned fascist world—we'll bury them one day. They'll get theirs. Just you wait." I pounded the table. And then, in silence, I stared into Halina's face and eyes.

"Halina," I said more gently, "you know I have to go now. When Hela recovers, we'll both join you here. Please be patient and wait. Please. I love you. Only you."

I hurriedly dressed, gave some money to Mala and Halina, and left with Ala to catch the first morning train back to Warsaw.

Franek was waiting for us at the station. "Jacku, the medicine's at Czyste Hospital, in the Infectious Disease Wing. It's being given only to wounded German soldiers from the Russian front. My contact says there's just one way to get it: steal it. The nurse in the wing is a girl from Poznan, a *Volksdeutsche.* We know her. She and the guard are friendly. We can depend on them."

I knew the Czyste Hospital well. In prewar times, it had served many Jewish patients. I was treated there myself for a fractured arm when I was ten years old.

Franek had arranged for me to visit the hospital at noon. "Don't forget your money and the gold coins."

I smiled and said, "And my Luftwaffe switchblade."

I walked along Jerozolimskie Boulevard, heading west in the direction of Towarowa and Wolska streets. I barely noticed the people rushing to work or lined up in front of the shops. My thoughts were still with Halina and our night together. The Germans had shattered my respect for humanity and decency, but in Halina I saw everything that was beautiful, pure, and ideal.

I walked in a daydream, reliving every touch and kiss. But as I saw the hospital in the distance, I forced all these thoughts from my mind even while realizing that I might never recapture them.

At the hospital gate, a German guard was checking people entering and leaving the grounds. I avoided the gate and walked along the barbed-wire fence encircling the buildings.

I scaled it and followed the signs to the cafeteria.

Suddenly a blue-uniformed worker with cleaning equipment appeared. "Follow me," he whispered.

I walked behind him and exchanged my valuable leather jacket for a blue work shirt. The contact, Jan, handed me his equipment and asked for the gold coins and the cash. I obliged. Jan then directed me to the operating and emergency ward, where Sister Eva met me with a slight smile and a strong *"Heil Hitler!"*

I followed her, spoke German, and pretended to be a *Volksdeutscher* employee. In her office, I started to empty a waste basket that she pointed to. Inside, I noticed a small box with the name "Jan" written on it. I took the box and shoved it down my shirt.

I looked around. Sister Eva was gone. I sensed a trap. My suspicions told me not to return via the same route. What if Sister Eva was working with the Gestapo?

I took no chances and dropped from the first-floor window to the ground. I made my way around several buildings to confuse anyone who might have trailed me and wound up at the cafeteria entrance. No sight of Jan.

I abandoned my cleaning gear and headed for the fence. It was now guarded by dogs. They scared me. I turned back and went for the gate. To hell with my leather jacket. Having come this far, I wasn't going to fail now. Hela needed the medicine. If they caught me, both of us would die.

But how to escape?

The hospital was full of Germans. The grounds were circled by barbed wire. The fence was patrolled by guard dogs. And a Nazi sentry was guarding the gate.

I decided that only a daring maneuver would work.

Still wearing the blue work shirt, I walked boldly through the gate and saluted with a loud *"Heil Hitler!"*

The sentry returned the salute and demanded my pass.

I didn't stop or turn around. I just kept walking.

"Halt! Halt!"

I started to run.

Shots rang out.

I raced down the street.

At the corner, I turned and spotted a passing trolley. I leaped aboard and was swiftly carried out of danger. I kept feeling the precious medicine again and again, to make sure it was still there. After several stops, I changed trolleys and crossed into the ghetto.

* * *

"Here, Doctor. Is this what you wanted?"

Dr. Grynszpan examined the medicine. "I don't know how you did it, but it looks like the real thing. Jacku, you're a brave kid, a *molodiec.*"

We found Hela in a semicoma, still running a fever.

"Izaakl, I sat here all night, crying and praying," Mama told me. "But deep inside, I knew you'd make it. Where would we be without you?"

Dr. Grynszpan smiled and whispered, "The prayers didn't hurt. But this should do the trick."

The next morning, Hela was fully conscious. She began to urinate. Her speech returned. Her blue eyes cleared. The fever subsided.

I felt victorious.

CHAPTER 13

In June of 1942, Hitler predicted that his Wehrmacht would crush the armies of the Soviet Union before the summer was over. By July, his mechanized divisions were deep inside Russia, massing before Stalingrad on the banks of the river Volga.

It was the third year of the war, and the Germans were celebrating one victory after another.

Meanwhile, the third year of life in the Jewish ghetto of Warsaw was harsher than ever. There was less food, more disease, more executions, and more people on the streets. Thousands of people were dying weekly, yet great numbers of refugees were arriving daily from all over Europe, swelling the ranks of the homeless and the starving.

The streets were beginning to look like battle zones as the hungry population preyed upon itself, scrounging and fighting for food. This confusion, in turn, gave the German propaganda units an excellent opportunity for their anti-Semitic designs.

One morning I was holding a meeting with Lutek, Shmulek, Hela, and some of my cousins behind the heavy wooden doors of our shop at Twarda 29. We were discussing a possible smuggling arrangement with Haim Benkart and his gang, when suddenly we heard strange noises coming from the street outside.

I looked through the peephole I had drilled in the door. People were running in panic. A moment later, I saw several German jeeps filled with SS troops pull up on the corner of Twarda and Panska streets.

The Germans jumped from the jeeps and began unloading cameras and filming equipment. Then they set up several tables and loaded them with food and liquor. Two more vehicles suddenly appeared: a black Mercedes limousine and a military half-track. A high-ranking SS officer emerged from the Mercedes, followed by several saluting staff members.

The half-track was filled with young Hasidic Yeshiva students, wearing black frocks, beards, and side curls.

The SS troops began herding the frightened students from the half-track and lining them up in front of the food-laden tables. Then they brought some swollen, starving children to the nearby sidewalk.

As I continued my vigil, the German intentions became clear. They had come to film a Hasidic "festival," complete with food, liquor, and dancing, while the starving youngsters watched.

At the command of the SS officer, the sordid spectacle began. While the Nazi cameraman moved around looking for various angles from which to shoot the scene, the SS soldiers forced the Hasidim to act merry at gunpoint. They made some pour liquor down their throats, others gorge themselves on the food, and still others dance with wild abandon.

The children on the sidewalk tried to snatch some food from the overloaded tables, but the SS troops kicked them away. The more "festive" the scene became, the louder the screams from the starving children.

On the sidelines, the Germans were having their own celebration. They were drinking, laughing, and ridiculing the Jewish "garbage."

Safe in my hideout, I watched the ugly sight with growing revulsion.

Soon the SS officer in charge became bored. He put on his spotless white gloves, adjusted his monocle, and barked an order to his aide. Then he disappeared into his limousine.

A moment later, staccato bursts of machine-gun fire erupted on all sides. The Hasidim fell in heaps where they stood. The swollen children were torn apart by bullets.

Within minutes, the Germans packed their cameras and equipment, gathered up their tables, and vanished.

In the square, they left behind a bloody mass of bodies. Human flesh and bones were mixed up with spilled liquor, discarded food containers, and garbage. The pathetic corpses of the ghetto children, their hunger now ended, lay scattered in the gutter.

The hungry kids never even got to taste the food. German bullets had riddled them just as they were reaching for the scraps. Their terrified faces registered their confusion. As they died, their eyes opened wide with astonishment. They seemed to be saying, "But I'm so hungry."

I longed for revenge. I wanted it more than anything. I would live for the day when we would have the power to humiliate these Nazi bastards.

Days passed, and my predicament grew worse. The deal with Haim Benkart didn't work out. I had no income, and no other smuggling route was opening up. The enormous expense of feeding my family, my cousins, my aunts, and my Grandma Masha was quickly depleting my reserves.

Halina was waiting for me on the Aryan side, but I was waiting for Hela to recover fully. She had made good progress but was still too weak to climb the cemetery wall. Mama insisted we delay a few more days. Despite my eagerness to be with Halina, I exercised restraint and waited.

Grandma Masha had been bedridden now for many months. From time to time, I'd visit, to cheer her and seek her advice. On each occasion, I'd bring her food and leave money with her daughters, Edzia and Pesa.

Now, with more time on my hands, I crossed the ghetto to Ostrowska Street. Carrying a bundle as usual, I entered my grandma's apartment. My aunts relieved me of the food as I walked into the bedroom.

Propped up against a large pillow, my beloved Grandma Masha was lying in a state of starvation. Her exposed ankles were swollen, and her eyes were strangely puffed.

"What the hell happens to all the food I bring here?"

Both my aunts stared at me in silence. Then Grandma Masha told her daughters to leave and asked me to sit down on the bed beside her. She caressed my face. Her frail hands trembled, but her delicate voice remained steady. She paused only to breathe, or to close her eyes as though praying for me to understand.

"Izaakl," she said, "it's a *sreife.* An uncontrollable fire is burning among us Jews. It's not the first time in our history. It's our sacred duty to save what can be saved and to continue our life and our people's existence."

She paused a moment to wipe her eyes. The years of hardship and tragedy had taken their toll; I knew she was wasting away.

I shifted my weight on the bed. I couldn't bring myself just to sit there and look at her sad face. I'd always regarded her as my symbol of continuity and inspiration. Now I was watching that symbol disintegrate. My Grandma Masha, my pillar of decency and morality, was dying.

I felt lonely and abandoned already.

"But Grandma, *Bobe,* I don't want to hear all that. Look at you, your eyes, your feet, they're swollen. Those big slobs out there are feeding themselves with your food." I was boiling with rage.

"My child, my Izaakl." She tried with her last strength to sit up. "May God save you and give you years. You have been God's angel to our family. You've brought me all you could spare. And you are only fifteen."

"But, Grandma," I interrupted, "you are swollen from hunger. Look at you!"

"Izaakl, listen. I'm your grandma, but I'm also a mother who must first feed her children, no matter what their age." She pulled me closer and kissed my forehead.

Her explanation failed to satisfy me. My aunts had been feeding themselves with the food and money I brought, while allowing their mother to starve. Bedridden, she was dependent on their mercy. And they'd been cheating her for months. Still, she had never complained. In a way, she had actually cooperated in their conspiracy.

Abruptly, I ran out of the bedroom and exploded at my aunts. I cursed and screamed. I grabbed my Aunt Edzia by her hair and dragged her into the room where my Aunt Pesa was waiting in fear. I slapped them both repeatedly.

"You bitches, gorging yourselves on my sweat, on my skin. Risk your own fat asses going across the wall." I grabbed Aunt Edzia's hand with a grip that made her moan and pulled her to the window.

"There, you see that bloody wall?" I continued in my rage, pointing through the open window. "Climb it if you want to eat, you parasite. If what I bring you isn't enough, then sell your flesh for more food."

Edzia screamed and began pounding my chest. She did not expect her young nephew to be so outspoken. I suddenly realized that my tongue was lashing out without mercy. I let go of her hand.

"Yes," she said, "we did spend most of your money on ourselves. Yes, we stole the food you brought for Grandma. But she knew what we were doing. She even pretended to be asleep to make it easier for us. She helped us do what our consciences kept telling us not to do, what we didn't want to do, but what our hunger and pain made us do."

She looked at me with frightened eyes. "We're still young, and maybe we can survive. But your grandma won't survive. We all know that. But nobody's ever dared say it."

Edzia burst into tears, fell on a nearby bed, and covered her face with her hands. She lay there sobbing while her sister went over to comfort her.

I didn't forgive them. I couldn't accept or understand their explanation. All I could think of was my Grandma Masha lying half-starved in the next room.

CHAPTER 14

I kept delaying my departure to the Aryan side. I wanted to be in the ghetto when my grandma died. I would have to arrange the funeral. I would never permit her to be buried in a mass grave.

Time and again, I was ready to go.

Time and again, I didn't go.

And then one day, it was too late.

Once more, the Third Reich interfered with my plans and my life.

I was part of a crowd waiting anxiously outside the *Judenrat,* the Jewish Community Council headquarters. Rumors had been circulating all day that important news was about to come out of the *Judenrat,* news that would affect every man, woman, and child in the ghetto.

And so we were standing in the street waiting. When the news finally came, it was bad.

That day, July 22, 1942, marked the beginning of the final solution for Ghetto Warsaw, for its hundreds of thousands of wretched inhabitants.

On that day, Dr. Adam Czerniakow, the chairman of the *Judenrat,* committed suicide rather than give in to further threats from the Nazis. He refused to sign the new mass deportation orders for the ghetto residents. The SS command immediately ordered distribution of the infamous *Bekanntmachung* wall posters to announce the new Nazi policy: resettlement in Russia for Warsaw's Jewry.

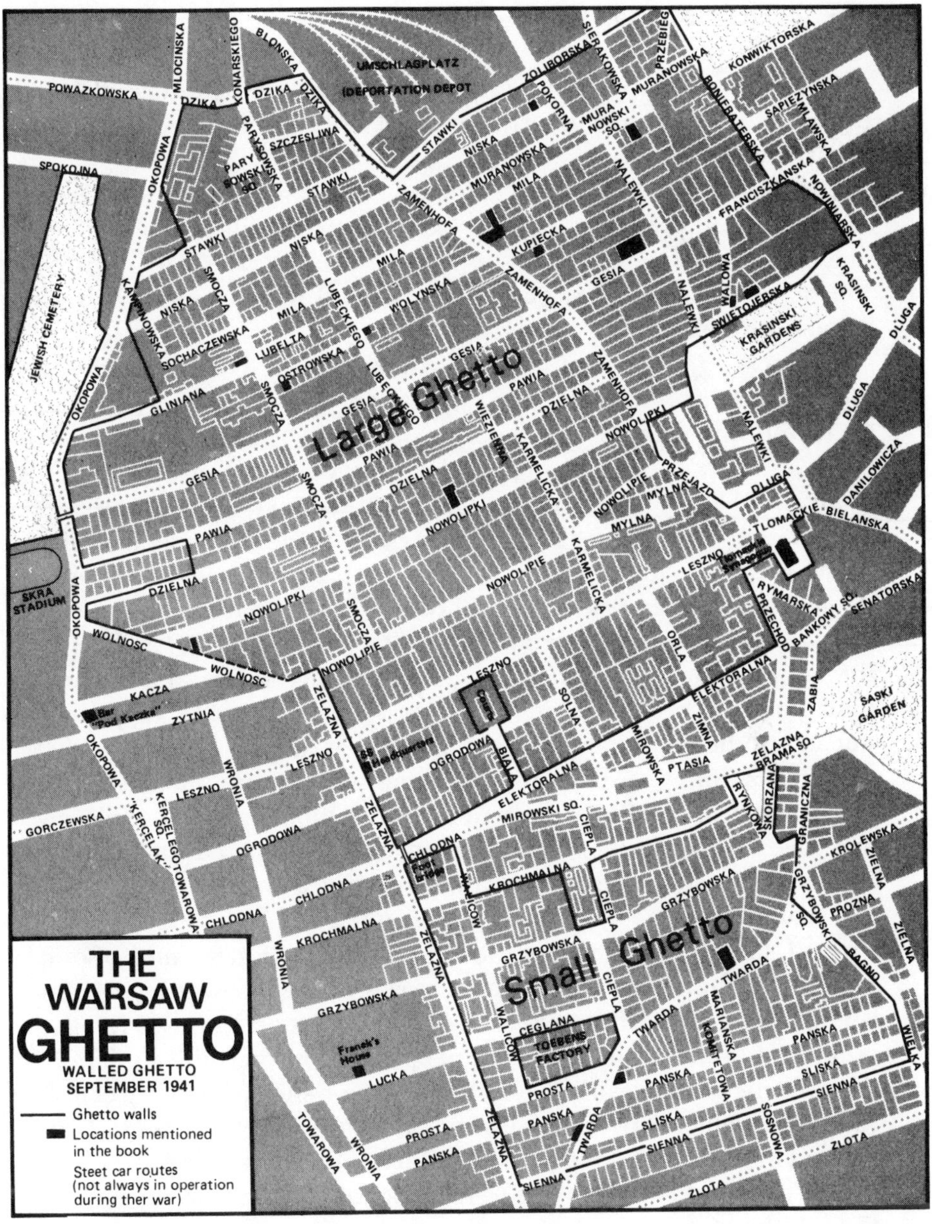
THE WARSAW GHETTO
WALLED GHETTO
SEPTEMBER 1941
Ghetto walls
Locations mentioned in the book
Steet car routes
(not always in operation during ther war)
Large Ghetto
Small Ghetto
UMSCHLAGPLATZ
(DEPORTATION DEPOT)
JEWISH CEMETERY
SKRA STADIUM
KRASINSKI GARDENS
SASKI GARDEN
TOEBBENS FACTORY
POWAZKOWSKA
SPOKOJNA
MLOCINSKA
KONARSKIEGO
BLONSKA
DZIKA
STAWKI
ZOLIBORSKA
SIERAKOWSKA
PRZEBIEG
MURANOWSKA
KONWIKTORSKA
BONIFRATERSKA
SAPIEZYNSKA
MLAWSKA
FRANCISZKANSKA
NOWINIARSKA
NISKA
MILA
MURANOWSKI SQ.
POKORNA
ZAMENHOFA
KUPIECKA
GESIA
NALEWKI
WALOWA
SWIETOJERSKA
KRASINSKI SQ.
DLUGA
OKOPOWA
SMOCZA
LUBECKIEGO
WOLYNSKA
SOCHACZEWSKA
LUBELTA
OSTROWSKA
GLINIANA
PAWIA
DZIELNA
NOWOLIPKI
NOWOLIPIE
KARMELICKA
WIEZIENNA
PRZEJAZD
MYLNA
DANILOWICZA
TLOMACKIE
BIELANSKA
LESZNO
RYMARSKA
PRZECHOD
BANKOWY SQ.
SENATORSKA
ORLA
ELEKTORALNA
WOLNOSC
KACZA
ZYTNIA
ZELAZNA
SOLNA
BIALA
OGRODOWA
MIROWSKA
ZIMNA
PTASIA
ZELAZNA BRAMA SQ.
ZABIA
MIROWSKI SQ.
CIEPLA
RYNKOWA
SKORZANA
GRANICZNA
KROLEWSKA
ZIELNA
GORCZEWSKA
KERCELAK
CHLODNA
KROCHMALNA
WALICOW
GRZYBOWSKA
PROZNA
BAGNO
WRONIA
TOWAROWA
TWARDA
CEGLANA
MARIANSKA
KOMITETOWA
PANSKA
SLISKA
SIENNA
SOSNOWA
ZLOTA
WIELKA
LUCKA
PROSTA

Dr. Czerniakow's death and the deportation decree—resettlement, the Germans called it—served only to further confuse the frightened and hungry people.

"The big city is crowded," the German propagandists proclaimed. "Hunger is widespread and epidemics rampant. Why not reside for the war's duration in the fertile areas of the Ukraine, now German-occupied territory?"

The message was reasonable, logical, persuasive. It was low-keyed and calculated. Resettlement offered new opportunities, a new life, a new beginning.

Resettlement was a way out of the ghetto. A way to escape the misery and hunger.

To back up their "honorable" intentions, the Germans offered ten pounds of bread, jam, and sugar to anyone who volunteered to go to the new territory. Thousands of starving people lined up to receive the food. The trip to the Ukraine was a secondary matter. What could be worse, they reasoned, than starving in the ghetto?

Then, to compound the confusion and set one Jew against the other, the Germans announced a variety of exceptions to the resettlement plan. They issued thousands of permits that exempted certain favored classes from deportation. The Jewish police, members of the *Judenrat,* the Pinkert members, the medical services, and the hospital staffs all received red cards for life. This meant they were needed in the ghetto and did not have to resettle.

Officials from various German business enterprises, such as Toebens, Schultz, and Hallman, sealed off entire blocks of houses, placed SS guards or gendarmes around them, and announced that anyone who owned a sewing machine could report for work in their factories. These Jews, too, didn't have to resettle.

In all, half the ghetto's population had exemption permits of one kind or another that enabled them to stay behind in Warsaw. Meanwhile, squads of SS troops searched the streets and houses for the other half of the population, the people without permits, to deport them. Some of the Jewish police, the *jamniks*—sneaky dogs, we called them—actually cooperated with the SS in the search in an effort to save themselves and their families from deportation.

The tactics of the Germans were designed so as not to set the entire Jewish population against them at once. They feared mass breakouts from the ghetto if everybody became alarmed at the same time.

As a precaution, the Germans circled the wall surrounding the ghetto, including the cemetery, with hundreds of additional heavily armed gendarmes.

Confusion and anarchy took hold. Brother was set against brother, sister against sister, husband against wife. No one knew what to do or how to behave. The German strategy of "divide and conquer" was exposing the depths of human selfishness as never before.

The first word received from the deportees was reassuring. It confirmed that a resettlement was indeed taking place. But this news was soon followed by other, more disquieting information. The SS, it was rumored, was forcing hundreds of deportees to write postcards home, urging those friends and relatives left behind to join the resettlement movement, to volunteer, to come to the land of peace and plenty—the Ukraine.

At the same time, a trickle of deportees somehow managed to make their way back to the ghetto. And they were telling other stories, strange tales, frightening tales, warning those who had remained behind not to leave the ghetto no matter what the Germans promised. They claimed that a Nazi extermination camp had been set up in Treblinka, near the town of Malkinia, some 125 kilometers northeast of Warsaw. They claimed there were gas chambers. And that the Germans were gassing to death all the Jews who were brought there.

People listened in silence to these horrifying revelations. They knew the Germans were capable of bestiality. They had suffered at German hands for years through deprivation, starvation, rape, robbery, pillage, torture, murder. They knew they could expect anything.

But putting people to death in gas chambers!

"It's impossible. Such a thing in the twentieth century? The poor souls telling these tales are sick, insane. They've invented the stories. They're mentally exhausted after all they've been through."

The rationalizations went on and on. No one wanted to believe such terrible news, such utter cruelty.

Most people dismissed the reports as fantasy.

I felt trapped. For weeks I'd been preparing to cross into Aryan Warsaw with Hela, to join Halina in Milanowek. But now the Germans had sealed the ghetto tighter than ever. They had closed the cage. And inside, they were hunting Jews like animals. They trapped them in the streets, cornered them in courtyards, seized them in cellars.

The massive deportation operation was like a gruesome game, with the outcome known only to the Germans. Once they caught the Jews, they dragged them off to the *Umschlagplatz,* the railroad sidings, situated just outside the ghetto at the edge of Stawki and Dzika streets. The depot was only minutes away from the ghetto wall and its exit. The SS command had chosen the location for maximum efficiency.

Out of the ghetto.

Into the cattle cars.

Off to the gas chambers.

On their way, the captured Jews never passed through any part of Aryan Warsaw.

For the first few days under the new Nazi policy, most people were preoccupied with trying to find ways to exempt themselves from resettlement. People were willing to pay any price for any permit, without regard to its validity or to whether it would still be honored the following day.

What passed for normal life in the ghetto ceased to exist. Stores, bakeries, medical services, cafés, restaurants, hidden schools, theaters, all were shut down.

As I expected, Mama became virtually hysterical. Day and night, she spoke of nothing but schemes to save the family. She searched frantically for miracles. She was unable to use reason or logic. She lamented her children's fate. And she blamed me for not having left the ghetto in time.

Most of her emotional outbursts, however, were directed at Papa. In actuality, Papa had given up on survival a long time before. His fanatical mania for decent living and self-respect infuriated Mama.

While the SS squads were busy hunting people outside, Papa had to have his daily shave and shower; his pants were pressed every morning. His books were neatly stored and cataloged, and he attended to them with loving care. These were his children. He had no fear and no suggestions. He never argued. He attended and talked only to himself, as if explaining his inaction to his own conscience.

I hated myself for not getting out of the ghetto earlier. I longed to be with Halina. I hardly slept at all. At night, lying in bed, I imagined being with her for a day, a week, a month.

I never believed, for even one moment, that the Nazis would ever allow any Jew to live, to breathe, to love. But my determination to survive and one day tell the world what the Germans were doing to us was at least as great as—or greater than—their will or ability to destroy me. I had to and would survive. I had to save Halina and Hela and so many more. But now I had run out of ideas.

I went to visit my Grandma Masha. Having reached the limits of her endurance, she was voicing her complaints directly to God.

"How much can a human being suffer? There's a limit, dear God. And we've all reached that limit. We must have sinned, oh, Lord. But enough is enough."

Still concerned only for her children and grandchildren, she urged me to save myself.

"Survive, my child. Survive. I'm too old, too sick. Don't worry about me any longer."

I knew this would be my last visit with her. I'd never see her again. I knew the murderous SS squads would reach Ostrowska Street, then order a Jewish policeman, a *jamnik,* to carry her down to a horse-drawn wagon filled with other invalids. And I also knew she wouldn't even survive the ride to the *Umschlagplatz,* much less the trip in a cattle car. I kissed her cheeks, smoothed her hair, and choked back my tears.

My aunts Edzia and Pesa were there, but their minds were centered on themselves. "Jacku, tell us what to do. Do you think we should volunteer? Should we join a shop? We have no sewing machines, and the lines in front of Toebbens' recruiting office are endless."

I'd been the hero of the family for so long. All my relatives considered me courageous and resourceful and were still appealing to me for help. But I felt powerless.

"Don't volunteer. Hold out. Hide." That was all I could advise. But it wasn't enough. They were too tired. Tired of hiding, of starving, of not sleeping, not bathing. They were tired of life itself.

For weeks, I dodged the SS squads. I kept my sister and parents hidden in the basement beneath our shop at Twarda 29. But the SS searches were intensifying each day.

The Germans now set quotas for the Jewish police. They threatened to deport them and their families if they didn't provide 6,000 Jews daily for resettlement. As a result, the *jamniki* ran frantically from house to house, searching, urging people to volunteer. They clubbed and kicked people into the streets, where the waiting SS squads seized them and marched them off to the *Umschlagplatz.*

Meanwhile, rumors kept the population's hopes alive.

"Russian bombers are on their way."

"American paratroopers are landing in Germany."

"Hitler has been assassinated."

People wanted to hear any kind of rumor. Rumors about battles, the Allies, the Nazis, rumors about decrees and permits. First, red permits were better than white, then whites were better than reds. People lived on rumors, never knowing whether what they heard or did was right or wrong.

One evening, I returned to find Mama in tears. She was hugging our old family shoemaker, Shmeel. He had decided to volunteer for resettlement with his two starving granddaughters.

"Zlatka, I have no strength to go on. It must be His will. As we pray on Yom Kippur, *der Oybeshter,* our God, directs and chooses who shall live and who shall perish. Zlatkeshi, He's picked us. He chose us to perish."

A year earlier, Shmeel's wife had died from typhoid. His daughter, the mother of the two girls, had recently been killed by the Germans while trying to cross the ghetto wall for food. The girls' father had escaped to Russia three years ago, and nobody had heard from him since.

"My dear Zlatkeshi, please understand," the shoemaker said. "Maybe in the Ukraine the girls will have a chance to live."

"No, Shmeel. The *yekes* are liars, murderers. They'll kill you and the girls, too. I won't let you go."

I watched old Shmeel arguing with Mama. I watched the confused faces of the fragile girls, perhaps eight or ten years old.

I choked back my tears as Shmeel turned to me. "Izaakl, you and your family. My customers for a generation. How can I leave my friends?"

He patted the girls' hair as they turned their eyes sideways so as not to face me, not to face life, humanity, or even the sun.

I remembered Shmeel sitting on a low stool in his basement workshop with his helper for whole days and nights. Their hammers in hand, an old shoe on an iron form, they spat and nailed. Shmeel had his mouth filled with wooden pins on his right cheek and small nails on the left, yet he always managed to talk as he worked.

"Reb Shmeel," I pleaded, "listen to Mama. Don't volunteer. Don't trust the Germans. Hide with us in our basement."

Shmeel shook his head in bewilderment and looked up to the ceiling, to God.

Mama locked the door and forced Shmeel and his granddaughters to remain with us overnight. But things didn't get better for Shmeel. And a few days later, I saw him and his girls, among other wretched Jews, marching off to an unknown future. They had finally surrendered to despair.

By now, the SS squads had abandoned all restraints. They were openly breaking into homes, stores, basements, and attics. The Jewish police were finding it more and more difficult to meet their daily quotas, to feed the *Umschlagplatz* and its waiting cattle cars.

But the more the danger mounted, the more I fought back. I knew we couldn't remain in hiding much longer. The SS and the Jewish police had already ransacked the rooms and apartments above us. It would only be a matter of days before they would return to search the basement and find all four of us. I felt chained to that basement, to Hela, to Mama, to Papa, to my people.

"Mama," I suddenly suggested, "why don't you and Hela apply for work at the Toebbens uniform factory?"

"You and your ideas!" Mama snapped. "You just want to get rid of us."

"That's not true, Mama. And you know it."

"No, we mustn't separate. The family must stay together. If God wills it, we'll all perish together."

"Mama, don't talk about death. Talk about life, survival. I want to live, and I want Hela and you to live. Tomorrow morning at five, we're going out to Toebbens."

"But what good will it do? We don't have sewing machines."

"Oh, yes, we do," I said. "I have two of them. I buried them a long time ago. And now's the time to use them."

"You buried the machines? You didn't turn them in? You must be joking!"

Mama was both laughing and crying at the same time. Hela was shaking me in her delight and surprise.

Shortly after curfew was lifted the next morning, Mama and I, with the sewing machines slung across our backs, took our places in line before the Toebbens plant on Prosta Street. Because of her recent illness, Hela remained at home. We didn't want to subject her to the pushing and shoving, the long hours of waiting in the sun.

The tension among the crowd was unbearable. It was common knowledge that SS squads often drove up and grabbed people waiting in line. So every time motorized traffic was heard, we all scrambled for cover in nearby houses. The SS didn't really care whether Toebbens had enough workers to produce uniforms. All they cared about was feeding the *Umschlagplatz.*

Suddenly Mama disappeared from sight.

"Mama! Where are you?" I screamed. She had been standing in line only about twenty or thirty people behind me. I was frantic. I had to find Mama, but I was afraid of losing my place in line.

In my heart, I continued screaming.

Mama, don't play games with me! Get back to your place in line.

Mama, I'm confused enough. I can't discipline myself much longer, pretend much longer, act much longer that I'm the kid with guts. Always cool and collected, always knowing what to do.

Mama, my insides are being torn to shreds! My stomach is bursting. I want to vomit. I want to shit. I want to sit down and just cry and cry.

Mama, I've had enough!

But my survival instinct commanded me to disregard my feelings and to convince myself that it was some other kid who wanted to cry and be taken care of. Some other kid who was soft and sentimental and scared.

This kid must fight his feelings, must fight for survival. Starting now.

I pointed my switchblade at the throat of a middle-aged man next to me.

"You! This is my place in line. Remember it! I have to go find my mother. I don't envy you if you give me trouble when I get back."

I scared the hell out of an innocent man.

"Yes, yes," he mumbled. "I haven't done anything. Please," he begged, "put that knife away."

I ran down the line. I passed ten, twenty, thirty, forty, fifty people. There was no sight of Mama. I panicked.

"Mama, where are you!" I screamed.

The people in line were not interested in answering me. They were concerned only with their own survival. What was another crazy hoodlum in the ghetto? Nothing new, nothing exceptional. The streets were filled with people gone mad. Children, abandoned and hungry. Teenagers, wild and furious.

I ran up and down the long line, my eyes aching, my face wet with tears. Suddenly I stumbled on a body. I barely glanced at it. Bodies in the street were normal sights in the ghetto. Bodies were usually disregarded.

But then my eyes fixed on the shoes. And the coat.

That's Mama's coat!

Why would they cover a body with Mama's coat?

Wild with fear, I snatched up the coat. And there was my mother, stretched out in the gutter. With her eyes closed and her face drained of color, she looked like the mummies I had seen in the museum as a schoolboy.

"Mama! Mama!"

I slapped her, harder than I intended.

"Mama! Wake up! You're not dead, wake up!"

There was no movement from her. I slapped her again. I shook her.

"Mama! Wake up, it's me, Izaakl!"

She stirred, ever so slightly. Then she opened her eyes and blinked.

You see, I woke you. I brought you back to life. I was talking to myself. *See how strong my will power is. If you want something strongly enough, it works.*

I helped her to her feet.

"Izaakl . . . I must have fainted. Everything was spinning—the sky, the people. And you were so far away. I didn't have time to call you. I just blacked out."

"It's all right now, Mama. I'm here. And you're all right. Let's get back in line."

Mama had indeed fainted, and strangers had simply covered her with her coat and left.

What was there to fuss about? Just another dead Jew in the gutter.

It was the sewing machine that mattered. Of course, they stole it from her. We never saw it again.

We returned to my original place in line. Several hours later, we were accepted for work at Toebbens. We had only one sewing machine, but we were lucky. We each got a permit.

And when I registered, I wrote Hela's name, not my own.

CHAPTER 15

Mama and Hela said goodbye to Papa and me early the next day. Holding official work permits, they had to move into the specially assigned and guarded Prosta Street block. None of us knew whether we'd ever see each other again. We didn't even know which of us was safer.

Hela cried when she embraced me. We held on to each other for a long, long time. We couldn't let go.

Mama for once sounded optimistic. "Maybe with God's help, this will work out, but, Izaakl, take good care of yourself and Father. Don't risk, don't take chances, you hear me?"

Papa and I would continue our dangerous existence in the basement. I knew it was only temporary, but we had no choice. Besides, I had to find a way to get to Milanowek, to Halina. But I couldn't leave Papa alone. He'd surely take his life, or be shot when found.

My mind wandered. "What about *Bobe?*" I wondered whether Grandma Masha was still in the hidden bedroom where I had left her, with food and water, or whether she was buried somewhere among hundreds of rotting bodies in a mass grave. I had a sudden urge to see her, to see if she was still alive, to see if the Germans had overlooked the door that I had concealed and blocked with a large wardrobe.

More than ever, I needed her wise words, her caresses, her consolation. I was in despair, I was powerless. Sometimes I felt like I couldn't take care of myself, let alone anyone else.

So I took some food with me and went to find my grandma. As I rounded each corner, I held my breath, fearing I would get caught.

I reached the corner of Ostrowska and stopped. SS and Ukrainian troops were everywhere, with machine guns and dogs. Hundreds of people, young and old, were standing in the street. They had been dragged out of their dwellings like animals.

I ran back a block to Gesia Street. It was deserted.

I entered the courtyard of the building next to Grandma's. Like a squirrel, I climbed the drainpipe to the roof.

In an instant, I was down the hatch, through the attic, and on the fourth floor of Grandma's house.

I stopped. A deathlike stillness filled the air. Not a soul. Not a voice. Not a scratch. Not a sound. The house was empty.

The people had vanished, and Grandma Masha was gone. I would never see her again.

I stood there, on the fourth-floor landing, and suddenly felt stripped and naked. My favorite human being was no longer there to comfort me. They had torn away from me a vibrant part of my heart and soul.

Abandoned and insecure, I couldn't accept my nakedness. Maybe she'd left a sweater, her old worn-out robe, or her long cotton skirt. Or perhaps she'd left her shawl, the one she'd knitted so carefully. Or her Bible, with the crumbling yellow pages. Or her eyeglasses, with the tired piece of string that hung from them.

I had to have something of hers. I had to hold on to something. Something familiar.

I ran down the steps to Grandma's apartment. Abandoned possessions cluttered the stairs. Rucksacks, bags, satchels. A teddy bear. A doll. Everything was scattered in confusion. The SS had shown no mercy.

The door to my Grandma's apartment stood wide open. I ran through the rooms to the last one, the hidden room. I couldn't believe what I saw.

A miracle! A miracle!

The SS had discovered the room, but they'd forgotten my Grandma Masha. Dressed in a white nightgown, her long, silvery hair swept wildly back, Grandma Masha was sitting in the center of the room in her favorite chair. Her glasses were perched at the end of her nose. Her Bible was in her lap. And she was scolding her almighty God.

"Reboyne Shel Oilom, Oh, Lord, isn't it already enough? What have you done to my children? No, no, it is enough. It must be enough. *Genig is genig."*

I ran to her side.

"Bobe, Grandma! It's me, Izaakl!"

She stared at me as though her God had responded to her. She pulled me down to her and kissed me, with tears streaming down her noble face.

"Izaakl, *rateve dich.* Save yourself. You must survive, my precious child. Survive! Survive!"

She repeated these words over and over, like a biblical commandment.

"But, Grandma, how can I? Hell is out there. The world's disappearing. Everything's disintegrating. How can I save myself?"

She pulled my face close to hers and looked at me with her large, deep-set eyes. They were the eyes of despair and tragedy, eyes that were set a thousand miles into her skull.

"Nein, nein, mein teieres kind. The world is disappearing for me, but not for you. Never for you. You must survive. You must! You're my last one. They're all gone. Satan has taken them all from me. Without you, everything is finished. My Izaakl, you must survive!"

She grabbed me tightly and we embraced, both of us sobbing uncontrollably. I was crying like a lost child, like the fifteen-year-old I really was.

We comforted each other, but not for long. Not long enough. Suddenly we heard the brutal boots and voices of the SS troops. Laughing and cursing, they were trudging up the stairs.

No, there had been no miracle, no divine intervention. The SS had not forgotten my Grandma Masha. They had just left her for later. They knew she had no place to go, no place to hide. Now they were coming up the stairs to get her.

"Quick, quick, my child, my dear one," Grandma whispered. "Save yourself. Get under the bed. Quick!"

Obediently, I squeezed myself under the huge old Victorian bed and lay there in a flood of my own tears.

Grandma Masha then sat down on the edge of the bed. She spread her legs and concealed my presence with her long white gown.

There was no more Sabcia, David, Yosek, or Srulek. No more Marylka, Sara, or Mietek. No more Heniek, Gershon, or Salcia. They were all gone. Brutally driven from their homes and hiding places by the Germans.

So now my Grandma was determined to save the last of her twenty grandchildren.

The Germans stormed into the room. In one swift motion, they grabbed her by the arms and pulled her off the bed. They dragged her through the apartment. Then, as I listened from my hiding place paralyzed with fear, they threw her down the stairs like rubbish.

They made a *shmate,* a rag, a piece of garbage of my precious Grandma Masha. My Grandma, who used to watch over me at my bedside when I was sick as a child, who used to caress me, gently feel my forehead for fever with her long delicate fingers, who used to lay her head on the pillow next to mine to help me fall asleep. I could hardly breathe through my rage. I felt an overpowering rush of strength. I could have taken the big bulky bed on my back, run with it down the stairs, and smashed it over their Nazi heads. I could have choked them with my bare hands, broken their necks on my knees.

I could have; I could have; but I didn't.

Instead, I lay under my Grandma Masha's bed for what seemed like an eternity.

"Grandma," I vowed, "I will survive. No matter what happens, I will survive. Grandma," I swore, "you shall never be forgotten. I must, I will pay them back."

When things had quieted down outside, I crawled out from under the bed and left the building. I headed up Smocza Street. I had to get back to Papa, to our basement. I needed a place where I could sort things out.

Suddenly a squad of armed SS men leading a column of people came out of Nowolipki Street. They were coming straight toward me. I turned quickly into Pawia Street.

Several armed Ukrainians appeared from around the corner. They began stopping people on the sidewalk. I looked back. Jewish police and more Ukrainians were behind me. I had nowhere to run. No courtyards. No doorways. I was trapped.

The Ukrainians began shoving me and the other Jews off the sidewalk and into the gutter. And then they marched us off toward the *Umschlagplatz.* In desperation, I looked for a possible escape route. But there was no way out.

In the distance, I saw Ostrowska Street. I turned to look at my Grandma Masha's house. I felt a sudden sharp pain in my ribs. A Ukrainian guard had poked me with his rifle butt.

"Idzi vpierod, yobany Zydok! Get moving, you Jewish scum!"

Prodding, pushing, and cursing, the Ukrainians hurried us toward the cattle cars. Still in pain, I saw for the first time the dreaded deportation depot. Situated just outside the ghetto walls, around the corner from Dzika Street, the former lumberyard had become the focal point for all of the ghetto's misery.

As the guards were herding thousands of wretched people into a long row of cattle cars, I saw the tragedy of Warsaw's Jews unwind before my eyes. Almost on top of each other, the people were being squeezed in, perhaps a hundred in each car.

I wondered how they could survive the long trip to the Ukraine under such terrible conditions. No, I decided. It's impossible. The Treblinka stories seemed more likely.

I watched as the Germans brutalized the children, the old, and the sick. I knew this trip would lead to agony and death. This was no treatment for people who were meant to live.

SS officers and their dogs were roaming the depot. Ukrainians were guarding the sidings. And Jewish police kept on filling the cattle cars.

I had expected the most barbaric treatment from the Germans and the Ukrainians, but the brutality of the Jewish police officers made me sick. It was revolting. I longed to wrap my hands around the throat of the short stocky Lejkin or the tall bearded Szmerling. And what about the snob, the so-called aristocrat Szerynski, the chief of them all, a convert who was kicked back into the ghetto? They were acting as though they would be exempt forever. Didn't they know that all Jews were condemned? The stupid bastards. Today in uniform, tomorrow in the cattle car.

Several people were showing their exemption cards. I joined them and pretended to be a member of the ambulance service. The cardholders were allowed to leave, but a burly SS man struck me across the face. *"Du Scheissjude!* Get back where you belong!" He shoved me into a column headed for the trains.

Again, I moved out of line. To my right, several injured people were lying on the ground, begging for help. I bent and tried to comfort them. I tried to look busy, to buy time.

The SS and the Jewish police ignored me. I got up and headed for the gate. A Jewish policeman raced after me. "Hey you! Where do you think you're going?"

"I'm part of the medical service."

"The hell you are. Get your ass in line!"

He pushed me with his club. Once more I was headed for the train.

I moved out of the column again. I returned to the injured people and bent over a bleeding woman. The same Jewish policeman came after me.

"Aren't you human?" I cried out. "This woman's my mother. Can't you see she's hurt?"

The *jannik* saw through my lie. He raised his club to strike me. I saw it floating over my head. I seized it and pulled him to the ground. With all my strength, and without mercy, I struck him with his own club. He fell unconscious, next to the bleeding woman. My heart was pounding. Had I been seen? Had anyone noticed? Would I be shot right then and there?

I grabbed his police cap and put it on my head. I waited for a bullet, a rifle shot. Nothing happened. I stood up, club in hand, and looked around. Nobody had seen me. Nobody was coming for me.

I strode off through the crowds. I passed the SS officers. I passed the Ukrainians. I passed the Jewish police. Nobody stopped me.

At the exit, I saluted the SS guards and walked through. No one touched me.

I was out.

CHAPTER 16

Pretending to be a policeman in my stolen cap and club, I was able to walk home through the deserted streets. My heart was pounding. I was scared to look back. I just couldn't believe that I was walking freely in the streets and was out of that inferno, the *Umschlagplatz.*

Back in our basement hideout at Twarda 29, I found Papa sitting quietly in a corner, like a prisoner in a dungeon. A small candle cast its flickering light on the pages of the book he was reading, *Ethics,* by Spinoza.

I started to speak, rapidly and excitedly, anxious to tell him everything I'd seen and been through. But after a few moments, I noticed that he was not reacting. He was listening patiently and politely, but not a word I was saying seemed to affect him. Not a sign of emotion crossed his face. No grief for Grandma Masha. No joy for my escape. Nothing.

"Papa, you haven't heard a thing I've said."

"Yes, my son, I heard. I've heard everything. But what's the use? Life's no longer worth living. . . ."

"Shut up, dammit! I don't want any more of your philosophy. All you can think of is death! I don't want to hear about death. I want to talk about life. I want to live. I am going to survive. I'll bury them yet!"

Papa remained silent. He looked at me sadly, then returned to his book.

Exasperated and angry, I lay down on my bed. What a sea of defeatists they were—resigned, disarmed, ready to give up. I had often thought about giving up myself. It would have been so much easier. But I couldn't. I had to survive, even when life seemed more painful than death.

My thoughts drifted and eventually found Halina. Countless times each day, I imagined our reunion. We would fall into each other's arms. We would make love all night, all day. We would pretend the world of hate and violence didn't exist. I dozed off, dreaming about Halina and about escaping from the ghetto. By dawn, I was determined that I must find a way out.

I'd escaped once from the *Umschlagplatz,* but I knew I couldn't push my luck. The SS were too diabolical, too anxious to capture every last Jew. I simply had to get out before it was too late. Then I would contact old reliable Franek and go with his daughter, Ala, to Milanowek, to Halina. Now that Hela and Mama were safe for the time being at the Toebbens uniform plant, where the Germans needed their labor, all that was left was for me to find a way over the wall.

I surveyed all the familiar escape routes: the cemetery, the rooftops, Wolnosc Street. By now they were all heavily guarded. I weighed the possibilities but could reach no conclusions. No way seemed safe. So early one morning, I set out to crisscross the ghetto, to search for an idea, an opening. I wouldn't rest until I found the loophole.

The streets were already swarming with SS troops and Jewish police, moving relentlessly, house by house, street by street. So I made my way through attics and over rooftops, peering down at the activity on the ground. The roof of a building near the guarded wooden bridge over Chlodna Street was a good vantage point. I was not far from the Leszno gate to the ghetto, and I could see Aryan Warsaw over the western wall on Zelazna.

Then I heard a commotion. Two trucks, partially filled with young men, were waiting at the corner below. Loud orders were being given, and several uniformed Germans were walking to and from the gate.

I was surprised. This wasn't a typical SS squad. These Germans were from outside the ghetto. They apparently needed a work force and were stopping people at the bridge, offering them jobs instead of deportation.

I ran down to a vacant apartment on the second floor, where I could see and hear better. The Germans were talking about a labor camp in Rembertow, about thirty kilometers away. I knew instinctively that if I could get on one of those trucks, I could get safely out of the ghetto. Then I would jump from the truck as it traveled through Aryan Warsaw.

But Papa was alone in the basement, and I wouldn't abandon him. I bit my lips hard. Time was critical. I had to make a fast decision. Risking everything, I took off and started running through the streets. I knew that if I met the SS, I was finished. But I wouldn't abandon my father.

Block after block, I ran. Hoping. Praying. Please, please don't let me meet any Germans. Finally, I burst into our basement.

"Papa! Quick! Get some things and come with me!"

There was something in my voice that couldn't be questioned. Something firm. Something commanding.

Papa grabbed his jacket and a book and another book.

"Papa, our lives are at stake, move!"

He picked another book, exchanged the first one. His books were his children; how could he leave any behind?

Without a word, I pushed him out the door. I moved fast, pulling Papa behind me through the backyards and alleys. Soon we arrived at the wooden bridge. The trucks were still at the corner.

Summoning all my courage and nerve, I approached one of the German guards. He was wearing an olive uniform with a red swastika armband.

"My brother and I are strong. We want to work."

For a moment, the German looked at me in surprise. "How old are you?"

I looked him straight in the eye. "Twenty."

He pointed at Papa. "And this one?"

"My brother? He's thirty."

Papa stood pale and speechless.

"Auf den Lastwagen. Schnell. Genug Juden! Abfahren."

He ordered us onto the rear truck. They had enough Jews.

Minutes later, Papa and I, together with about a hundred other men, were on our way to Rembertow. As we bounced along through

Warsaw's Aryan streets, wild escape ideas bounced around in my head. But several guards were sitting up front with machine guns. To attempt escape now was far too risky.

Fear and logic clashed with my desire to be free; fear and logic won. I decided to wait and find out what Rembertow was like. I'd find another chance to escape. First, I'd see where Papa would wind up.

It took less than an hour to reach the camp, where we were immediately assigned to manual labor gangs. Several hundred men were working at the site, building huge gasoline storage facilities for the Germans. *Volksdeutsche* civilians were supervising the project. I was relieved to see no SS troops, no striped uniforms, no walls, not even a barbed-wire fence.

The day passed rapidly. At night, we were taken to a small compound of three wooden barracks surrounded by a wire fence and guarded by older Germans. Compared to conditions in the ghetto, we were now in heaven.

The food at the camp wasn't bad. The work was hard, and the treatment depended on the foreman. Being *Volksdeutsche,* the civilians all spoke Polish. I soon found I could do business with them. I became friendly with Willy, a plump pumpkin of a man, our *Schachmeister,* or chief foreman. Jewelry, I discovered, interested Willy. I began to trade him the watches and rings that some of us had managed to hide in return for favors.

The atmosphere at Rembertow, although disciplined, in some respects resembled the climate of a civilian work project. During the afternoon, street vendors would appear at the work site and hawk their wares of lemonade and native Polish foods. The foremen would call a break and allow the workers to buy refreshments.

One afternoon, I met Mietek, an old buddy from my smuggling days. Mietek was several years older than I and had a reputation in the ghetto as a big-time operator. We were glad to find each other alive.

Before long, Mietek took me into his confidence. "Jacku, how'd you like to break out?"

Without hesitation, I agreed.

"I knew you would," he said. "Now, listen. I've got a plan." Mietek lowered his voice. "Look across the road to your left."

I looked.

"You see that motorcycle with the sidecar?"

I nodded.

"That belongs to one of the engineers. Every morning, he parks it there at exactly the same place."

"So what?"

"So this," Mietek said. "The dumb *yeke* never takes the key. Look and you'll see it in the ignition."

"You're right. I see it."

"Now, all we have to do is hop on and disappear."

"But how do you operate it?" I asked. "I've never driven a motorcycle."

"There's nothing to it. I'll drive. But the trick is getting to it fast. What do you say?"

The plan sounded simple enough, but the stakes were very high. If we were caught, the Germans would shoot us on the spot.

"Once we're out of here," Mietek continued, "we can dump the motorcycle and get to Warsaw on foot. We can use the side roads. It'll be safer and probably just as fast."

"What about my father? I can't leave him here."

"Take him along," my friend said. "He can sit in the sidecar. But I gotta know tonight, because I'm taking off tomorrow."

To my surprise, Papa didn't oppose me when I told him about the plan. On the other hand, he didn't agree, either. I felt that when the time came, I could push him into it.

The following afternoon, during the commotion of the lunch break, Mietek moved close to me. "Now or never," he whispered.

I grabbed Papa's hand. "Okay, Papa. Let's go." I started forward, but Papa froze.

"What's the matter?"

"I can't, Jacek."

"What do you mean, you can't?"

"I can't. That's all."

"Dammit! Let's go, Papa! Now's our chance!"

"No! You go, Jacek. Please."

Mietek was growing nervous.

"Papa, please!"

Papa stood paralyzed. He wouldn't budge.

A moment later, Mietek was walking across the road—alone. I watched him, a brave young Jew, cool and purposeful, risking death for freedom.

He had fifty steps to go. Forty. Twenty. He walked slowly and deliberately, so as not to attract attention. Now he was on the motorcycle.

He tossed a quick glance in my direction, then turned the key in the ignition. The engine roared, and Mietek zoomed down the road in a cloud of dust.

I envied him.

"I couldn't do it. I'm just not made for such adventures," Papa was repeating to himself over and over. He felt guilty and could not look me in the eyes.

I felt a sudden wave of compassion for him. He had lived so much longer than I, read so much more. His disillusionment with life had to be that much greater than mine.

"It's okay, Papa. Tomorrow's another day."

"Tomorrow, if you have the chance, go without me. I mean it, Jacku. I do."

Mietek's escape triggered a change in the camp. The number of guards was doubled. Supervision was tightened. And privileges were canceled. Still, I had to find a way out.

The opportunity finally arrived when Willy, my greedy foreman, had to make a trip to Warsaw for special provisions. I promised to lead him to money and jewels buried by deported Jews if he'd take me along for the ride. Willy agreed.

I said a quick goodbye to Papa and climbed aboard the open platform of the truck leaving for the capital. Willy sat in the cab with the driver and an armed guard.

As the truck approached the outskirts of Warsaw, I steeled myself for action. The guard had placed his machine gun on the ledge of the window behind him, pointing the barrel in my direction, and was talking to Willy and the driver.

That guard was my key to success. If he didn't notice me, I could be free in minutes. I tensed as the truck approached the outskirts of Warsaw, and I kept an eye on him. I knew every street and corner. Everything was familiar: the buildings, the courtyards, the stores, the people.

Slowly, I crept along the open platform to the end of the truck, where I pretended to straighten a huge rain tarpaulin that was draped over some cargo. The trio of Germans in the cab paid no attention to me. They continued talking. The truck slowed as it turned into a busy intersection. I made my move.

I rolled off the platform, turned into the block from which we had come, and disappeared among the pedestrians. A short while later, I was on Lucka Street, at Franek's door.

Ala and her mother once again greeted me warmly and graciously. They offered me a bath, a hearty breakfast, and a change of clothes. Ala was radiant with joy. She told me that Halina was safe and well, but very worried about me since she hadn't seen me for many weeks.

Franek arrived at noon. We had a brief conversation. Then he drew me into another room and confided that he'd joined the Polish underground. "Here's my gun," he said as he pulled from his shirt a brand-new Parabellum pistol. "It's for you, Jacku. Use it well."

I looked at that "fortune," that shiny instrument that meant power, revenge! I stared at the gun and at Franek. I really felt like saying, "You are crazy to part with it."

But I didn't. And Franek wasn't crazy. He was Papa's true friend, who would sit endless hours with him debating the progress of civilization. But the two men, once both profound pacifists, had differed dramatically in their dealings with the current reality.

This gun was a miracle. With trembling hands, I touched it. "It's mine, really mine, *Panie* Franku?"

"Of course, it's yours. Our forces have been in touch with your resistance people behind the wall. They tell us the deportations are just about over. Most of the Jews are gone, but not all. There's a hard core left that the SS can't find. They're concentrated in a tiny area—the central ghetto, they call it. You know, of course, the Germans reduced the size of the ghetto?"

"How many Jews are left?" I asked.

"I don't know. Rumors say more than a quarter million were deported. But those who are left are arming themselves. They're young people, like you. They've decided to fight it out."

I felt a surge of pride. Armed resistance. *Jewish* armed resistance.

"They're building underground bunkers. They've formed a Jewish military force."

The more I heard, the more my excitement mounted. "Franek, I want to be there. I want to join them."

Franek put his arm about me. "I knew you would, Jacku. I knew you'd want to fight back. And we do, too. We'll join forces. We'll organize and fight them right here, on this side of the wall."

He turned and walked to the window. "The Germans took all those thousands of Jews and murdered them in scientific death factories. There was no resettlement in the Ukraine. It was all a pack of lies. The people were sent to Treblinka, a huge extermination camp. There the beasts gassed and burned everybody—men, women, children; the old, the young, the sick. Everybody. Then they threw their ashes into pits."

Franek's voice shook with anger.

"Are you sure, Franek? Are you really sure this is happening?"

"Yes, Jacku. Many Polish rail workers report the same unbelievable thing. A number of Jews who escaped from Treblinka also tell the same story. In fact, the new Jewish underground, the ZOB, sent special agents to investigate. And they also found the stories true."

I was trembling. I couldn't believe it. I didn't want to believe it. Death factories? Scientific death factories? But then, I thought, it was in character with all the Nazi cruelties I already knew of. It was so efficient, so German.

I was seething. I had to hit back. I was excited by the idea of armed resistance. I'd fight them in the ghetto. *I would have my revenge.*

But first I had to reach Milanowek and see Halina. I knew she was brave and that she would join me. We would return to the ghetto and never be separated again. We would fight the Germans. Even if we had only our fists, we'd fight.

CHAPTER 17

Milanowek looked more peaceful than ever. The early fall colors, the golds and browns and rusts, beautified the Polish countryside.

I felt freedom in the air.

I breathed deeply and stopped often to look around. How beautiful nature was in the Aryan world!

Ala, holding my hand, walked silently beside me. She was puzzled by my strange behavior, but she didn't say a word. How could she understand what it meant for me, a ghetto slave, to be walking freely down a country road, unafraid and alive?

Everything was quiet near the cottage. Not a sound. No smoke from the chimney. No sign of human existence. But we knew that Halina and Mala were there. Ala unlocked the back entrance. We walked in, closed the door, and waited. We looked around to see if anyone had followed us, then went down to the basement, where Halina and Mala threw themselves at me, hugged and kissed me, and screamed for joy.

Tears rolled down Ala's rosy cheeks as she hugged us all. She wanted so much to be a part of the celebration. Halina and Mala took her hand, and they all danced together while I stood and watched in bewildered amusement.

They locked the doors and windows and spread themselves out on the floor to listen as I filled them in on the news from Warsaw. They no longer believed that any Jews remained alive. They had heard cruel and depressing rumors during their infrequent trips to the marketplace, rumors that left them entirely without hope. Our meeting was a mixture of joy and sadness.

Halina couldn't keep her hands still for a moment. She sat near me, touching me, petting me, and feeding me my favorite candy, the *Krowki Pomorskie,* a local delicacy from Milanowek.

Mala bombarded me with questions and fears about her family. I had nothing specific to tell her. I did not know their fate. But she wouldn't give up. She refused to accept that they might have perished.

"I can't believe it. It's too horrible."

Ala tried to comfort her. She tried to ease the pain for everyone. She was the youngest of us, and the only non-Jew. A sensitive Christian soul caught up in a Jewish tragedy.

I had planned to take Halina and Mala back to the ghetto, and this was what they expected me to tell them. Instead, I told them about the beginnings of a Jewish underground resistance, that I'd have to return to the ghetto alone at first to check out conditions and then arrange to take them there later. I showed them the pistol Franek had given me. "I'm getting one for you, too, Halina. It's the only way. It's the only thing left to do."

Halina was overwhelmed by these new developments.

"You mean a handful of poor, hungry Jews are going to take on monster Germany? How?"

Mala and Ala stood beside us, speechless. What I was saying seemed to make absolutely no sense to them.

"Yes, Halina. We'll fight them out in the open, on our ghetto streets, from our windows, from our roofs and attics. We'll fight them with sticks and bottles. With rocks. With guns."

"God, it sounds so exciting and so frightening, Jacku," Halina said. "I can hardly believe it. I just hope you'll give me some of your courage. I'll need it." She threw her arms around me. "I can't wait to start, to make you proud of me."

We went upstairs. It took all night to share our love, our excitement, our uncertainty about the future.

It took all morning to say goodbye.

That afternoon, back in Franek's apartment, I rehashed my decision to return to the ghetto. Franek admitted that what he knew about conditions behind the wall came mainly from rumors, and he warned me not to depend entirely on what he told me.

"By now, you know the Germans better than any of us. Follow your own mind, your own instincts. That's my advice." We shook hands and embraced. "You know you can always count on our house, Jacku. It'll always be your home, as well."

He wanted to walk out with me, but I held him back. "No. From here on, I've got to go it alone. You've done enough for me. I'll try to call you, if the phone still works. If not, I'll come back and get Halina myself."

With the pistol in my shirt and food in my rucksack, I was on my way. I was in fighting spirits. I headed for the Jewish cemetery, the area I knew best. From there, I'd cross back into the ghetto.

I walked along Zelazna Street on the Aryan side of the wall. Where a few weeks ago heavily armed Germans patrolled the street, now only a gendarme or two idled away their time. It must be finished in there, I thought. It's all so quiet.

I entered Okopowa Street, passed the corner of Kacza Street, and stopped. A sign was swinging gently in the breeze: Restauracja Pod Kaczka. My feelings stirred. But nothing else.

I walked up the steps. A wooden board nailed across the door carried the words, "Property of the Third Reich," plus a warning: "Death penalty for anyone entering without permission." I went around to the rear entrance. Another board with the same notice. Everything was quiet inside. No voices. Only memories.

In my mind, I saw Jadzia's radiant face. Then her father's—*knajpiarz* Maciek. True Christians. If only there were more like them, I thought. I wondered where the Germans had sent them. I wondered whether they were still alive.

A light rain was now falling from the cloudy September sky. I spent an hour or so at the Evangelical Cemetery. It was still wise to wait for darkness for what I had to do.

To cross the wall, I picked the spot where the gang and I had often stopped. There was a huge monument adjoining the wall. Its inscription said, "E. J. Wedel, Father and Founder of the Wedel Chocolate Works." Climbing that monument brought you halfway across the wall. Yankele would always stop at the top, touch the Wedel monument, lick his lips and exclaim, "Fucking bastards, *yekes,* now come and get me. I'll die a sweet chocolate death."

"Hey, Yankele," I once said to him, "even if I wrapped you as a gift for Satan, he'd send you back to this world. He hates sweet stuff." The gang had roared with laughter.

It wasn't far from there that Yankele had fallen from the tree, gunned down by the SS. I wondered how many thousands of other Yankeles were dying every day in the German death factories.

At dusk, I climbed the wall into the Jewish cemetery. I decided to spend the night in the Radzyminer Rabbi's *ohel,* the one I'd used for hiding in my smuggling days. Was it only a year ago? I remembered the excitement and creative energy that went into our gang. I remembered that despite the constant danger, there was a sense of adventure, a sense of pride that we were outwitting the Germans while helping to save our families. But mostly I remembered and longed for the sense of possibility, of youthful optimism, of hope for the future that inspired us and kept us going.

Gone now. I was the oldest boy of fifteen in the world.

Early the next morning, I walked carefully along the cemetery paths. I zigzagged back and forth, keeping a watchful eye out for German patrols. At the entrance gate, I noticed two Pinkert guards. Hundreds of unburied corpses were piled high everywhere around them. Bodies were stacked on either side of the gate and along the nearby wall. It looked like they'd been there for weeks.

The guards were surprised to see me walking toward them.

"Where's my friend, Shmerl?" I asked. "He was working here, a big shot. Where is he?"

"Where'd you come from? And what are you talking about?" one of the guards replied.

"Shmerl, the Pinkert chief. My friend, Shmerl. You must've heard of him."

The two men looked at each other in bewilderment. "The SS rounded up all the Pinkert men and their families a few days ago. We were left to attend burials. Our families are gone, and we eat and sleep here in the cemetery. We're afraid to leave and go back into the ghetto. All the streets are empty. Only Germans and Ukrainians roam the streets."

"But the Jews, there have got to be some Jews left," I insisted.

I threw countless questions at them which went unanswered. They stammered and trembled, incoherent in their fear. But they did finally confirm the rumors that a small ghetto remained. There were a few inhabited streets left, perhaps Zamenhofa, Gesia, Mila, Niska. . . .

I waited in the cemetery for the friendly darkness of night. With my gun ready, I slipped by the cemetery gate and made my way cautiously through the empty streets.

I headed up Gliniana, past the place where we used to play soccer. I walked by my Grandma Masha's house on Ostrowska Street. I choked back my tears and raced down the street. I dodged shadows, hid in doorways; I listened for every suspicious sound. My gun was always ready. It gave me security and, even more important, dignity.

Suddenly I heard many voices; voices of men, women, and children.

I ran into the nearest building, climbed the stairs to the attic, crossed the roof, and descended into an adjoining courtyard on Mila Street. The yard was filled with Jews.

I was overjoyed to find so many still alive. But my happiness was short-lived. Only minutes later, SS troops and Ukrainians appeared. Cursing and shouting orders, they began driving everyone out of the yard with their rifle butts.

I turned and tried to flee the way I'd come, but my path was blocked by the SS. I'd risked my life to get here, and now I was trapped again. The SS had sealed off two whole blocks of Mila Street, from Zamenhofa to Smocza. Troops were patrolling the sidewalk, while the Jews were being herded into the gutter.

I soon discovered what was going on. Now that most of the Jews had been sent to the death factories, the Germans were liquidating the ghetto's once most privileged class, the people who held the coverted special exemption cards. They were mainly Jewish police, *Judenrat* employees, cemetery workers, and other collaborators. They had done the dirty work for the Germans, and now they were no longer needed. Their turn had come. The Germans had called this "privileged" area of the ghetto the *kociol,* the boiler. It was a private SS joke, for this was where they planned finally to "boil" the "good" Jews. But now that I was standing among them, I didn't know whether to rejoice at seeing these sons of bitches getting what they deserved, or to regret that the last of Warsaw's Jews were being gathered for their final trip.

I walked around, witnessing scenes of torment. Distraught mothers were trying to comfort hysterical children; well-dressed men were arguing with each other about whom to blame; elderly women were huddling together, looking feeble and pathetic. Most of the police had already discarded their caps and uniforms. An overwhelming feeling of guilt was hanging in the air. I was sure I could touch it if I tried.

I listened to a desperate argument between a young man and his wife. The woman was screaming at her husband. "You're no good! You deserve the *Umschlagplatz!* You thought my mother wasn't good enough to hide with us. Now we're all here. Even you, Mr. Big Shot!"

The man, a former police lackey, was weeping. "I just tried to save you and the children." He fell to his knees and held on to his drowsy twins.

Nearby, I saw a *jamnik* trample his police cap and strike his head with his club. "Mama! Mama!" he screamed. "Forgive me! I was so stupid! So selfish!" Blood was streaming down his face, but he continued to rant and rave. "No! I can't live! I shouldn't live! I don't deserve to live!"

Finally, I grew weary of pushing my way through the mass of people. I lay down in the gutter among all the other wretched human beings and dozed off into a troubled sleep.

A burst of machine gun fire, an SS alarm clock, awakened everyone at dawn. A squad of Germans was setting up tables at the corner of Mila and Zamenhofa streets. I moved closer through the mob of people to see what was happening.

The Jews from the "boiler" were being marched off somewhere to the left, in the direction of the *Umschlagplatz.* At the same time, a selection was taking place. A bespectacled, middle-aged SS officer, using a whip, was directing some of the healthy young men to the right, away from the *Umschlagplatz.*

"Los! Schnell! Alles rechts!"

A number of screaming SS men were hurrying the bulk of the bewildered men, women, and children off to the left—pushing, shoving, and beating them with rifle butts and whips. The cruelty showered on these formerly privileged Jews was unmatched by any I'd previously seen.

Now, more than anything, I wanted to be tapped by the selecting SS man's whip, to be directed away from the *Umschlagplatz.* I knew in my heart that all the others were going off to their deaths.

I feared the cattle car depot, but I was ready for it. I had the gun, and I intended to use it at the right moment. I was way up front now, anticipating the moment of decision, when I felt the SS man's whip pass over my hair. Simultaneously, someone grabbed my arm and yanked me to the right. I was standing with those chosen to remain behind.

I watched as the other Jews were marched off to the railroad sidings.

Hauptsturmführer Geipel stood on a table in the street and adjusted his spectacles as he looked over the group of "selected" young people gathered before him. A number of SS soldiers, weary from their strenuous Jew-whipping duties of the morning, lounged at ease on the fringes of the group.

Now a young SS aide to Geipel barked a command: *"Achtung! Achtung!"*

A volley of machine gun fire burst into the air. An immediate silence fell over the street. Then Geipel began to speak.

"This is a very lucky day for you. You've been chosen to serve the Third Reich. Each of you is part of a team—*die Werterfassung.* Your mission is twofold—charity and cleanliness. First, you will be helping Germany's poor. Winter is coming, and you will be providing *Winterhilfe.* Second, you will be helping to clean up the filth your friends have left behind."

The irony of this crazy situation was almost too much for me to bear. *Hauptsturmführer* Geipel was speaking to us almost in the manner of an athletic coach delivering a pep talk to his soccer team. We, a "lucky" group of tormented Jews, were to remain in the ghetto for an indefinite period. We were to select, assemble, and help transport to Germany all the possessions—the furniture, clothing, bedding, rugs, china, toys—left behind by the almost half-million Jews the Germans had sent to their deaths.

I felt like screaming, "Murderers, sadists!"

But I didn't.

CHAPTER 18

"There is nothing to fear," the German posters announced. "Resettlement is ended. All Jews can now live in peace. There is no need to hide. Come join the German work units."

The new Nazi *Bekanntmachung* was plastered everywhere, both in the so-called "wild" areas of the deserted large ghetto and in the few populated streets of the new central ghetto.

A new wall was built down the middle of Gesia Street, with a gate on the corner of Zamenhofa. The SS requisitioned an entire block on Niska Street as residences for *Werterfassung* workers. The first house near the wall was Niska 4. I moved in, choosing a comfortable four-room apartment for my quarters.

To underscore their good intentions, the Nazis announced the construction of a new kindergarten for all young children who might still be in hiding. Thousands of people suddenly began to emerge from nowhere—cellars, attics, secret rooms, sewers. Somehow, they had managed to hide from the SS squads through the months of deportations. About forty thousand people converged on the new central ghetto.

They were mostly young, militant, and ready to fight.

After a few days at the *Werterfassung* storage depot, working with a *Kommando* unit that loaded furniture from vacated Jewish apartments into German trucks, I managed to get assigned to a station job. I became assistant group leader at the huge storage center at

Zamenhofa 44. This group repaired and cleaned furniture before its shipment to Germany.

My new job gave me the opportunity to lead a double life. I was legally employed by the SS, while illegally smuggling arms, food, and construction supplies for building bunkers.

I liked the irony of the setup. We were getting ready for the final hour, preparing for a huge confrontation, right under their Nazi noses. We were getting ready for revenge, defiance, and psychological warfare. At last we were going to try to beat them at their own game.

All night, in my dreams, I made plans and designed schemes.

I dreamed that I was leading a new gang, a gang of teenagers.

I dreamed of a huge bunker deep under the foundation of Niska 4: a bunker with guns, Molotov bottles, food, supplies, and tricky entrances. A bunker full of Jews.

I dreamed of Halina and Mala, of Mama and Hela, of Papa. Of gathering them all together.

I dreamed that Lutek and Shmulek were alive somewhere. Along with some of my cousins and aunts. And my Grandma Masha.

I dreamed and tossed and sweated and dreamed some more.

But early in the morning when the weak October sunlight shone through the worn-out shades of my bare bedroom, I stood up from my soaked mattress and stared out the window in anger and bitterness. I was standing there all alone. That was my reality.

It was at that moment that I resolved to head for the Toebbens workshops to get Mama and Hela. That would be my first assignment.

I talked to Halina in a coded telephone conversation.

"Please, Jacku, please don't make me wait any longer than that. I want to be with you. I've got to."

"It'll be any day now. I've still got some things to arrange. Then I'll be ready. No more than a few days. I promise you. I must get Mama and Hela first. Please be patient."

My task seemed impossible. To reach Toebbens, I would have to cross about two miles of deserted streets that were patrolled by SS troops, gendarmes, or Polish police. Anyone found in the area without permission was immediately shot. In fact, a number of Christian

Poles had been executed recently for venturing into the area to steal valuables from the empty ghetto houses.

Then I would have to enter the guarded Toebbens enclave, get Mama and Hela out, cross the wild ghetto again, and, finally, pass through the central ghetto's gate without a permit—all by nightfall, before curfew.

I knew that only a bold and daring plan would work.

And I had one. As a Polish policeman, a blue, I could easily march through the empty streets. All I had to do was acquire the uniform, the holster, and the cap.

I wandered a few blocks in and out of the empty houses, avoiding the German patrols. Finally I spotted a pair of blues on Leszno Street. They were approaching an abandoned bar at the corner of Solna. I quickly entered the bar through a side window and waited till the blues came closer. Then I deliberately broke some bottles. They stopped and drew their guns.

"You in there," one of them ordered. "Come out with your hands up!"

The blues peered through the window, trying to see into the darkness. Holding a bottle, I staggered toward them, pretending to be a Christian kid who was drunk.

"Hey, boys," I said, my speech slurred. "I thought these filthy Jews were supposed to be starving. Goddammit! The place is loaded! There's a cellar back there full of stuff, champagne, cognac, vodka. You wouldn't believe it!"

The policemen ignored me. "Just keep your hands in the air and step outside!"

"Dammit!" I insisted. "C'mon in and take a look! Christ! There's cases o' stuff!" I opened the door and staggered backward. "C'mon. Lemme showya the cellar."

The blues entered the bar warily. They leveled their guns at me. I held my hands up and continued my act. I believed their guns were unloaded, but what if things had changed? I couldn't be certain.

"It's back here, boys. The stairs're back here." I moved to the rear, to the darkest part of the bar.

Suddenly one of the blues turned a flashlight on me. "Goddammit! If this is a trick, you won't walk outta here alive!"

"No trick, Christ! I swear it!" I opened the cellar door and pointed. "Down there. It's all down there. Cases 'n' cases. C'mon, I'll show ya."

The blues hesitated. I could sense the conflict in their minds. They were intrigued by the prospect of finding hidden treasure. But how could they trust me?

"We'll stay here," one of them said. "You bring up a case. And no funny business."

I knew my time was running out. "Okay. I'll be right up."

I took a step or two down, then wheeled around with my gun drawn. I acted tough.

"Hands up! This one's loaded!"

The blues dropped their guns and raised their hands slowly into the air. I'd taken them completely by surprise.

I grabbed the flashlight and quickly shoved the blues down into the pitch-black cellar. "Keep your mouths shut, or I'll blast your brains out!"

The two men, both middle-aged, begged for mercy. "Please. Please don't kill us. We're fathers."

"I mean business," I said. "Just do what you're told, and you won't get hurt."

"Yes, yes. Anything you say."

I ordered one of them to strip. Within seconds, I was clothed in his uniform.

"Please don't take our guns," they pleaded. "We'll lose our jobs. The Gestapo might even shoot us. Jesus Christ, be merciful."

I let them keep their empty weapons, but I took a belt and holster to complete my disguise. I looked like a real blue. I locked them both in the basement, straightened my policeman's cap, and walked briskly up Solna Street. I passed two German patrols, saluted smartly, and smiled. At the Toebbens gate, I walked straight through and saluted the guards. Once inside, I walked to the gate of the former Commerce School and boldly asked the *Volksdeutscher* guard for assistance.

"I'm looking for a certain Jewess," I told him. "I have an arrest order for her." I showed a slip of paper with Mama's name on it.

He nodded and took me to the first floor where the Jewish foreman brought my frightened mother to the front of the workshop. I spoke roughly to her. "Yes, that's the one, *parch Zydowa,* filthy Jewess. You're under arrest!" I wanted everyone to hear.

Mama stared at me. She wanted to scream out and touch me, but I clamped my hand over her mouth and pushed her out of the building and across the empty street. I didn't let her talk or turn around until we reached her flat. Once there, we embraced and clung to each other. She felt so thin and frail in my arms. She cried and laughed and looked in amazement at her son, "the policeman."

I asked about Hela.

"My Izaakl, my Izaakl. If only you had come a few days earlier. Last week, on *Kol Nidre* eve, these German sadists raided the night shift where all the young girls worked. They marched them straight to the *Umschlagplatz.* Hela was still weak from the typhoid, you know, but she remembered what you taught her: always try to escape. And that's what she did. She and some other girls tried to run for their lives right outside the gates. And the SS gunned them down. These bandits who kill and murder young kids!" She broke down and sobbed.

I crashed my fist into the wall. "Dammit! Dammit! If only I'd come a week ago, Hela'd still be alive. The bastards! I swear. I swear, Mama. Someday they'll pay for it!"

I explained my plan to her. "You're in my custody now, Mama. I have orders to deliver you to the central ghetto. You don't know me. You've never seen me. Don't talk. Not a word. Just look sad, or cry. I might be rough to you if we meet any *yekes.* But it's the only way."

I put on my police cap, checked the loaded gun in my holster, then marched her to the Toebbens gate. I saluted the German gendarme.

"Herr *Feldwebel, eine Judin verhaftet.* One Jewess arrested." He waved me on. We had gotten through with no trouble.

For the next hour and a half, I steered Mama through the old ghetto streets. I shoved and kicked her whenever German patrols passed. Finally, saluting the sentry again, I shoved her through the gate of the central ghetto. No one questioned me.

I headed straight for my apartment in the Niska Street enclave. Once there, Mama was in ecstasy. She hugged and kissed me. She embarrassed me, marveling at the way I looked and at how I'd smuggled her safely through such danger.

"I knew you'd survive," she said. "I knew you'd find a way." But then the tears returned to her eyes. "My Hayele, my darling Hayele, murdered in cold blood . . ."

Throughout the night, I soothed and comforted her. I told her about Papa. About Halina. About the *Werterfassung* operation.

"I can get a job for you at the storage center," I told her. "It'll make you more legitimate, just in case of SS raids."

"Anything you say, Izaakl. You're the expert in this war. You're the professor."

I took her to another room in the apartment. "This room is for Papa. Soon I'll bring him back, too. I've even prepared some books."

And then, with a feeling of manly pride, I showed her the room I would share with Halina. This was the first time I told her about our relationship. She didn't take me seriously.

"Still children and already in love. It's the war." She shook her head. "Even love's been turned upside down. It's your world, Izaakl. But only for as long as the Germans allow it. So go ahead. Be in love. May God bless you!"

CHAPTER 19

The three backyards of the storage center at Zamenhofa 44 were huge and long. Spacious underground shelters lay beneath them. In prewar days, these were used for storage by local bazaar merchants. As head of a new smuggling gang, I was now using these underground labyrinths to reach several connecting tunnels that led to Kupiecka and Nalewki streets.

Rudy Mietek, or *Geiler Motl,* as he was nicknamed, was my right-hand man. Muscular and manly, Rudy had red hair and hundreds of freckles, which practically covered his face. He came from a Hasidic family and, at the age of sixteen, was already a nonbeliever.

Rudy talked for hours with Mama, trying to convince her that there was no God; and that if there was one, He was on the wrong side.

"My whole family, especially my father and grandfather," he said, "were God-fearing people, faithful followers of the famous Gerer Rebe, a saintly rabbi. Yet the Germans slaughtered them all. Where was God then? I'll tell you something else. When the Germans come for me, I'll die with my hands at their throats! If I go to the grave, they'll go with me."

Rudy was tough. He hid in cellars, jumped roofs, and escaped from the *Umschlagplatz* twice. And when he finally was herded into the cattle cars, he jumped the train on its trip to Treblinka.

I remembered the night he arrived back in the ghetto. I had

When I was on the Aryan side only days before the Warsaw ghetto uprising, I visited Franek, a Christian friend of the family. My picture was taken wearing the boots I was so proud of. Years later, when I looked up my old friend, I found that he and the photo had both miraculously survived Warsaw's destruction.

This photo of my parents was taken about the time I was born. My father Aron had the distant blue eyes of a dreamer; my mother Zlatka was the practical one in the family.

My younger sister Hela was only eight when this picture was taken. Like all Jewish children in Warsaw, she was soon required to grow up very fast.

This picture, taken around 1910, shows my Grandma Masha when she was about forty years old. She and five of her nine children were visiting her brother in London.

Even the Germans laughed when Crazy Rubinstein told jokes and performed his antics on the streets of the ghetto.

Many of the smugglers who risked their lives bringing food into the ghetto were very young children.

As you can see from the expressions on the faces of these children who have been caught smuggling by a German soldier, they well understood the dangers of their occupation. Whether they survived the next twenty-four hours in the hands of the Gestapo is questionable.

The first victims of the Nazi regime were children. Disease, starvation, and the terrors of separation from their parents quickly took a deadly toll.

This is one of the *ohels,* or mausoleums, that were built to honor the memory of saintly rabbis. When our gang was using the cemetery as a smuggling route, we often spent the night of our return from the Aryan side hiding in an *ohel,* waiting to join the mourners in the first funeral procession the next morning.

Here you see the brick wall that separates the Jewish cemetery from the Evangelical Cemetery. If the submachine guns of the Germans patrolling the cemetery didn't catch up with us first, all we had to do was climb one of those conveniently located trees and we were out of the ghetto and into Aryan Warsaw.

The picture on the left is of the Tlomackie Synagogue in Warsaw and was taken at about the time my choir sang there. The other is the rubble of the synagogue after SS General Jurgen Stroop blew it up in May 1943; then he declared Warsaw to be *Judenrein,* or free of Jews.

The total assault to squelch our rebellion against the Germans that took place on the Warsaw ghetto during late April 1943 was directed by the German brigadier general of the SS, Jurgen Stroop, using experienced combat troops.

In the later stages of the fighting, the Germans decided simply to burn down a huge area in the middle of Warsaw. We never believed that they would go to such extremes just to get their hands on a few thousand Jews.

As we emerged from the smoke-filled bunkers, the Germans rounded everyone up. Most were executed on the spot, but a few were sent to concentration camps. The man bending over in the background is being tortured to make him reveal the location of the bunker in which his friends are still trying to hide.

The top photo is a view of the Warsaw ghetto before the uprising; at the bottom you see the same area after the unbelievable destruction delivered by the Germans during the fighting.

Motorcycles like these, with machine guns mounted on the sidecars, patrolled our long column during the forced march from Flossenburg concentration camp to Dachau. Anyone who slowed up or dropped out of the line was shot. I captured this cycle from SS guards fleeing the approaching American tanks. I'm in the sidecar (replacing the machine gun!), and another survivor of the march is on the cycle.

After liberation, a group of us formed a band called The Happy Boys and toured refugee camps and hospitals all over Europe where survivors were being treated. Making music again helped me take my mind off my own losses.

After my mother and I were separated at Majdanek, she continued to believe that I would survive—although I never dared believe the same thing about her. So she was happy, but not truly surprised, to find me again when the war was over. This picture of us was taken a year or so after liberation.

I am standing by a tree in the Jewish cemetery. My gang of boy smugglers climbed the tree, went over the wall, and landed in the Evangelical Cemetery, which was part of Aryan Warsaw. One of the kids was killed by Germans here; they opened fire as he, the last one to go over the wall, was trying to escape.

On revisiting Warsaw recently, I found that one of the covers of the sewers that I used as a travel route during the ghetto uprising had been turned into a monument to remind future generations of those desperate trips in and out of the ghetto.

In Warsaw today there is an impressive monument to the victims of the Holocaust. It reminds the world of man's potential for inhumanity. I always lay a wreath there when I visit Warsaw.

watched him talking to a group of kids in one of the Mila Street courtyards.

"Believe me, you schmucks, they are killing everybody. They have gigantic gassing camps. Let's fight them to the death, *yatn*. Let's fight them with our fists, with rocks, sticks, knives. Let's make them bleed like we do."

He was filthy, unshaved, and tired from the long, risky trip back to Warsaw. Impressed by his fighting spirit, I grabbed his lapels.

"Hey, kiddo, big talker!" I challenged him.

"Get your hands off me." In a flash, his switchblade shone in front of my eyes. I let go and smiled.

I knew then that Rudy was my kind of a guy.

Then there was Yosek, who, like Rudy and me, was sixteen. Lean and delicate, Yosek had a subtle manner that balanced Rudy's explosive character. But there was nothing subtle about his determination to avenge his brother's murder at the *Umschlagplatz* only a few days earlier.

The two boys had been raised at Dr. Korczak's orphanage on Krochmalna Street. When the SS hauled Dr. Korczak, his staff, and the children to the cattle cars, Yosek rebelled. He climbed the wall behind the railroad tracks and escaped. His younger brother was gunned down right behind him.

But I was closest to the third member of the gang, Shmulek Grinberg, my former smuggling accomplice and Mala's brother. I had found him only a few days earlier, when out of curiosity I had stopped at the Swietojerska Street complex and asked around for the Grinberg family. To my amazement, Mrs. Grinberg and Shmulek were still in their old dungeon of an apartment. They were just barely existing.

They promptly accepted my invitation to join Mama and me on Niska Street. And using my friendship with Fritz Rosen, the foreman at the storage depot, I got Shmulek a job there.

With his unique personality and background, Fritz, a German Jew, was a rarity in the ghetto, and he and I became friends. In his early thirties, he lived with his beautiful wife, Rita, and their four-year-old son, Kurt. His boyhood friend from Berlin, SS *Untersturmführer* Helmut Werner, watched over him. Wherever Werner went, Fritz went. In charge of the *Werterfassung's* furniture division, Werner appointed Fritz as the foreman.

Every day Fritz brought Rita and Kurt to work with him; he was afraid to leave them behind at the Niska Street enclave in case of SS raids. Rita acted as Werner's secretary, and Kurt was placed in hiding during working hours.

SS officer Werner was a precise and theoretical Nazi who considered Jews unfit for survival. Fritz and Rita Rosen were the only exceptions. Often, in secret, they even lunched with Werner in his second-floor office. But Fritz understood the truth: ultimately, as a Jew, he would share the Jews' fate. So he helped us whenever he could; the resistance must go on.

Our strategy was to smuggle furs, silver, and other valuables that we found in the abandoned ghetto apartments. We'd bring the loot into the storage depot by hiding it in pieces of furniture. Then we would transfer it for sale in Aryan Warsaw, through the underground shelters and specially constructed tunnels or sewers. With the funds we acquired, we bought a variety of supplies on the black market: guns, ammunition, gasoline, food, bunker gear, batteries, and other necessities. We brought everything back with us through the same underground system.

My contacts in Aryan Warsaw in that fall of 1942 were mostly the familiar dealers at the Kiercelak Market. Franek was my arms supplier. He had become a respected member of *Gwardia Ludowa,* the left-wing Polish underground. And old Stas and his son-in-law, Antek, were back in business with the Wolnosc Street *melina.*

Finally, the day arrived when I was ready to bring Halina and Mala back to the ghetto. On a dreary October morning, I was perched high in a tree at the Jewish cemetery, waiting. My gun was loaded, and I had a clear view of the area all around me.

The stillness was eerie. A light rain was falling. Soon I saw three figures approaching on the Aryan side. Franek stopped at one of the monuments in the Evangelical Cemetery. He kissed the girls goodbye and pointed to the spot where I was waiting. As I started down the tree, I saw him wave.

A moment later, the girls were over the wall and in my arms. Quickly and quietly, we walked through the thick rows of monuments, stones, and bushes, heading for the *ohel,* the mausoleum. Once inside, I took Halina in my arms, stared at her face, and began to lick her salty tears. We held each other tightly. We kissed and stared at each other. Each time Halina began to say something, I would shut her up.

"Just hug me, just kiss me," I murmured. She understood me so well, so easily.

Often I had dreamed of her flirting with other men. I imagined her forgetting me, not wanting me. I imagined my beautiful Halina, loving, kissing other boys. It was absurd; it was illogical. She hardly had any contact with other men. Yet I was madly jealous and imagined the unimaginable.

We left the cemetery at dusk, in semi-darkness, and made our way through the empty streets of the wild ghetto.

"In case of trouble," I warned them, "run for the first courtyard and up to the attic. I'll stay behind and shoot it out if I have to."

I showed them the gun I was wearing in the holster beneath my leather jacket.

"When do I get a gun?" Halina asked. "You promised, Jacku. Remember? Franek told me to tell you he'd have two *spluwy* next week. One's for me. Okay?"

"Okay!"

Mala shook her head in amazement. "You mean you could actually kill, Halina? You could really do it?"

"Sure, Mala. I've thought about it a lot. For my mother and father and all the others. I'd shoot those beasts right now if I had the chance!"

"Shut up, both of you," I ordered. "Just follow me. We're crossing Smocza Street now. Beyond that is the central ghetto." I pointed to the new wall. "You can hear the noise already."

We climbed the wall and hurried to the Niska Street apartment, where a big feast awaited us. Mrs. Grinberg and Shmulek hadn't seen Mala in over two years. Their reunion was tearful, joyful, and painful, all at once. They kissed and hugged each other. They spoke separately and all together. They moved about excitedly. They sat. They stood. They ate and drank.

I introduced Halina to Mama. Yes, she remembered the skinny little girl from Swider but could hardly recognize this beautiful young woman. And I introduced her to my gang—to Rudy, Yosek, and Shmulek.

The festivities lasted till well past midnight, when I made my final toast, perhaps my tenth of the night: "There's one person missing—

Papa. I promise to have him back from Rembertow in a week. Let's drink to that."

I kept my promise the following Saturday. Franek arranged things with *Schachmeister* Willy at the Rembertow camp. Enough zlotys and gold coins persuaded him to send Papa back to Aryan Warsaw in one of the supply trucks. I waited at a prearranged spot, then simply walked off with him while the guard looked the other way.

Before returning to the ghetto, we stopped for lunch at Franek's apartment on Lucka Street. The sight of his old friend boosted Papa's spirits. He thanked Franek and his family profusely for their many noble deeds.

That same evening, I helped Papa over the wall and back into the ghetto. We all gathered again at the Niska Street apartment and had another celebration. But Mama broke down when she recalled Hela's murder. "Only fifteen, and cut down by those murderers," she kept repeating.

With my gun in one hand and a bottle in the other, I called for revenge. "From now on, dammit, we fight back and spill some German blood! We'll make it run as red as ours. Let's drink to that!"

Rudy drew his gun, and we embraced. We drank from the same bottle and swore to fight, to avenge.

Gunshots interrupted our celebration as I instructed Halina in the use of the new P.38 caliber pistol I had just given her. She handled it beautifully, with pride and expertise.

"Every bullet is a diamond," I told her. "But you are the most precious gem of all."

She kissed me passionately. "It's the best and most wonderful gift you could have given me, Jacku. I'll make you proud of me, you'll see. I'll fight like a man. I swear I'll have no mercy on the Nazi bastards."

Our behavior, our bravado, and our drinking shocked my parents and Mrs. Grinberg, who looked at us with astonishment. Our words sounded so strange to them. They were intimidated and confused. They wouldn't accept weapons in their house. I had to assure them that we would keep the guns well hidden, locked in the new bunker we were building.

We had excavated the bunker ourselves. Working slowly and meticulously every night after curfew, we had disposed of several tons of sand and gravel. We had poured it all into nearby sewer openings. Then I'd smuggled a Christian over from the Aryan side to help with the work; he was an expert in cement mixing and masonry.

We planned two hidden bunker entrances. One was through the bathroom floor of our apartment. From there, it was necessary to slide down the sewer pipe into the basement below the foundation.

The other entrance, which was more complicated, needed a tunnel, which was almost completed. The tunnel ran to the edge of the courtyard, where a large garbage bin was cemented to the pavement. Outfitted with oil, dried fruit, dried bread, cans of sardines, pickles, a kerosene cooker, lamps, a dozen Molotov bottles, and whatever meager medical supplies we could find, the bunker would hold us through a six-month siege.

Ours wasn't the only bunker. Construction was going on quite openly in almost every backyard. The central ghetto was becoming increasingly independent, a Jewish armed camp in the middle of the Third Reich. After the underground had executed a number of collaborators, the Jewish and Polish police didn't dare enter the ghetto streets in uniform. Those who did risked being found with bullets in their brains. SS officers and gendarmes also entered the ghetto now only in armed groups. They no longer took their leisurely strolls to entertain themselves with Jewish blood.

Halina's practice session and instruction continued quietly in our room later that evening. I watched her standing there, the gun securely in her hand. She was a real sight—tough, aggressive, yet feminine and graceful. A wide smile graced her lovely face. She wore one colorful scarf tied smartly around her throat; another was knotted in her long blond hair. Her large blue eyes provoked me, and she always left the top buttons of her blouse undone.

I loved her flirtations. "Halina, what guy could ever resist you?"

She came closer to me and whispered in my ear. "Don't you dare ever try. It's all yours, you know. All of it."

I grabbed her silky braids and pulled her close to me. "So what are we waiting for?"

"Love me, kiss me, hit me," she teased. "But don't you ever ignore me."

We laughed and played, and I buried my face in her hair. I inhaled her fragrance. We embraced with joy and declared our love a thousand times.

That night, we couldn't fall asleep. We made love, we lay awake, talking and dreaming about ourselves and each other. We were in a world of our own. We fantasized about the future, about what we really wanted: a normal human existence. The most exciting things we could imagine were to walk together in the Saski Park, to take snapshots of each other, or just to lie somewhere on a beach, without the deep gut ache that had become a part of our bodies.

Suddenly Halina took my face in her hands and looked deeply into my eyes. "Jacek, will you marry me someday?"

"Of course, Halina, someday. We'll always be great together. A team."

But then my enthusiasm faded as I began to consider our reality. I was leaning on a huge pillow that covered almost half the bed. The kerosene lamp was low in oil, and its wick, short and worn, gave a true reflection of our temporary underground existence.

I saw myself in the blue-green mirror of her eyes. In it, I was big, overpowering, enlarged into another dimension. I wanted to live up to that dimension, to surround her, to envelop and protect her. Yet I was frightened by her question. It came from wishful thinking, which I had learned not to allow myself. Throughout the almost three years in the ghetto, I had survived by battling and suppressing my fantasies and my emotions. So often I had recoiled in pain. So often I had become bitter. I was already shattered, overwhelmed with disappointment and disillusioned with life, society, people.

I dreaded becoming like my father in his complete apathy. Never did I want to be as disappointed in life as he was. In front of my eyes, a vibrant, intelligent soul had turned into a vegetable. I didn't want that to happen to me. I wanted to live, to survive emotionally as well as physically.

"But there are no rabbis left," Halina interrupted my thoughts. "And besides, what would a wedding be without a beautiful long white gown?"

I didn't answer.

"Jacek, will there ever be any rabbis again?"

I still didn't answer.

"I wonder if it's possible to marry without my mother and father," she continued thoughtfully. "Is an orphan entitled to the same wedding as other girls? With flowers and a ring and a canopy? And a honeymoon and lots of beautiful gifts?"

Halina turned away from me and gazed out the window into the star-filled sky. I turned off the flickering kerosene lamp. The moon was shining on our faces and our half-nude bodies, its brightness not yet extinguished by the brutality in which we had to live. And even that occurrence wouldn't surprise me now, I realized.

"Jacku, your mother would be against our marriage. Wouldn't she? She hates me."

"Halina! How can you say that? Mama doesn't hate you. She doesn't hate anyone but the Germans."

Halina turned to look at me again. I could feel her tension rising. "I wish my mother was here right now, screaming at me. But you know, she never did scream. I was more afraid of my father. Jacku, please don't laugh at me. I really want to get married someday and have a baby.

"Did I ever tell you how all my dolls were taken away?" she continued softly. "Some were burned or broken. Some were sent to Germany for German children to play with. Even my favorite ones. But now I want a child that I can care for and protect. One that will grow up and be free to travel far away from here, to the other end of the earth!

"Oh, you don't have to tell me, I know I'm dreaming. I know it's silly to think like this. But I can't help it. I want to live. I want to give birth to new life. That mess out there—that's not what life's about. It can't be. Tell me I'm right, Jacku! Tell me I'm right."

She was pointing to the ghetto wall, visible through the window. "I know there's a better, saner world somewhere. There has to be! Answer me, please, Jacku." Her voice was shaking, and she was sobbing.

I put my arms around her, and we held each other. Our silence was filled with the answers I couldn't give her.

CHAPTER 20

On a cold November morning, Halina and I were standing in front of Stas's place in Aryan Warsaw. We were back on the old Wolnosc Street *melina,* waiting for Rudy and Yosek. They were coming across, through the Jewish cemetery, with furs, silver, and damasks. We had successfully returned to the smuggling business.

With our loaded guns securely tucked into our clothes, we no longer feared the *szmalcowniki* as much. A tall young man, accompanied by four grim-faced companions, sauntered down the courtyard past us. The tall fellow and I exchanged glances. Suddenly he stopped.

"Jacek Eisner! *Servus!*"

"Artek Milner from Panska Street!"

We greeted each other with open arms. Artek and I had been neighbors and had attended the same school before the war. I invited him and his buddies into Stas's for a chat. We hadn't seen each other for more than two years, and we had a lot to catch up on.

"Jesus, Maria! What's going on?" Stas exclaimed as we all marched into his living room.

"It's okay, Stas. They're friends of mine. We just want to talk a bit."

Stas looked worried and uneasy. He wasn't used to having his apartment crowded with armed Jews. "Please don't make it long," he begged. "The Germans—"

"Screw the Germans!" I interrupted.

Stas looked at me helplessly and quietly left the room.

Artek was two years my senior and strikingly handsome. With his six-foot frame, blond hair, and blue eyes, he had no difficulty passing as a Christian. The pride of a prosperous textile merchant, he was the youngest of three sons. His two older brothers had escaped to Rumania and then to Paris before the Germans sealed the ghetto. I introduced Halina to him. She flushed and didn't look at him directly. He was obviously an experienced charmer. He smiled and kissed her hand lightly. I was definitely jealous.

Artek and I had a sense of each other's activities, but neither of us revealed anything or asked any embarrassing questions. Instead, Artek pulled out a wad of money. "I'm looking for a machine gun—a Schmeisser. Do you think you can get one?"

"A Schmeisser?" I stared at him with incredulity. A machine gun. I thought it ridiculous even to look for one.

"I'll see what I can do," I said. "Give me a few days."

"Good. Meet me at Mila Twenty-five, Sunday at 6 P.M. I'll be at the backyard entrance. Get ready, Jacek; big things are in the making."

I gestured to the bundle of bills in Artek's hand. "With that kind of cash, it shouldn't be too hard. Hitler himself would sell me one."

Everyone laughed.

The encounter with Artek marked the beginning of my real association with the underground. Until then, I'd been an armed smuggler with a bunker to my credit, like many others in the central ghetto who also had guns and bunkers. But a few—just hundreds—belonged to the organized underground. They were dedicated, determined young men and women. And both Halina and I were about to join them.

I could hardly wait for Sunday. Everything about Artek seemed exciting and glamorous. The way he dressed. The way he spoke. His money. His bodyguards. I sensed a clear fighting purpose about him. Halina counted the days with me. However, I made it clear to her that I wanted to attend that first meeting alone.

But what about the Schmeisser? Where in the world could I get a machine gun? With little expectation, I contacted Franek, my arms supplier. To my utter surprise, he said he could manage it. In fact, one had just been stolen from an SS depot. It would cost a thousand dollars. A fortune. I knew Artek wouldn't be able to raise that kind of money. But at least I had an offer.

On Sunday, at 6 P.M. sharp, I showed up alone in the backyard of Mila 25. I crossed the yard once or twice but didn't notice anything unusual. People were coming and going in the street as always. Suddenly a shabbily dressed man, apparently the janitor of the building, appeared and approached me.

"Are you lost, young fellow?"

"No. I'm just waiting for someone."

"Come and wait in my place."

The man opened the basement door and invited me in. After some hesitation, I followed him inside.

Artek appeared out of nowhere.

"Right on time, Jacek," he said. "I like that."

"Hey, Artek, quite a setup you've got here! A janitor in charge, and you're the landlord."

Artek smiled but didn't respond. Meanwhile, the "janitor" peeled off his fake mustache. I recognized him then as one of Artek's bodyguards. Now, we entered a subbasement through a hatch that had been concealed by a heavy credenza. After descending by ladder, I found myself in a well-furnished room filled with young men—and only one girl.

Artek wasted no time. "This is Jacek Eisner," he said, "our new man." Then he turned to me. "By the way, where's Halina?"

"I wasn't sure you wanted women here."

He smiled. "Don't be a *yold,* old-fashioned. Some of the girls are as good as us." He pointed at his girl friend, Roza. "Some are even better."

A slim brunette with black Spanish eyes stepped forward, smiled, and shook my hand firmly. "Where is Halina? Artek talked so much about her."

I didn't have time to explain. Janek Zloto, Artek's right-hand man, burst in with a smile. "There's an attractive blonde in a leather coat upstairs who insists she's expected here."

Artek climbed the ladder and returned seconds later with Halina on his arm. I blushed with embarrassment as he introduced her as the gang's first blond female member.

Halina embraced me awkwardly and apologized. "I couldn't stay behind," she said. "I just had to be a part of things."

Artek called the meeting to order and formally announced our acceptance into his underground group. Not a word about the organization, its leadership, or its aims. Everything remained a secret, and I didn't ask questions. I figured that's the way it should be.

I stood up and told him about the Schmeisser. Artek walked over to me and asked me to repeat myself. I assured him it was all on the level. With unrestrained joy, he kissed both my cheeks and ordered the gang to celebrate.

"But, Artek, you don't understand. It's a fortune. They want a thousand dollars!"

Artek laughed and swirled a bottle of vodka. "God, Jacku! Don't you know a machine gun has no price in the ghetto? It's priceless!

"Don't you worry. For a Schmeisser, the money'll be here."

Showing his appreciation, Artek instantly appointed me one of his two lieutenants, in the same rank with Janek Zloto, his righthand man. I insisted, however, that I be allowed to continue my own smuggling operation. I felt I still needed to be the boss of something.

At the end of the meeting, Artek ordered Halina and me to show up on Mila Street at 7 A.M. the following Sunday. It was to be our first underground assignment. Not a word about its nature. And no questions allowed. In the meantime, Artek and I prepared to meet at Franek's place to bring back the Schmeisser. Taking no chances, we made our way separately to Lucka Street on the Aryan side.

Franek couldn't believe his ears when I telephoned him earlier to tell him we had the money. "Just be in my apartment. I'll make the arrangements."

Now, tense and anxious, we sat in the attic with a pack of dollars and waited for the Schmeisser to arrive. Every sound in the street set our nerves on edge. Every step in the hall brought us to our feet. Our guns were ready, our minds alert. We expected the worst, perhaps a trap.

Three hours later, at dusk, two young Poles showed up escorting a German deserter in civilian clothes. The transaction was swift and efficient. As they counted the dollars, we examined the weapon. A few moments later, they were gone, and we owned a brand-new machine gun.

"A thousand dollars!" Franek said. "If our people had it, we'd have kept the gun ourselves. What a find!"

Artek was beaming. He kept turning the Schmeisser in his hands every which way, literally kissing the deadly steel weapon.

"Jacku," Franek suddenly said. "I must tell you something. We're getting out of here. All of us, the whole family. I have a feeling we're being watched. So please don't come here any more. Contact me in Milanowek. Don't ever forget I'm your friend. You can always count on me. And give my best to your parents."

We embraced and parted.

Jew and Christian.

Both in danger.

CHAPTER 21

A light snow was falling Sunday morning when Halina and I met with Artek and his gang at the Mila Street *melina.* Artek explained the business at hand. "It's simple. Just a toll-collection operation. Anyone who wants to use the tunnels has to pay a toll. Judge for yourselves how much each person can pay. Jacek and Halina, take five men with you. Use your guns if necessary. Nobody gets through without paying."

Artek turned to me and whispered, "On such a dull job, the Schmeisser gets a rest. But now, at least, you'll see where some of the money comes from."

Sunday, considered a day of rest, was the only day when both the employed minority and the "wild" majority who lived in hiding used the streets freely. Hundreds of individuals passed through the two tunnels to and from the brushmakers' enclave, where perhaps a thosuand or more people worked. Stationed at the Walowa Street tunnel entrance, I demanded and received "donations" all day long.

Collecting money at gunpoint was new to me. Until now, I had risked my life by smuggling to earn money for arms. Most people gave freely, once they learned where the money was going. They were proud to have a Jewish fighting force in their ghetto. Some, however, grumbled. They called it blackmail. But everyone admired Halina. She collected more money than anyone else. With her leather coat, riding pants, boots—and gun—she was irresistible.

They called her "the Jewish *shikse.*" And the bills piled up by the thousands in her straw bag.

By the end of the day, the gang had collected more than one hundred thousand zlotys—enough to buy half a dozen Molotov bottles and several guns. This was the first of many such collection assignments for Halina and me. Most of them were on Sundays. But sometimes, when we needed money urgently, we appeared in the tunnels on midweek evenings between six and nine o'clock curfew.

One day, Artek took me aside and told me to prepare for a major assignment.

"I want you to find Kronenberg and execute the prick."

"Kronenberg? The Jewish police officer! You want me to get rid of the son of a bitch? You really mean it?"

I stood there staring at Artek; my excitement had immobilized me for a moment.

Kronenberg. I knew the name well. I had seen him in action at the *Umschlagplatz:* kicking the old, the sick, the mothers with infants into the cattle cars as though they were garbage. Jewish life meant nothing to him. And that bastard knew that they were heading towards their deaths.

"Artek, that's great!" I exclaimed. I ran to discuss the assignment with Halina and with my gang.

Rudy was overjoyed, but I had to calm him. "Hold it, Rudy," I cautioned. "It must be thought out with brains and executed with finesse. He's got the protection of German gendarmes."

Kronenberg had been discovered hiding with his girl friend and sister in an apartment next to the Gesia Street gate. Halina and I surveyed the building. We studied his apartment, noted his movements, made a record of his schedule. Then I developed a plan of attack. I decided to enlist my friend Yosek's help. I needed his talent for climbing roofs and drainpipes. I picked the day—Sunday—when the crowds in the streets would provide cover for us in case of trouble.

Halina, Yosek, and I entered Gesia 20 via the roof. Because gendarmes were guarding the front entrance of the building, we went through the adjacent building to the rear on Kupiecka Street. Inside, Halina and I made our way, barefoot, down through the attic. Outside, Yosek climbed down the drainpipe. At a predetermined moment, gun in hand, he burst through Kronenberg's window.

"Don't make a move, or I'll blast your brains out!"

Simultaneously, I kicked open his front door. "Hands up! Quick! Not a sound out of you, or it'll be your last!"

Kronenberg, seated in pajamas near his sister and girl friend, stared at us in shock. We'd taken them completely by surprise. All three rose, their hands above their heads. The speed and suddenness of our attack kept them from alerting the Germans outside.

Pointing her gun at them, Halina ordered the girls out of the room. "Into the bedroom. Move!"

Kronenberg fell to his knees and begged for mercy. "Please don't hurt me. Please. I meant well. I really did. I'm sorry. I only tried to save my family."

I moved closer to him with my gun pointed at his head.

Yosek stationed himself outside the bedroom, and Halina began to read the prepared text of the underground's "sentence."

"For crimes against the Jewish people, innocent men, women, and children . . ."

At that moment, Artek appeared from nowhere. He knew Kronenberg well. Both had been ghetto big shots, though on opposite sides.

In a mocking voice, Artek reminded the now pathetic man of his former arrogance and cruelties. "Do you remember when you whipped the children into the cattle cars? Do you remember the old man you kicked down the stairs? Do you remember . . ."

Kronenberg held his head low to avoid Artek's eyes, the eyes of a witness turned judge. He begged and pleaded for his life. "Please don't kill me. They made me do it. I'm sorry. I'm sorry . . ."

Artek could stand no more. He fired at close range. Kronenberg slumped to the floor. Artek looked sad but relieved.

I ordered Halina and Yosek to get back up the stairs. They warned the girls in the bedroom to stay put and keep quiet. Then they ran from the apartment. I finished off the still-struggling collaborator with a bullet in the head. Within minutes, we were all on the roof, crossing back to the Kupiecka Street building.

Artek went his way. Halina, Yosek, and I went ours.

At my Niska Street apartment, a huge Chanukah dinner had been prepared. It was the eighth and final day of the celebration of the Maccabean miracle, the Jewish festival of lights. Mama, Papa, and

Mrs. Grinberg were waiting for us. They had no inkling of where we'd been or what we'd done.

They could never have imagined that we had become killers. In our own defense. For our revenge. For our survival.

CHAPTER 22

In January 1943, Heinrich Himmler, the chief SS hangman, visited Warsaw. Enraged at still finding a ghetto there more than three years after Germany had conquered Poland, he ordered its immediate liquidation.

The Warsaw SS district leadership promptly sent several hundred troops and some battalions of Ukrainians to accomplish the task in a week. Only a few months earlier, they had deported about four hundred thousand people. They assumed that the remaining forty or fifty thousand would pose no serious problem. Of course, the Jewish police were no longer available to help, since they, too, had recently gone the way of the cattle cars. Nor could the Germans count on any other Jewish collaborators. But these were minor problems . . . so they thought.

In the early hours of January 18, well-rested German troops entered the ghetto through the Gesia Street gate to round up the Jews. Moments later, they marched straight into a shower of Molotov bottles and bullets.

The Germans had entered the ghetto in their usual way, firing guns in the air and screaming for all Jews to come out of their buildings. But we weren't the usual Jews. Most of the women, children, sick, and elderly were gone. Those who remained were young, determined, and prepared to fight. We knew that death was the only possible outcome. We knew that we couldn't win, that the battle would

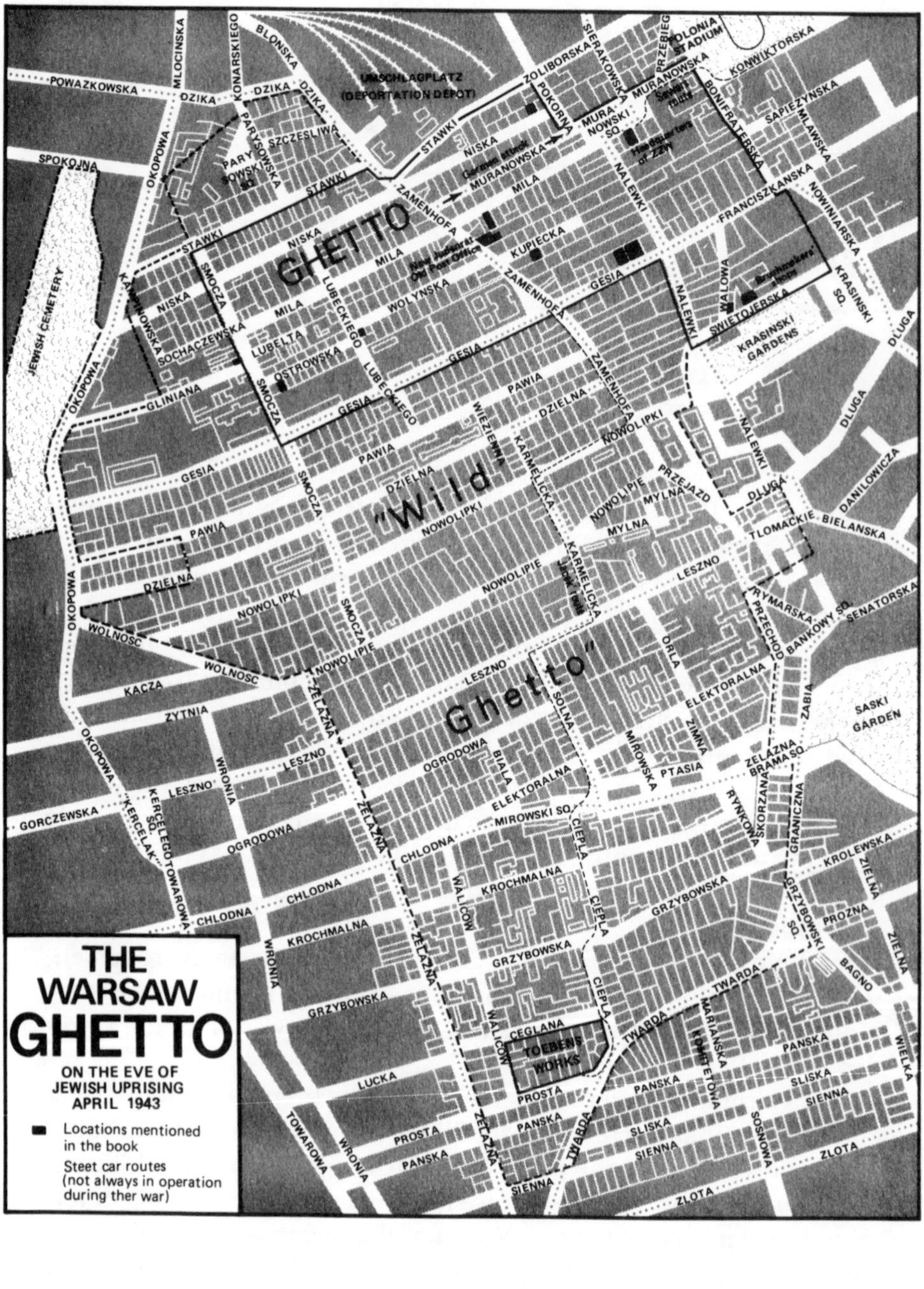

THE WARSAW GHETTO
ON THE EVE OF JEWISH UPRISING APRIL 1943
Locations mentioned in the book
Steet car routes (not always in operation during ther war)
UMSCHLAGPLATZ (DEPORTATION DEPOT)
GHETTO
"Wild Ghetto"
JEWISH CEMETERY
POLONIA STADIUM
KRASINSKI GARDENS
SASKI GARDEN
TOEBENS WORKS
POWAZKOWSKA
DZIKA
SPOKOJNA
MLOCINSKA
OKOPOWA
KONARSKIEGO
BLONSKA
PARYSOWSKA
PARYSOWSKI SQ.
SZCZESLIWA
STAWKI
NISKA
MURANOWSKA
ZOLIBORSKA
POKORNA
SIERAKOWSKA
PRZEBIEG
MURANOWSKI SQ.
KONWIKTORSKA
BONIFRATERSKA
SAPIEZYNSKA
MLAWSKA
FRANCISZKANSKA
NOWINIARSKA
NALEWKI
MILA
ZAMENHOFA
KUPIECKA
GESIA
WALOWA
SWIETOJERSKA
KRASINSKI SQ.
DLUGA
SMOCZA
LUBECKIEGO
WOLYNSKA
LUBELTA
OSTROWSKA
SOCHACZEWSKA
KAMIONOWSKA
GLINIANA
PAWIA
DZIELNA
WIEZIENNA
KARMELICKA
NOWOLIPKI
NOWOLIPIE
PRZEJAZD
MYLNA
TLOMACKIE
BIELANSKA
DANILOWICZA
LESZNO
TRYMARSKA
BANKOWY SQ.
SENATORSKA
PRZECHOD
WOLNOSC
KACZA
ZYTNIA
ZELAZNA
ORLA
SOLNA
ELEKTORALNA
ZIMNA
MIROWSKA
ZABIA
ZELAZNA BRAMA SQ.
WRONIA
OGRODOWA
BIALA
PTASIA
GORCZEWSKA
KERCELAK
KERCELEGO SQ.
TOWAROWA
MIROWSKI SQ.
CHLODNA
CIEPLA
SKORZANA
RYNKOWA
GRANICZNA
KROLEWSKA
ZIELNA
KROCHMALNA
WALICOW
GRZYBOWSKA
GRZYBOWSKI SQ.
PROZNA
BAGNO
CEGLANA
TWARDA
MARIANSKA
KOMITETOWA
PANSKA
WIELKA
LUCKA
PROSTA
SLISKA
SIENNA
SOSNOWA
ZLOTA

eventually end in our annihilation. We counted on no help, no allies, and no miracles. But we also knew we could wait no longer. We would be the first civilian people in occupied Europe to rise openly in the streets against the Germans.

On the third day of fighting, rumors began to spread that the Germans had retreated. Halina, Rudy, and I left our rooftop positions and headed for Kupiecka Street, where we heard unusual activity on the next block.

We climbed to the roof of Kupiecka 11 and looked down into the backyards of Gesia 6 and 8. A squad of SS troops were gathered around several large horse-drawn platforms. Together with their fellow companions in murder, the SS men in the building, they were in the process of liquidating a makeshift ghetto hospital. Before our eyes, the SS soldiers were tossing screaming patients out of the second-, third-, and fourth-floor windows. And on the ground, the loading squad was piling the bodies on the platforms. The continuous screams were horrifying.

At last, Halina found her voice. "Good God! Are we just going to stand here and watch this slaughter with folded arms?"

Rudy and I drew our guns and crawled to the roof's edge. We took aim and were about to fire when suddenly I pulled back.

"What the hell can we do with just pistols?" I said. "We'll only alert them, and they'll come after us with machine guns. Rudy, go get Artek with the Schmeisser. We'll have our own massacre of these bastards!"

Rudy disappeared on the double; Halina and I took up positions in the attic. Meanwhile, the slaughter outside continued. Some of the patients tried to flee down the stairs, but the SS gunned them down.

As we watched from the attic windows, a husky blond German on a balcony grabbed a child who couldn't have been more than two or three. The boy was screaming and covering his half-naked body with his hands.

"Hans!" the German yelled to his comrade. "Let's see how good you are."

He threw the boy into the air. Hans raised his automatic and blew the child apart.

"Bull's-eye! You owe me a bottle of champagne!" He raised his weapon in the air and roared with laughter.

I felt like shrieking. Rudy now reappeared with Artek and Janek Zloto.

"Jacek, you and Rudy cover me," Artek ordered. "Halina, you and Janek keep the staircase clear."

"Can't I see the bastards get it?" Halina asked.

"Do what you're told!" I snapped. Halina disappeared.

Now a fresh group of SS men entered the yard.

Artek whispered, "It's now or never," and aimed his Schmeisser, spraying a barrage of bullets. Within seconds, half a dozen Germans were lying in their own blood. The panicked horses began to gallop in all directions. Rudy and I opened fire with our pistols.

"Dammit! This is what I've been waiting for!" Rudy shouted. "This is worth living for! The SS on the run!"

I was in ecstasy. "Look! Their blood's as red as ours!"

Now the Germans regrouped and began returning our fire.

"They're shooting from the windows!" Artek yelled. "Let's get the hell out of here! We've done all we can."

As SS fire ripped the air on Gesia Street, I led the way through the tunnel to the cellars of the storage center. We remained there until dusk. We emerged to find the Germans gone. They had withdrawn, taking some of their wounded. Only the wall and the Gesia Street gate were still being guarded.

After three days of raids, the SS managed to deport only several hundred victims. And the price they paid was high. They lost a number of armored vehicles, and many German soldiers lay dead or wounded in the streets.

Throughout the fighting, SS *Obersturmführer* Konrad, the new commander of the *Werterfassung,* had forbidden any SS troops to enter his domain, the Niska Street enclave. Shrewder than his predecessor, he wanted to keep his *Werterfassung* post for as long as possible to avoid being sent to the Russian front. He wanted to save himself and get rich. If, in the process, several hundred Jews managed to survive, it was no great tragedy to him.

Despite Konrad's protection, I took no chances. I ordered everyone to stay in our Niska Street bunker overnight. Halina, the gang, and I remained on the roof to keep guard. I knew the Germans might return at any time to complete their mission—to make Warsaw *Judenrein,* free of Jews.

Mama greeted me that evening with anger and scorn. "You young *shnieks,* rebels, will only bring more trouble upon us. Who are you going to fight? The German army? And besides, who ever heard of Jewish boys with guns? It's disgraceful! What will you grow up to be, gangsters? I want no guns in my house!" she screamed.

Papa continued the lecture in a calmer tone. "The miracle of today, the German retreat, is God's work. Fate. Jews do not take fate into their own hands. You young fighters want to change the world. We Jews have lived through almost two thousand years of persecution. This is not the first time we've been hunted. Look at our past, the Crusades, the Spanish Inquisition, the Czarist pogroms. We survived them all without guns. Guns are not our way."

I gulped down a glass of vodka to keep from exploding at them. "You ought to be proud of us. You ought to bless us for what we're trying to do. I've read your books about the Spanish Inquisition. How can you compare it to the present slaughter? Back then, a Jew was allowed to emigrate, and most left Spain for other places where they could survive. It's possible that you and I are descendants of those survivors. But now, Papa, listen to me. Don't shut your ears and mind! Can I leave Poland now? Will the Germans let me go?"

My parents and Mrs. Grinberg sat in silence. I wasn't finished. "Something else you may have forgotten about. During the Inquisition, Jews could convert and still live—like the Marranos. But not now! Look at Franek's neighbors. They were born Catholic. Their grandparents converted fifty years ago. But the Germans still killed them in Treblinka. They weren't Aryan enough. And do you know that now more Jews and Jewish property are being destroyed in one week than in all three hundred years of the pogroms put together! You're comparing stones to Mount Everest. We can't treat every disease with the same medicine. This is a new enemy. They're out to destroy us completely. Once and for all!"

My voice rose. "Can't you see? Prayers aren't enough. Your ancient methods won't save us. Maybe the truth is you'd rather die than let us kids take over! You're all blind to reality. All you know is how to appease, to compromise, to pray. You're defeatists. And I'm through with you!"

Rudy tried to calm me. "What do you expect from them, Jacku? My pious father, in his *tallis,* was still praying for the Messiah when the Germans shoved him into the cattle car. I screamed at him, 'Papa, let's try to escape! Come, follow me!' But all he could say was,

'No, this is God's will. Only the Messiah can change things.' So you know what happened? The Messiah never came to him. But the Germans sent him to the Messiah, through the chimneys of Treblinka! That's the way they want us to be.

"Hell, no! A new kind of Jew is being born right here, right now. In the Warsaw ghetto!"

The impasse—the gap—between the younger and older generations continued. Neither side budged, but we felt more certain than ever that our path of resistance and rebellion was right. So life in the ghetto continued as before. Everyone waited for the final day of reckoning.

The gang and I continued our smuggling forays with more zest than ever. We acquired guns, Molotov bottles, gasoline, and other much-needed equipment for our bunker.

One day in March, Artek assembled his entire gang for an important announcement. His voice rang with pride.

"From now on, we're part of the militant Beitar Revisionist fighting group called ZZW, under the leadership of Rodal and Frenkel. The ZZW isn't as big or numerous as the ZOB under Anielewicz, but they're more militant and better armed. They have good connections with the Polish AK underground. I chose the ZZW as the group for us to join. I'm sure you all agree with me."

Domineering and dictatorial, Artek allowed no discussion of the subject. If he wanted it that way, so it would be. I always admired the Beitar movement. As a boy of twelve, I belonged to its youth movement, and I liked the thought that we had become linked with the mainstream Jewish underground resistance. We were no longer just another splinter group. Halina was all smiles. She congratulated Artek and promised to fight wherever and whenever needed.

Artek's outfit by now numbered more than forty members. It had long ago absorbed my small gang. And though I still maintained direct control over my group in the *Werterfassung* smuggling operation, we all continued under Artek's command as before.

Many of our supplies, however, went directly to the ZZW Muranowski headquarters. And, in case of an all-out action, it was understood that Artek would surrender his outfit to the overall command of Frenkel and Rodal.

By the spring of 1943, the German high command realized that time was working against them. The remaining "rabble" in the ghetto had taken advantage of every passing day to strengthen and fortify their positions. Clearly, the attempt to liquidate the "Jew scum" in January had failed.

SS General Jürgen Stroop, an experienced guerrilla and partisan fighter, was given the task of annihilating the Jewish "vermin." By mid-April, he had amassed thousands of German troops, dozens of tanks and armored vehicles, and countless artillery pieces just outside the Warsaw ghetto wall.

They were waiting for Stroop's order to attack.

CHAPTER 23

It was Sunday, April 18, 1943, Passover eve. Halina and I had just returned from our collection posts in the brushmakers' tunnels.

"We just got word from the AK Polish underground," Artek greeted us in a serious and tense voice. "The SS will surround the ghetto tonight. They're mechanized, in battalion strength."

Halina and I turned pale and looked at each other in silent anxiety. "Is it definite, or just another rumor?" I stammered.

"I don't know," answered Artek. "Let's go to headquarters. They probably know more by now."

We wasted no time and went with Artek to the bunker on Muranowski Square that was headquarters for the ZZW.

"So, once again they've picked a Jewish holiday to destroy us," Frenkel commented as we filed past the serious young people guarding the "store" entrance. "Maybe they're trying to tell us something. Maybe they want to show us that God doesn't give a damn."

This was my second meeting with the ZZW leadership. Frenkel impressed me as being a very intense and serious thinker and planner. But it was Rodal, a former Hasid, who seemed to be the life of the unit. In his late twenties, he was both passionate and eloquent, with fearless, alert eyes. A long-time Beitar member, he was spokesman for the group. At our recent induction ceremony, he had explained the major ZZW goal:

"We must fight the Germans, not just because they're killing and torturing our people. Not just because they're brutal and sadistic. Not just because they're evil. We must fight them as a symbol for posterity to show that even in the face of certain death, with hardly any weapons, a handful of Jews had the guts to stand up to the mighty German army."

Rodal had been inspiring then; he was no less so now. He confirmed the AK reports and called upon everyone to make the coming clash their last glorious battle. "We'll make them pay dearly for every position, for every Jewish life. We'll make Muranowski Square a flaming sign of our defiance."

Later that evening, in his own Mila Street bunker, Artek gave us our final instructions. "Jacek, take your people to Zamenhofa 44. Gather all the Molotov bottles, guns, food, and fuel stored there. Then get it over to the main ZZW bunker. We won't fight here on Mila Street. We'll leave that to the ZOB units. We'll concentrate on Muranowski Square. Meet me there before sunrise."

News of the impending battle spread rapidly through the ghetto. Distressed and anxious people were milling around in the streets long past curfew. Most had already made preparations to spend the night in their bunkers or to take up fighting positions.

Back in my apartment, I prepared my parents for their bunker existence. With Mrs. Grinberg, Halina, Mala, and the others who were to share our bunker, we practiced descending through the floor entrance concealed under the toilet opening of our street-level apartment.

As my gang and I were about to leave on our mission, Mama suddenly became alarmed. "Where are you all going? This whole thing's crazy. What do you expect to accomplish? The *yekes* will only murder you. This fighting's nonsense. You're committing suicide!"

"No, Mama. It's the only way. Remember what they did to Hayele, and to all the others. This time, at least, we'll take some of them with us. I'll be back as soon as I can. We just have to collect our supplies."

We departed before dawn and headed for the Zamenhofa 44 depot. A few stars still glimmered in the sky.

"Rudy, you and the others wait for the rickshaws at the end of the tunnel," I instructed. "We'll meet you there."

At the depot, Halina and I stealthily entered the building via the roof and attic. We peered down into the yard. Two gendarmes were still there. "They must've been forgotten," I mumbled.

The Germans were packing their gear into a rickshaw, preparing to head into the street. I recognized them both.

"We've got to get their weapons and uniforms," I whispered.

"I'll go down the stairs," Halina said, removing her boots. "You get them from the yard."

"Good. We'll hit them from both sides. Make them think they're outnumbered."

Moments later, shoeless and silent, Halina leveled her gun. *"Hände hoch! Halt!"*

The Germans dropped their rifles. Their arms shot into the air.

I appeared. "No one moves! *Kein Tritt!*"

We faced the two Germans, pointing our guns straight at them. A bewildered look appeared on their faces. Their lips were moving as though they wanted to say something. They must have felt these were their last seconds. Yet they couldn't believe it. They had been our steady guards at the storage center for the last several months. They had been the masters of our life and death, and now, suddenly, it was the reverse.

We knew them well; they were middle-aged fathers or grandfathers from small Bavarian towns. They had never done anything cruel, but I was certain they would kill or torture Jews if ordered. Halina turned to me.

"Are you going to kill them?" Her voice was defensive, her face ambivalent.

"No, we'll let them go if they give us their weapons and uniforms."

Halina was relieved, and so was I. Killing was not our specialty. Halina covered me while I gathered their rifles, belts, and pistols. I shoved them toward the basement. "Off with your clothes! Quick! I don't want to kill you."

The men started to undress.

"Faster! *Los!* Before I tear those uniforms off your backs!"

I saw mistrust in their eyes. They didn't believe me. They were certain I would kill them. They couldn't imagine any other outcome. Suddenly one of them hurled his boots at me while his comrade hurled himself at Halina. She opened fire. The German slumped down the stairs. A fountain of blood spread over his belly as he tumbled into the basement.

I jumped at the other German. As I landed on top of him, I pulled the trigger and emptied my pistol into his chest. He let out a scream, and his body slumped motionless before me. Both Germans tumbled into the basement.

I looked at Halina. She was trembling. It was the first time she'd ever shot to kill. "It's not so easy," she murmured. "How can they do it? Why is killing so simple for them? Are they really so different from us?"

"Cover me while I check them out," I interrupted. "We've got work to do."

I tied up the badly wounded gendarmes and left them to their fate. Then we swiftly loaded their gear on the rickshaws and took off for our rendezvous.

"Two rifles and ammunition!" I said. "Wait till Artek sees this!" Rudy was jumping with excitement.

For the next two hours, we worked feverishly, loading everything we thought important. As daylight arrived, the gang and I pulled into Muranowski Square with our rickshaws. They were piled high with equipment and supplies.

We had accomplished our mission.

The ZZW leadership had chosen the buildings on the south side of Muranowski Square, at the corner of Nalewki Street, as our main line of defense. The buildings there were mostly four- to six-story dwellings. Their roofs afforded an unobstructed view of the square and provided good cover for the two approach streets of Mila and Muranowska. Walls blocked the streets to the northeast. Accessible only from the rooftops, the Nalewki Street buildings were strategically favorable. They were easy to defend, and they protected our rear.

Artek had assigned Halina and me, plus about twenty others, to cover the roofs and attics of buildings five, seven, nine, and eleven. Then Frenkel asked Artek for two special youngsters. Artek didn't hesitate. He turned to Halina and me. "Hey, *cwaniaki,* you're elected. You're gonna make history! Get up on top of number seven. And you, Rudy, get up there behind them. Cover number five to the right. The first Jewish battle flag's going up, maybe the first in two thousand years!"

I could hear the pride in his voice.

"Protect that flag with your lives," Frenkel said, looking squarely into our eyes. "Even if it's in shreds, protect it!"

With pistols and Molotov bottles, Halina, Rudy, and I, as well as several other young fighters, started up the six stories to the roof of number seven, the tallest building in the area. The higher we climbed, the higher our spirits soared.

The view from the roof was breathtaking. The spring sun was shining with full force. Not a cloud marred the sky. Below us stretched a peaceful sea of rooftops.

A handful of young men and women began tying our colors to a chimney. They made a hole in the roof to hold the pole firm. A moment later, the blue and white flag was flying over Warsaw.

Halina rushed to touch it. She moved her fingers over the Star of David. "I'm so proud, Jacku. I'm full of goosebumps and chills, just being a part of it."

I drew her close. We looked at each other, at the flag, and out over the rooftops. Artek approached from behind. "Okay, kids. We've got a job to do. We need your brains now, not your emotions."

"Yes, I understand," Halina said, wiping her eyes. "It's just . . . it's just the first time I've ever seen a Jewish flag."

Artek moved closer. "I know what you mean. It's not just the flag. It's this whole damn thing. It's all coming to an end."

"But I want to live!" Halina suddenly cried out.

Everyone turned to stare at her.

"We *are* going to live, Halina. You, me, and everything Jewish. We're going to give the Germans hell! We're going to survive. We'll see them buried yet!"

She drew close to me and took a deep breath. And then she smiled. "You're right. We will fight, Jacku. And we'll outlive those Nazi pigs!"

Rodal, Frenkel, and Janek Zloto checked the flag. "If only we had a camera," Frenkel said. "What a picture for the world to see."

April 19 passed rather uneventfully for the ZZW resistance. ZOB units did most of the fighting that first day. Scattered battles took place throughout the ghetto. Muranowski Square remained firmly in Jewish hands. And the beautiful blue and white flag, with its Star of David, fluttered in the wind.

Throughout the day, Halina and I listened to the gunfire that came mostly from the brushmakers' section. Then, just before darkness, the Germans, feeling unsafe, withdrew beyond the ghetto walls.

That night, in my parents' bunker at Niska 4, we rushed through the Passover seder, the ritual that recalled the liberation of our ancestors in ancient Egypt. Knowing that our final battle now would surely end in death, not freedom, we still drank to life. *L'Chaim.*

The story of Moses and Jewish slavery was a fairy tale compared to our present danger. "What we need is another miracle," Rudy said with a touch of bitterness.

"If one of us survives to tell it all," I replied, "that would be miracle enough."

After the seder, we emerged from the bunker and returned to our positions at the ZZW stronghold. Artek intercepted us. "We just got a message from the AK. They're in an uproar because the Polish national flag isn't flying beside the blue and white."

"What can we do about it?" I asked.

"We just had a meeting at headquarters. And all of us agreed. The red and white belongs up there. They're sending us a flag tomorrow at noon."

Artek ran his hand through his hair. "Jacek, you know the sewers best. You'll guide the messenger through."

He paused and looked at Halina. Then he turned back to me. "But only you. Halina and the rest of your gang remain at their rooftop stations."

Fierce battles raged in the ghetto Tuesday morning. It was the second day of the uprising. But Muranowski Square had still not been assaulted in strength.

At about ten, I kissed Halina goodbye and took off on my mission. With gun in hand, I entered the sewer on Muranowski Square's southeast corner. Although I was a veteran smuggler, I'd never ventured through the sewers in that part of town.

My assignment was to take me to the Polonia Soccer Stadium exit on Konwiktorska Street, next to the mental institution. This was an easily recognizable location, with light street traffic, not too far from the ghetto walls. At my point of entry, I left a petrol lamp hanging from the inside of the manhole cover to guide me on my return. Then, with my heart beating rapidly, I slowly made my way through the stinking tunnels. After a while, my route became more familiar.

But I noticed that the level of mud and sewage was reaching above my knees.

That's not the way I remember it, I thought. Something's wrong here. At every turn, every junction, I was sinking deeper in the grimy water. As my progress slowed, my reflexes sharpened. I was fighting my fears, desperately disciplining myself to avoid panic. Though terrified at the thought of drowning like a sewer rat, I was determined to reach the exit and bring back the Polish flag.

Suddenly I heard a sound—a sort of sobbing, wailing sound. I held my breath. Could it be a cat? No cat could survive in here. I got out my gun and switched on my flashlight. There, caught in the beam of light, was a young exhausted girl, desperately clinging to the wet sewer wall. Her body was curled around a thick rope that was floating in the murky water.

"Who are you? What are you doing here?"

The girl didn't turn around. She bent her body still more, almost into a sitting position, with only her head and arms visible above the sewage.

"I'm not Jewish," she pleaded. "My uncle's a priest in Praga. Please save me. I'm sick. I don't want to die here."

I grabbed her hair from behind and spun her around. Not Jewish? Well, maybe, I thought—she's blond, green eyes. "How'd you get here?"

Without answering, she grabbed my scarf and held on tightly.

"Okay, come on," I said. "Let's walk. Hold on to me."

"No, I can't. I'm sick. My feet. I don't feel them."

I picked her up and looked straight into her eyes. *"Amhu? Swojska?"*

I felt her tremble as she heard the words.

"Yes, I'm Jewish. I've been here since Monday. I wanted to get out of the ghetto. Everything was on fire. Our house. The bunker. My parents have Christian friends in Praga. They thought I could pass on the Aryan side. Please help me get there. I'm lost. I know I'll die here."

I felt her grasp loosen. I saw her eyes close. I slapped her several times. "Stay awake and hang on."

With my gun in one hand, the flashlight in the other, and the girl on my back, I continued to trudge through the sewer. The slimy water was almost waist-high. Each time I'd stop to rest, the girl would brace herself on my neck. "No. Please don't leave me. Please. I'll die."

After a while, she began to talk.

"My name's Sala. I'm sixteen. The Germans killed my parents and I'm all alone now. And I'm scared. I don't want to die."

"Sala, I'm your brother and friend," I said. "And you're going to live. I'll tell my friends you're Aryan, and they'll help you get to Praga."

Slowly, I made my way forward, guiding myself by the faint rays of light seeping through the manhole-cover vents. I stopped at each one to listen. Soon I heard the chatter of Polish and the sound of traffic. I knew we had reached the Aryan side.

In the distance, I saw a bright ray of light penetrating the darkness. I was sure a manhole cover had been removed. Perhaps this was a trap. Were SS troops waiting there for me? Dismissing my doubts, I moved toward the light. Suddenly I heard a voice and an echo: "Kazik."

I took a deep breath and waited. It was the name I'd been expecting. I began to walk forward. Again, the voice and echo.

"Let me get into firing position," I whispered to Sala, who was now clutching me frantically. I was still not certain of my safety.

As I peered ahead, a young teenager began to lower himself into the sewer through the bright hole above. The boy couldn't see into the darkness, but I could see him clearly.

"Kazik," I called.

"Kazik," he repeated.

The right name wasn't enough. He had to show me the flag. Kazik unbuttoned his shirt, and I saw his lean body wrapped with a red and white cloth. "Hey, who's that?" He motioned to Sala as his eyes adjusted to the dark. "You were supposed to come alone."

"It's okay," I said. "She's Christian. I found her in the muck."

"Holy Mother Czestochowska! What a filthy mess!"

"She's a smuggler from Praga," I explained. "She got lost in the sewers."

"All right," Kazik replied. "We'll take care of her."

He raised his head to the sewer opening. "Hey, Wacek! We found a girl down here. She needs help. We've got to get her to Praga."

As we lifted Sala out, I gave her a knowing smile. "Mother Mary saved your life, Sala," I said for all to hear. "So don't forget to go to church."

With the girl gone, Kazik and I spoke freely. We were two teenagers with a common cause. Kazik's orders were to deliver the flag personally to the ghetto. He wouldn't hand it over to me. So we both set out to make our way back through the sewers.

I cautioned him about the risks. "Muranowski Square may be full of Germans."

But Kazik was undeterred. The AK had ordered him to deliver the flag as a symbol of help to the fighting ghetto, and that was what he would do.

I admired his disguise. He was dressed as a city sanitation department employee. So were his accomplices outside the sewer opening. It looked so legitimate.

During the slow return, we became friendly. We knew many of the same people, smugglers and black market dealers, especially at the Kiercelak Market.

To Kazik, this was all an adventure. He hated the Germans, but unlike myself, he wasn't fighting for survival. He wasn't a Jew.

Now we reached the flickering lamp and waited. Artek's instructions were that we should not emerge on our own. We waited impatiently. Not a sound. Only distant gunshots. It was almost 6 P.M. when we heard voices. The cover began to move. I pushed it up and crawled out to find Halina waiting. She kissed me while Artek was pulling me up. I was filthy and smelled terrible, but that didn't bother her. I introduced Kazik, who was in a hurry to get back.

"He must reach the Aryan side before curfew, and there are only three hours left," I explained.

Artek promptly escorted him to the roof of number seven. Within minutes, the Polish red and white colors were flying beside the Jewish blue and white.

Two symbols of resistance against all odds.

CHAPTER 24

On Wednesday, April 21, the Germans in battalion strength began to assemble their armed might on Muranowska Street. They had deployed their infantry all along the walls of the houses. Their vehicles were in the center of the street. A half-track with signal equipment, surrounded by three armored vehicles, was set up a short distance from the square and would serve as mobile headquarters. Apparently General Stroop was taking personal command of the impending battle.

I saw him from my rooftop position at Muranowska 20. Artek had posted me there to report on German strength and movements. Had I possessed a machine gun, Artek's Schmeisser perhaps, I could have killed the bastard.

Precisely at 9 A.M., the tanks, armored cars, and howitzers opened a merciless assault. They were after the buildings on the south side of Muranowski Square—number seven in particular, where the Jewish and Polish flags were flying.

By noon, the ZZW fighters decided to counterattack from the rear; they lacked the means for a frontal assault. About twenty-five young Jews, some in SS uniforms, crossed the Mila Street buildings to the south side of Muranowski. One by one, they moved toward the attics and roofs. The SS troops, anticipating such tactics, aimed steady bursts of machine gun fire at the buildings behind them. Nevertheless, the Jewish fighters, armed with Molotov bottles and some Sten submachine guns, managed to get through. At a given signal, they bombarded the street below.

Havoc hit the SS. Several vehicles, including a Panzer half-track, caught fire. From my roof position, I saw the storm troopers running for cover. I yelled to Halina and Yosek, "Look at the supermen running; some of them are on fire."

After a while, the SS regrouped. Two snakelike columns of Germans swarmed down the street, hugging the buildings. Simultaneously, SS machine gunners directed heavy fire at the upper floors of the Muranowski Square structures.

Some of them were burning.

Now the SS began an assault on the street-level stores and the lower floors. A fierce battle developed. The Jews threw all they had at the SS. In several buildings, the Germans managed to reach the first floor. Each time, they were driven back behind their Panzers. In such close fighting, the entrenched Jews had the upper hand. Even though various floors were burning, they still managed to attack from the windows and attics.

While the battle raged, Halina and I were on top of number seven, guarding the flags. We were there all day—dodging bullets, watching the fighting, smelling powder, inhaling smoke, extinguishing flames. None of the SS managed to get up that high.

By late afternoon, General Stroop ordered a withdrawal. The Germans pulled back into the safety of the Aryan world. The battle was temporarily halted. In growing darkness, we climbed down from the roof. Muranowski Square, although still smoldering, was overflowing with excited ZZW fighters.

On the third evening of the uprising, the ghetto was still fighting in high spirits, with most of its population unharmed and still in their bunkers.

So far, we were in good shape. Artek ordered us to clean up. Scattered fires were smothered, and the wounded, including several SS troopers, were cared for. When we were through, Artek winked at me. It was a signal that Halina and I could take off to my parents' bunker at Niska 4 for the night.

"Hey, *yatn,*" he warned, "not later than five A.M. Tomorrow won't be so easy. Stroop'll be back in even greater force. We do embarrass him, you know."

* * *

Early Thursday morning, General Stroop returned with more troops, heavier artillery, and more armor. German guns pounded Muranowski Square for hours. At noon, the infantry assault resumed. Shells exploded. Walls collapsed. Windows shattered. Debris rained into the streets.

Some floors in each building were burning. The roof next to the flags was smoldering.

Halina and I, choking and black with smoke, clamped wet handkerchiefs over our mouths to help us breathe. The intense heat forced us from number seven to number five, next to Rudy's post.

Still our flags were flying. Shells had torn them. Bullets had pierced them. Their edges were charred. Their fabric shredded. But despite everything, our colors were up there, defiantly challenging the Germans.

Now the SS were fighting their way into the buildings.

"Let 'em have it!" Artek shouted.

Everyone on the roofs opened fire. Most of our fighters were scattered through the blazing buildings. They were firing from rooms, from windows, from attics, from stairs.

But the German artillery fire and machine-gunning took their toll. A number of Germans reached the third and fourth floors. They were waving small flags to their command cars in the street.

On the roof, I was firing while leaning on the gutter pipe, pressing my body into its depth for protection. Suddenly Halina screamed: "Jacku! Look!"

A German helmet had popped through the hatch. Then another.

"Hold it! Don't fire!" I ordered.

We ran behind the chimney and watched. With a sudden thrust, two SS men crawled onto the roof. They looked about cautiously. Then, crouching low, they headed toward the flags. I waited, watching for any more Germans to emerge. None appeared.

As the soldiers approached the flags, I signaled Halina. We stepped from behind the chimney, our guns blazing. Both men rolled to the edge of the roof and disappeared into the smoke-filled street below.

A volley of hand grenades erupted from the hatch.

We held our breath as the deadly sticks rolled off the roof or exploded in the air. Apparently the SS hadn't given up. Soon the Germans had a machine gun mounted right at the roof opening. They began spraying bullets in a circle. Everyone on the roof scrambled for cover, except Rudy.

With bullets flying above him, Rudy, clutching a Molotov bottle, rolled to the edge of the building. In an instant, he lowered himself down the gutter pipe. A moment later, a roaring explosion rocked the roof. The machine gun in front of us collapsed into the attic. In its place, a cloud of smoke swirled skyward. Rudy came crawling back.

His face was streaked, his hair disheveled, his breathing uneven. We pulled him to safety.

"I got the bastards!" Rudy said excitedly. "I did it! Right through the window. An attic full of *yekes!*"

The words came tumbling from his mouth. Nobody interrupted. Nobody budged. He had saved the flags and all of us.

Late in the afternoon, General Stroop called the battle off again. The Germans left the ghetto once more.

Artek, Rodal, and Frenkel came up to congratulate Rudy. But there wasn't enough strength for celebration. Nor enough time. Most of our positions were in ruins. The day's fighting had resulted in a heavy toll of wounded and killed. Those not hurt were busy tending to those who were. Also, our reserve supplies in the bunkers were running low. We were especially short of long-range weapons.

Halina and I spent hours searching for arms and gasoline at the half-burned Zamenhofa 44 depot. We found little. Disappointed, we returned to the ZZW stronghold. Frenkel and Artek were talking to the group, planning for the next morning's battle. By now, some of the initial enthusiasm had faded. Our fighters were exhausted. They desperately needed rest.

This time, Artek wouldn't allow Halina and me to leave for my parents' bunker. Instead, he assigned us to guard duty. We, too, needed rest badly, but we trudged up to the roof and stretched ourselves out near the flags. The hot air from the smoldering roofs around us made us feel even sleepier.

Rudy, Yosek, and Shmulek wandered over from their nearby positions. They sat down and formed a small circle near the chimney. My whole gang was now together, seeking comfort from each other's presence.

"Artek'll probably keep us here for two or three more days," I said. "Then we'll move on."

"If we're still alive," Rudy commented.

"You did all right today, Rudy. So let's talk of life, not death. Anyway, there's no sense worrying about that now."

I turned to Shmulek and Yosek. "You guys'll have to make up your own minds about leaving or continuing to fight, when the time comes. But the most important thing to remember is *survival.* We've seen that the Germans can bleed. We also know they can be scared, just like us. They can suffer and die. And we've proved that Jews can and will fight.

"So when all this is over, I want to live. And I want all of you to survive, too."

Rudy shot to his feet. "Goddamn it, Jacek! So you want us to survive? Well, big shot, I got news for you. You can take your survival and shove it up your ass!"

Halina, Yosek, and Shmulek stared at Rudy in shock. I was also taken aback.

"Where's everybody?" Rudy continued. "Where are all the Jews? What did they do to them? You and your survival! Hanging on to life at any price! Where do you get your passion to go on breathing when everyone we knew and loved has been murdered? Do you think you're better than everyone else? That you have special connections to God? Well, the fact is, He wants no part of you! Don't forget, you're a Jew! And He, my father's Messiah, is right now dining in Berlin. In partnership with them! Survival? What for?"

He pulled his pistol from under his shirt. "You see this, Jacek—that's all I want. To empty this gun into their German bellies. To blow them to pieces. And the last bullet, the last one I'll pump into my own brain!

"You can survive, my friend. And after it's all over, the world will put you in a museum so people can stare at you, the last Jew, civilization's tribute to an extinct species. A museum piece. An antique. Where are they? The Americans, the Russians, the English? Our allies! Not even a leaflet to tell us: Hello! Sorry! Something! Anything!

"Well, fuck civilization! Fuck the museums! Fuck their culture—their opera houses, their music halls, their libraries! Fuckin' hypocrites, all of them. I'll blow them all to pieces! Just give me a big enough bomb."

Rudy was now screaming at the top of his lungs. His voice was hoarse, his eyes wild. Halina buried her face in her hands. Yosek and Shmulek sat speechless. Suddenly Rudy stooped, seized a Molotov bottle, and ran to the edge of the roof.

"Wait, Rudy!" I called. "Let me talk to you!"

"To hell with you. To hell with everybody! I don't give a damn any more." Rudy waved his pistol and shook the Molotov bottle over smoky Muranowski Square. "You fuckin' *yekes!* Just come 'n' get me. C'mon. I'll blow you all to pieces!"

Rudy's boots were on the edge of the roof, on the gutter pipe of the six-story building.

As he continued to rant against the Germans, I crawled toward him and clenched my legs around his. I jerked him, and he fell backward into my lap. I swung my body on top of him, grabbed the Molotov bottle and handed it to Shmulek, who had silently followed me.

"Rudy, Rudy," I yelled, "you crazy bastard! To die is easy. Don't you think I know that? To survive and outlive these animals and their Reich. That's the game!"

I held on to his wild red hair and spoke to him with all the passion I could muster. "You and I must survive to see them buried in their own pool of hatred and blood! Fight them. But don't commit suicide, you idiot!"

A rope fell next to me. I looked up and saw Artek at the other end of it. Shmulek and I wrapped the rope around Rudy's body. But there was no longer any contest. Rudy's passion and hysteria had given way to helplessness. Within seconds, we had him back next to the chimney.

Artek said nothing. He simply patted Rudy's head. Then he took the Molotov bottle and disappeared down the attic, heading for the subterranean bunker.

Halina lay next to me, her head in my lap. Her blond hair shone in the moonlight even though it was filthy with soot and ashes.

Shmulek turned to Rudy and Yosek, interrupting the stillness. "Hey, *yatn,* let's leave the lovers alone. Come on, let's walk." They reloaded their revolvers and disappeared along the roofs.

Halina was tired, but she could not fall asleep. She opened her eyes intermittently as though to assure herself that I was still there. I bent down and kissed her sooty face. We embraced wordlessly. We were engulfed with love, desperation, regrets, sympathy, anger, and fear: fear of being separated, fear of having to decide about tomorrow, fear that the night would come to an end.

Halina pulled me close to her and planted her lips deeply into my mouth. Our lips parted only when we were out of breath. Seeking the warmth of each other's bodies, we ignored the devastation surrounding us and made defiant, passionate love, perhaps for the last time.

Our lovemaking ended with tears rolling down our black, soot-covered faces.

The night turned long and bleak. My soul, my spirits, and my feelings were as murky and depressed as the dark cloudy sky. Propped against the chimney, I was sitting with my back to the flags. I didn't want to turn around, to acknowledge that the symbol of our existence was in shreds.

Halina dozed in my lap as I played with her hair. I exhausted myself, searching for an answer. I heard my voice addressing God. *"Adojshem, Adojshem, Eil Rachum Vechanun;* Oh, God, Lord of mercy and compassion." That was my solo piece from the Tlomackie Synagogue choir. It was my grandma's favorite; I had so often sung it for her. My voice carried that serene, liturgical melody out over the burning ghetto houses. I sang and cried and felt that I was alone with God.

And as the sun began to rise and the night's darkness slowly lifted, I saw them all sitting around me—Halina and Rudy, Yosek and Shmulek—all listening to a voice from the Tlomackie choir. A voice that cried out, "Oh, God, Lord of mercy and compassion."

CHAPTER 25

The SS entered the ghetto the following day through the Dzika Street gate. There was an easily identifiable command car, but no sign of General Stroop.

From my rooftop position, I watched the Germans arrange themselves in an arc in the streets around Muranowski Square. There were more armored vehicles, more artillery, more machine guns, but fewer infantry than before. I wondered what it all meant.

I noted the number of SS vehicles and guns. I memorized their positions. Then I reported to Artek.

"It sounds like they're gonna blast us to hell," Artek said. "I've got to tell Frenkel. We lost almost forty youngsters yesterday. We can't afford the same today."

Carrying his Schmeisser, he took off for the ZZW bunker. Before long, he was back. "Rodal and Frenkel have decided to pull back. They figure the *yekes* intend to level Muranowski Square."

"What about the flags?" I asked.

Artek looked straight into my eyes. "Every hour the flags fly is another victory for humanity, for Jewish dignity."

"Okay. I'll stay behind with Halina. We'll stay up there as long as possible. How many Molotov bottles can you spare?"

"Not many," Artek said. "The AK keeps promising supplies. But they claim they can't get through. I don't trust them. No more than ten or twenty percent of what they promise is actually delivered to us.

You'd think they'd open another front on the Aryan side to help relieve some of our misery. But no. They're just like the rest of the world." Artek spat in disgust.

Halina lit a cigarette and placed it between his lips. She smiled at him. His battle-weary, dirty face exploded with a smile. They hugged each other.

"But don't you guys worry," Artek went on. "Some of us are also staying. We'll back you up."

Our conversation was suddenly interrupted by exploding shells. The SS attack had begun. We returned to our respective positions. All morning, the Germans pounded away. Chimneys toppled. Floors collapsed. Flames soared. Halina and I crouched together on the roof of number seven. Buildings were smoldering around us. The smell of powder was in the air. The ghetto reeked of desolation.

By midday, the Muranowski Square buildings were once more on fire. Flames reached the rooftops. We retreated to the backyard buildings.

Suddenly the artillery stopped. Once again, the Germans were putting their infantry into action. The bombardment had been so intense that most building interiors were either on fire or engulfed in smoke. The Germans expected little opposition.

With gas masks on their faces, a small detachment of SS infantry made their way across Muranowski Square. They were concentrating on only one building—number seven. It was obvious that their objective was to capture the flags. Without opposition, they quickly reached the upper floors and attic of the building.

On top of the adjoining buildings, Artek was holding us back. He wanted the SS to go all the way. We watched in suspense, waiting for the hatch to open. Finally, half a dozen SS men emerged from the attic, one by one. When they stopped coming, Halina, Rudy, and I attacked, firing from three sides.

The SS were taken completely by surprise. Within seconds, every last one of them was dead. The roof was quiet, and our flags were still up. But the cloth was in shreds. Strips were hanging down like heavy tears, the tears of a people in agony.

I motioned to Halina, and we crawled slowly to the edge of the roof. We peered over and saw the square filled with smoke. We couldn't tell whether the Germans were still there. But we did see a single SS man who had fallen from the roof. His body was folded grotesquely over a sign that hung outside a former butcher shop and advertised to the German "butchers": "Meat, Salamis—S. Wolff."

Halina and I looked at each other. We began to smile. Then we both burst into loud laughter. We looked at each other, our faces filthy with smoke. We looked at the scene below. We kept laughing and laughing.

After three full days of fighting, Rodal, Frenkel, and Artek were still alive and in good spirits. But the same couldn't be said for their young fighters. They had suffered a heavy toll of dead and wounded. Bunkers were in bad shape, smoke had penetrated everywhere, and reserves of bullets and Molotov bottles were nonexistent.

When darkness fell, Artek's nod was enough to send my gang and me away for the night. The Germans had again left the ghetto for the safety of the Aryan side. Jews began to emerge from their hideouts.

They were crawling out into the open spaces, seeking a safer street, house, or bunker, one that was not yet on fire. On that night, few oases were left. People found no safety. They walked about in a daze. They were seeking comfort, reassuring one another that perhaps the fires and the smoke would clear by daybreak, that perhaps their attics or bunkers would be habitable again. They dared not think otherwise, since no alternatives were left. Only death or, at best, a cattle-car ride to the gas chambers.

When we reached Niska Street, I became worried. It had been forty-eight hours since I'd seen my parents. The street was quiet and deserted. And the yard at Niska 4 was strewn with rubble and smoking rubbish.

With growing trepidation, I entered the bunker. In an instant, all my concerns vanished. Everyone was there: Mama, Papa, Mala, Mrs. Grinberg, and all the neighbors who had been hiding with them.

Bedlam broke out. Everyone tried to speak at once. It was both heartwarming and depressing. My gang and I had been given up for lost. Now we had returned from the dead. There were tears and laughter. Kisses and compliments. Mama, as usual, bemoaned her fate. Mala and Mrs. Grinberg, as usual, tried to calm her down. Halina tried to assure Mama that life was still possible. But Mama wouldn't listen.

Everybody wanted to get out, but they were afraid that the SS would be waiting for them on the streets. They were afraid to remain in the bunker, but they were even more afraid to leave it. Our arrival renewed their spirits and gave assurance that Jewish life had not yet been extinguished. We, the young fighters, were tangible proof of it.

But the bunker had become a nightmare. We'd prepared and planned for many possibilities, except this one. We hadn't foreseen the problem of stifling smoke from burning buildings.

I was no longer certain of survival within the close confines of the bunker. But there was nothing any of us could do about it except hope and pray that the house above us would not be burned to the ground. I did insist, however, that everyone leave the bunker for some fresh air.

"Get out. Get outside right now. Take a walk. It's safe now. Take advantage of the dark. The air will do you good."

Slowly, everyone trooped into the open yard. They wandered around and looked at all the wreckage. Niska Street was in shambles. If morale was boosted at all by the brief excursion outdoors, it was only temporary.

Early that morning, SS officer Konrad, escorted by an armored detachment, had appeared on Niska Street. Through loudspeakers, he urged all workers from the *Werterfassung* to come out of hiding. He personally would guarantee their safety. They would all be transported to a labor camp, where they could work and live in peace. The alternative, he proclaimed, would be the firing squad.

Several hundred people had appeared, again falling prey to German promises. But the majority, in the thousands, refused to be lured forth. As soon as the volunteers had been marched off to the *Umschlagplatz,* howitzers began systematically to bombard each building along Niska Street, setting them all on fire. By nightfall, the shelling ceased. Most people were still in their bunkers.

Our appearance at some of the neighboring bunkers gave a few individuals the courage to venture out. Many, however, couldn't make it. Their bunkers had filled with smoke, and the people inside had choked to death. Some, in attics, had been burned alive. Others had been killed jumping from the windows.

A dazed remnant of survivors walked about seeking safety, not knowing where or how to find it. Many who no longer had bunkers to return to searched desperately for other places that might provide them with yet another day's survival. The confused and panic-stricken people instinctively followed the more confident ones, hoping to be led to safety by the time tomorrow's dawn broke.

The bunkers that were still safe were now filled to capacity. Their occupants were prepared, at gunpoint, to halt the entry even of relatives and friends. To allow them in would mean giving away some of the precious air that they themselves needed to breathe. Thus, the human tragedy unfolded all night long in the burning streets and smoldering courtyards.

Our own bunker, now somewhat cleared of smoke, was once again filled with all its occupants. Halina, my gang, and I stayed only temporarily, for a few hours of badly needed sleep.

I had a very difficult time with Mama. Having hated the bunker from the very first day, she was now anxious to leave it. She hung on my shoulder and shouted, "You'll see, my son, you'll see, one day you will find me buried here. Remember my words. Don't leave me here. Don't leave your mama in this ugly hole."

Her wailing tore into my guts. I knew that Mama was right, but I also knew that outside she'd be gunned down or collapse in shock or pain. What choice did I have? I took a deep breath and forced myself to act unmoved.

For several more days, my gang and I maneuvered our way back and forth between the Muranowski Square battle stations and the bunker. But that, too, came to an end on Wednesday, April 28.

For more than a week, the SS squads had suffered heavy casualties without achieving any noticeable victory over the Jews. Now General Stroop decided to change his tactics. Instead of battling the survivors house by house, block by block, he simply began to bombard the ghetto day and night with artillery. Even planes appeared over the ghetto roofs, dropping hundreds of incendiary bombs. Whatever had been partially burned before soon was completely engulfed in flames and smoke.

Muranowski Square was a complete inferno. The burning streets were a spectacle for miles around. Even the tough, organized fighters, or what was left of them after ten days of battle, were now undecided as to what steps to take. Only about forty ZZW fighters had survived. Frenkel was still alive, but Rodal had been killed. Of Artek's people, only Janek Zloto was still at his side. Artek, with his Schmeisser, had accounted for dozens of German casualties. But he was far from satisfied. He was angry that the blazing inferno made contact with the enemy virtually impossible.

Finally, zero hour arrived. All the ZZW bunkers were empty, smoked out. Our flags were gone, burnt, together with the roof of number seven. And those still alive were totally exhausted.

Black with soot and ash, our clothes torn to tatters, we assembled for a final meeting in the middle of Muranowski Square. Artek, as always, was charming to Halina. Even in the worst hours, he had a smile or compliment for her. Now he addressed us all sadly.

"I haven't much to tell you. You all know as much as I do. There aren't many of us left. We've lost a lot of good kids, good fighters. But we're going to try and make it out through the sewers."

"The sewers are flooded," I interrupted. "They flooded them not long ago."

"I know. Still, we have to try. If we get through, we can join the AK partisans. They've been telling us to get out for the past several days."

"And what about the tunnel?" I asked. Everybody looked at me. The tunnel was ZZW's secret arrangement; none of us had ever been there or been told the location of its entrances or exits.

"The tunnel is gone as well," Artek replied. "The SS now knows about it." He shrugged his shoulders. "Only a couple of days ago, we could've made it. But you know me and Frenkel. We had to keep fighting. And now the *yekes* finally got smart. They'll probably bomb the ghetto for another week or so, then comb it for the leftovers."

Everyone was silent for a moment. Then Artek turned to me. "Well, Jacku, this is it. I'm glad we met."

He hugged Halina and kissed her cheeks. "You're a fighter and a lady. I hope you and Jacek make it." Halina was in tears, clinging to Artek.

"Why the goodbye speech?" I broke in. "We may still follow you through the sewers."

"Yes," Halina joined in, "maybe we'll go with you."

But his reply was firm. "No. Getting out with us is too risky. Our chances are pretty slim. You guys—especially you, Jacek—have your parents and a bunker that's still okay. Stay in it as long as you can. Use the sewers as a last resort."

All our arguments failed to change his mind. Artek had made my decision for me. Still we kept talking, delaying the moment we would have to say goodbye.

Finally, we were on our own. We started for the bunker on Niska Street. Halina was so exhausted she could barely move her feet. I had to help her walk. We stopped and looked back at the smoky square. Artek was still standing there with Janek Zloto, waving goodbye.

Halina, Yosek, Shmulek, Rudy, and I stood transfixed. Each one of us was afraid to talk, to say anything. Each one of us was afraid to cry.

CHAPTER 26

Even the elements were against us. A sharp wind hurled the hot, foul air through the streets. We had no water, only parched throats. A sea of flames swirled around us.

SS troops were stalking the ghetto as we tried to make our way to the sewer entrance on Muranowski Square, our last hope. The constant German bombing and shelling had finally forced us to abandon our bunker. Acrid smoke had filled the air, making it impossible to remain there any longer.

The streets were corridors of flame. Using knotted bedsheets, people were lowering themselves from windows and balconies. Some were falling to their deaths. Others were on fire, living human torches.

We walked in the middle of the street as chunks of flaming debris crashed around us. I sensed the danger from the roving SS troops. I couldn't see them. But I knew they were there, ready to pounce on us at any moment. We made it to the southeast corner. The square was shrouded in smoke. I knew the sewer entrance well, but I couldn't find it. Mounds of burning timber and rubble were everywhere.

"We've got to find it," I insisted. "We've got to."

"The hell with the sewer!" Rudy said. "It's a deathtrap, anyway."

Rudy, tense and impatient, was eager for a final shootout with the SS. He wanted to finish it all right then and there. I grabbed his shirt, pulled him close, and started to yell. "Either you follow me, or you get the hell out of here! You want to commit suicide? Well, I don't!"

He pushed me away, kicking me in the stomach. I pulled him to the ground. We struggled with each other as everyone around us watched in silence. With all my strength, I pulled his head between my knees and began hitting him with my fists. Rudy was stronger than me, but he did not really fight back. His powerful frame accepted my blows, allowing me to simmer down.

And then we heard the unmistakable German command. *"Hinlegen! Hände hoch!* Hands up!"

SS troops emerged from the smoke. Like gas-masked ghosts, they pointed their machine guns at us. I shot to my feet. Rudy started to turn, grabbing his pistol, ready to open fire.

"Alles hinlegen!"

"Don't shoot, Rudy," I said. "It's useless." I stepped in front of him and seized his arm. No one said a word. Even my talkative mother remained silent.

The commanding SS officer, his mask off, ordered us all to be searched. Then they shoved us to the ground with our hands behind our heads.

"Verfluchte Banditen! I'd like to finish you off right now. But you're lucky. You're going to the *Umschlagplatz."*

"There's still hope," I whispered to Halina and Rudy. "Let's wait. If we start something here, we're finished."

We sat in the square for what seemed like hours. The SS brought more captured Jews to join us. At last, when we numbered about fifty, the SS officer ordered us to our feet. We marched through the flaming ghetto for the last time.

The *Umschlagplatz,* about 600 feet wide and 500 feet deep, stretched before us. Dozens of empty cattle cars were standing on the tracks in the distance. German officers were directing the show from an SS command booth near the entrance.

A long, low barrack on the left combined with two smaller barracks on the right to form a "V." On the roofs rested several heavy machine guns, manned by Ukrainian troops. The guns were aimed down at the center of the compound where we were standing among hundreds of others.

Thus far, we'd all managed to stay together. Seething with anger and hatred, Halina and Rudy were waiting for their moment of revenge. I had my hands full trying to pacify them.

"We must all stay together and be in the same car," I whispered to Halina. Then I turned to Rudy. "Goddammit! I see the foolish plans in your eyes. Don't even think it. We'll get a chance to jump from the car. I know we can do it."

I begged him and the others not to succumb to their emotions. "No heroism. Not now, please."

Mama prayed, cursed the Germans, and deplored Jewish fate. Papa stood motionless and resigned.

I took a deep breath and marveled at the discipline of those around me at the *Umschlagplatz.* No begging. No screaming. Just erect young people; fighters who took pride in their courage; people determined to fight again at any opportunity.

No Jewish policemen were shoving us, beating us. No one to be ashamed of. We had wiped out all the *jamniki.*

Suddenly several SS officers approached us. Mama's bent form displeased one.

"Straighten up so I can count! You pig!" His whip crashed down on her head. Mama screamed with pain. I wanted to leap at the sadist's throat. But I didn't budge. Survival, that was what counted.

I felt something behind me. Halina was pushing a pistol into my hand. I held the weapon behind me as the SS men passed.

"How in hell did you hide it?" I asked.

"Never mind. Use it, Jacku. Go on."

"No. I'm not ready to commit suicide. Not yet."

The words had barely left my mouth when a series of shots exploded. The SS officers fell to the ground. More shots came from all directions. Pandemonium broke loose. I dropped to the ground, pulling Halina and Mama with me. German soldiers were falling around us. Others were running for cover.

"It's all lost now, Halina!" I screamed above the commotion. "You can have it your way."

I pulled out my pistol and emptied it at the running SS men. The machine guns on the roofs sprayed the compound. Bleeding people were everywhere. No one knew who was hit. Everyone stayed on the ground, piled one on top of the other.

Two SS men lay near me in a pool of blood. Bullets whistled over me. I pushed Halina's head down to protect her with my body. The shooting lasted no more than a few minutes. A half-track suddenly appeared. SS soldiers leaped off with whips and dogs.

"Up! Up! Everyone up! *Los! Schnell!* You scum, you bandits."

People scrambled to their feet. Dogs barked. The SS shouted. I grabbed Halina to make sure she stayed with me. Mama was on her feet before I was. Papa refused to stand up. He had had enough. Mama and I pulled him to his feet.

Dozens of angry SS men were now running through the *Umschlagplatz.* They were herding everyone to the cattle cars. Anyone unable to move fast enough was shot. Frantic people were helping each other into the "safety" of the train.

Still together, we all managed to board the same car. A moment later, the huge steel door slid shut. The darkened car fell silent. Overcome with grief, fear, and exhaustion, everyone sat motionless on the floor. Even Halina was in shock. But Rudy and I couldn't sit still.

I looked through the small wire-covered windows. At least a hundred dead or wounded Jews were lying in the blood-soaked yard before me. German medics were tending to a few bleeding SS men.

We can't survive, I thought. They won't let us. It's impossible. Seventy million Germans. Millions of Ukrainians. And millions of other anti-Semites. They're all out to get us. We're all alone. Even God's on their side. A sudden anger swept over me. I grabbed Halina and shook her.

"Listen to me. Listen. You've got to promise to fight. No matter what happens, you can't give up. You hear me? You've got to survive. You've got to. Promise me."

She looked at me sadly. "I promise, I promise."

The brief uprising had forced the Germans to load the cattle cars much faster than usual. Only forty to fifty people, therefore, were locked in each car, instead of the usual eighty to a hundred. The extra room made us more comfortable and allowed us to move around. Mama, Papa, Mrs. Grinberg, and the Altmans, a couple in their thirties, were the only adults in the car.

The guards climbed to the roof of our car, and the train pulled away from the *Umschlagplatz.* It was about 8 P.M.

As the train headed east, the gang and I held a hurried conference. East meant Treblinka. This was confirmed when we crossed the double-decker Vistula Bridge, *Most Kolejowy.* Treblinka meant the gas chambers.

"It's less than a five-hour ride," Rudy said impatiently. "If we're gonna do something, we'd better start right now." With his bare hands, he began to tear the wire away from one of the windows. "They won't get me. I promise you that. If your head gets through, your body'll follow."

Shmulek volunteered to be the first to try and reach for the door latch and break the seal. I pushed him aside. "You're not long enough. I'm taller."

I carefully eased my head, then my body, through the narrow window. Rudy and Shmulek held on to my ankles. After a few minutes, I signaled them to pull me back in. I was exuberant, even though it was windy and cold outside the moving train, and I made a good target for the guards on the roof.

"We can and will break that seal and open the door," I said. "I'm sure of it."

At least twenty kids lined up to try to break the seal. We all wanted to survive. For the next hour and a half, more than a dozen tried their luck. Some even went out two and three times.

"The seal's gone!" Yosek finally shouted. "The latch is unhooked! We can open the door!"

Excitement shot through the cattle car. Escape was possible.

As the train rolled along the Vistula River, I saw the huge POW camp of the former military barracks in Deblin. My excitement increased as I realized that we had guessed wrong. We were not heading for Treblinka. We were heading southeast, and that meant Majdanek. That was good news only because the trip would last much longer. Jumping would be safer late at night or early in the morning when the guards would be tired.

Soon, Rudy, Shmulek, and I pushed the heavy door back a few inches and excitedly inhaled the clean night air. After a brief discussion, it was all set. We would begin jumping at 3 A.M. About thirty teenagers, both boys and girls, were going. They were all ready to take their chances to seize this opportunity to escape, try to survive so they could fight back again.

Mama kept walking through the darkness, looking for her son. She had to touch me every now and then, to make sure I was really there.

As we sat and waited, Lajzor, who was in his late teens and had jumped the train to Treblinka eight months before, gave us some pointers. "Don't leap. Be soft. Give in to the ground. Roll down the embankment into the grass or shrubs. And make sure there's a forest nearby, where you can disappear quickly."

We listened attentively. We exchanged addresses of Christian friends in Warsaw with places to hide. Ordinarily, it was dangerous to divulge names, but by now we were all one family. As 3 A.M. approached, the tension became almost unbearable. Mama was on the verge of hysteria.

"Why did all this happen to me? Who cursed my children? God, why have you forsaken us?"

Her cries got louder; her eyes got wilder. I was afraid that she was losing her mind. We all tried to soothe her. We feared that the screams would be heard by the guards on the roof. But suddenly she collapsed and then fell into a deep sleep.

Halina and I joined the others. The moment of decision had arrived. I pulled the door back a few feet. The sound of the train on the tracks rushed in. We were rolling through open country. A wooded area was visible.

The first to go was Rudy. With his belt tight around his coat, he hugged everyone and said goodbye. And he rolled swiftly out and down the embankment. I was sorry to part with him. I'd grown to love him.

Lajzor was next. Then Yosek. He smiled, but I knew he really wanted to cry. We held on to each other for a moment.

Now the first girl, Anka Anielewicz, stepped to the door. She'd worked at the storage center. I knew her and her sister well. She stood tall and erect. Not a word came from her. Just a smile, a handshake, and she was gone.

So it went for more than an hour. About twenty were now gone. The car was almost half-empty. Suddenly, machine-gun fire shattered the night. Escapes apparently had been taking place from the other cars as well. The SS guards were now wide awake and aiming at those who were jumping. In the dark, it wasn't easy to detect the shadowy forms dropping from the train.

"Let's throw a coat beforehand, then jump a few seconds later," I suggested.

The ruse worked. The guards began firing at the coats instead of at the jumpers. At least half a dozen were still waiting to go. Shmulek was next. Then Halina and I.

Mrs. Grinberg kissed her son. She'd already lost her husband and two other sons. Shmulek was her youngest. She had no more tears.

Shmulek, though, was battling his emotions. He needed strength to jump. His mother sensed his need. She crawled to the door with him and caressed him. I threw out a coat. Shmulek rolled after it. Mrs. Grinberg covered her face, as did Mala.

And then, as if she'd suddenly received a divine message that her son was about to disappear, Mama woke up. She leaped at me and wrapped herself around my feet.

"Don't, Izaakl! Don't jump! You'll kill yourself. The *yekes* will kill you. God! What'll happen to me? How can you leave your Mama like this?"

Halina and I stared at her in amazement. I was awed by her forcefulness. Mrs. Grinberg and Mala tried to intervene, but it didn't help. The others resumed jumping. There was more machine-gun fire while I was on the floor wrestling with Mama.

Suddenly the train screeched to a halt. We all fell forward. Mama released me and rolled away. The SS guards climbed down from the roofs. They slid the doors wide open and sprayed each car with bullets. Then they shut the doors and resealed them. Minutes later, we were moving again.

I crawled to Halina, then to Mama and Papa. They were unhurt. So were Mrs. Grinberg and Mala. But not all were that lucky. The Altmans and several youngsters were wounded and bleeding. Halina and I tore up some shirts and bandaged their wounds. Then we sat down, weary and depressed.

Not a word was uttered. All our friends were gone, but we were still in the trap. We were too tired even to contemplate what to do next. Mama came over and sat near me. She held and caressed me. She said nothing. All that mattered to her was that we were still together.

CHAPTER 27

The early morning sun pierced the small rectangular windows of the cattle car. I saw Papa near the one we had opened earlier the night before. In his hands, he was clutching the only book he had managed to hide, Spinoza's *Ethics.* In this ugly cattle car, on the way to the gas chambers, Papa was straining his eyesight studying humanity, wanting so badly to understand it.

I moved closer to Halina, feeling her warmth. I kissed her eyes, her ears, her neck, her lips. I held my breath and covered my face with her golden hair. I wanted that moment to last forever.

Though still half-asleep, she moved herself closer to me. I was sitting in an almost empty corner, holding her in my arms, when, with a huge roar, the train came to an abrupt stop, jarring us apart. I pulled her back to me, and we held on to each other even more tightly. Halina stared into my eyes and moved her hands across my face. She kissed me and urged me to survive and to remember her. We swore to meet again.

The train was rolling onto a siding that would bring it to the unloading platform. This area, called *Plage Laszkewicz,* was formerly an aircraft repair center which now served as the reception depot for the huge concentration camp, Majdanek. Voices from outside brought us all to our feet. I helped Mama get up. She kept asking where we were. She seemed burdened with guilt.

"You see, they're all dead now. I saved you, Izaakl. Jumping was suicide. Don't you agree? Don't you?"

"No, Zlatka," Mrs. Grinberg said. "Don't say that. It was fate. It was my son's fate to jump. It was your son's fate to be with you." The two women embraced.

"It's all insane," Papa said. "Civilization has gone mad. I pity them. I pity them all. It's such a disgrace. They should all be ashamed."

The cattle car doors were suddenly rolled back. *"Raus! Raus! Verfluchte Bande!* You cursed lot! Out of the car!"

Buckets of water were tossed into the car. I grabbed Halina and Mama to help them out. The others followed. I stood erect, soaking wet, and saw hundreds and hundreds of captive people milling around in a huge open area. Two low barracks were off to the right. On the left, a wire fence separated the area from two similar compounds. The distant one contained five long barracks, divided by fences. The closer one contained a huge hangar and several smaller barracks. In the distance, I saw several guard towers, each with machine guns directed at us.

In the center compound, SS men with whips and dogs, aided by Ukrainians and former Jewish POWs *(yentzes),* were pushing, whipping, and kicking the Jews. Men, women, and children were being ordered about—right, left, forward—all in total confusion. The SS, it seemed, were giving the orders. The Ukrainians and *yentzes* were carrying them out.

Our group, from the Warsaw train, was relatively small and subdued. The other group, over a thousand, had just arrived from Holland. Most of them were totally bewildered. Many were screaming for their loved ones who had died in the cattle cars. They had been packed in like animals, a hundred or more to a car. Many had collapsed, crushed, never to recover. Others had just choked to death.

A vapor of human stench and sweat was still wafting from their train. Some of the people were half-naked and wild with hysteria. They looked in amazement at the relatively calm and well-dressed *Warszawiaki,* the Jews from Warsaw. They probably wondered if we had come from a resort. The mixture of the two trainloads was fascinating. People of different backgrounds and experiences, all committed to the same destiny, the gas chambers.

Then the SS gave orders for the separation of males and females.

People converged into a huge mass as families and friends tried to stay together. I stood there in the crowd, mentally isolated, my eyes searching for a way to keep Halina and Mama with me. I had been hit twice already. Halina had tasted the whip as well, but she was still clinging to me.

I looked at Mama, and she stared back at me. Her expressive eyes pierced right through me. I could sense her inner turmoil. I could feel her anguish. But I couldn't speak. Instead, I grabbed her face and kissed it. I pulled her to me, wanting to embrace her.

I felt no response. She was stiff and unmoving. Suddenly she pushed me away. Violently. Cruelly. Coldly.

Then, with equal suddenness, she drew me back. She held my face on her cheek and in a trembling voice commanded, "Izaakl, my child, my son, save yourself. Live. Survive. Don't worry about me any longer. I'm your murderer. What did I do, what did I do? You would have jumped, if not for me. I'll never forgive myself. How could I have known the hell that's here?"

Her breathing became rapid. She kissed me repeatedly. Then she pulled a knotted handkerchief from her bosom and shoved it into my shirt.

"This is my jewelry. Save yourself, Izaakl. Forget me. You're young and brave. You will survive. I know you will. I'll die in peace because I know you'll outlive these murderers."

Then, abruptly, without another word, Mama pulled away and disappeared into the crowd. Halina and I, tightly clutching each other's hands, tried to go after her. But she was moving rapidly, not looking back.

A few moments later, the crowd devoured her, just as it had earlier swallowed up my father, Mrs. Grinberg, and Mama.

Only Halina and I were still united. With all our strength, we tried to resist the surging force of the crowd, the whipping, and the shoving. But how much longer could we go on? We looked into each other's eyes, trying to absorb each other's souls, to become one. We embraced in a tight and desperate grip.

"Halina, Halina," I said. "You have to survive. We'll meet in Milanowek, in Franek's cottage. Wait for me there. And never forget that I love you. Never forget. Survive, and wait for me."

"Yes, Jacku, yes. We'll meet again. I love you. Survive, and be strong for me. I'll always love you.'' Her voice faltered; her eyes were filled with tears.

The SS whips, the dogs, and the terrified crowd were more powerful than our love. Within seconds, we were separated.

Suddenly, as though a fairy tale had come to life, a beautiful white horse and rider appeared in the distance. I couldn't believe my eyes as I watched the animal gallop closer and closer. In the saddle was a majestic, monocled figure in an SS general's uniform decorated with red velvet lapels, topped by a striped SS cap. A long white cape lined with red satin floated behind him. Several SS officers, using their whips and guns, cleared a path for the ''emperor.'' Standing in the stirrups, he rode through the masses of ''rubbish,'' assessing the scene. He seemed satisfied. He jerked the reins, causing his horse to rear up on its hind legs, then motioned with a white-gloved hand.

Within seconds, a handsome white pony appeared, carrying what looked like the ''heir to the throne,'' a young boy who could not have been more than ten or eleven years old.

The ''emperor'' motioned again with his white-gloved hand, and the boy, in a white uniform and shiny black boots, dismounted. He was holding a small whip in one hand, and there was a holster strapped to his side. He walked to a platform and stepped onto it. Then, in a clear but childish voice, he began to speak. In Yiddish!

''My name is Srulek. And I'm from Lodz. This is my 'grandpa,' the great General Globocnik!''

The name was familiar. Globocnik was Himmler's chief executioner in southern Poland. The first to introduce the gas van in Belzec and Sobibor for the purpose of human extermination.

I saw that most of the people around me were now quiet. They were stunned. Males and females were in separate columns in front of the two long ugly barracks.

''You see these barracks in front of you?'' the boy continued. ''They have showers for *Entlausung,* to disinfect your filthy bodies. My grandpa, the general, has told me to assure you that only water comes out of these showers. He gives you his word of honor. And so do I. This isn't a trick. Believe me, and you'll live. Don't be afraid. Don't hesitate to take the *Entlausung.* If you refuse, there'll be a bloodbath right here.''

He emphasized the point by drawing his pistol and firing several shots in the air.

The whole thing was too much. I thought I was hallucinating. I couldn't believe what was happening. A brainwashed Jewish child, adopted by the "kind general," leading his people to their slaughter. How diabolical!

I looked at the buildings before me, the *Entlausung* barracks. They were long wooden structures with too many windows. I wondered what was happening inside them. Is that what gas chambers look like? So flimsy. So ugly. Just simple wooden shacks. Plain barracks that won't arouse suspicion. Why should anyone be afraid to enter simple wooden houses?

But what about all those windows? Why are they sealed and taped? Is it to stop the air from getting in? Or to stop the gas from getting out? Once you're inside, everything is sealed—the doors, the windows, your fate. It's only "to disinfect your filthy bodies." How reassuring!

Thousands of people were now standing in front of the barracks. One for males. The other for females. German propriety. German morality. German treachery. The Germans had tricked us so many times before. Why wouldn't they do it again?

I was sure it was a trick. The more deception, the less resistance. The less resistance, the easier the killing. Little Srulek was just another German weapon.

"Don't believe him," I whispered. "He's lying. Don't trust him. Don't go in the barracks. They're gas chambers."

The men and women just stared at me and said nothing. Their silence frightened me.

"Listen to me," I begged them. "Don't be fooled. They'll kill you in there!"

The Dutch Jews began whispering to one another. I didn't understand their language, but their faces revealed their thoughts: I must be crazy. What I was saying was too terrifying to believe. I must be a Warsaw rebel, a troublemaker.

A beautiful young woman pushed her way through the crowd to stand in front of me. She was holding a child in her arms, a girl, perhaps three years old. The child was extremely frightened. Her head was buried in her mother's bosom.

"Just follow my instructions and you'll soon be out of here," I heard Srulek repeat. "They're just showers—nice clean showers."

The woman looked at me in silence. But I could see in her eyes an unspoken plea: Save me. Save my child.

I looked beyond her. In the crowd, I could see some of the youths who'd been with me on the train from Warsaw. They, too, were urging the people not to believe the little bastard.

A sudden burst of machine-gun fire ripped the air. People began falling before Srulek. Apparently, the little monster had grown impatient with the lack of response and had signaled for his promised bloodbath. As pandemonium broke loose, the beautiful woman in front of me thrust her child into my arms. The frightened girl refused to go. Screaming, she threw her arms around her mother's neck. The mother tried to disengage her, but the child was clinging for life.

Several whip-wielding SS men now began shoving people near me. They were herding them toward the barracks and a monocled, round-faced SS officer standing there in a white doctor's uniform. The "doctor" was making a selection, choosing who was to live and who was to die.

The mother with the child could sense what was coming. She seized her daughter's long braids and brutally pulled her hair. The child shrieked. Her grasp loosened from around her mother's neck. And the mother placed the child in my arms.

The mother's eyes again spoke to me: "You, young stranger. Please help my child. Shield her. Smuggle her through the selection. I don't know how to do it. I don't want to die. I'm young. Alone, I can make it. I can arouse the male instinct of the man who has my life in his hands. He won't sentence me to death. You'll see. He'll point me to the left, to life."

"But she's not my child," I cried. "And I don't know how I can save her!"

We were handing the small living parcel back and forth between us, when the mother spotted a blood-spattered raincoat on the ground. She picked it up, brushed the dirt from it, and tossed it over my shoulder.

I read her mind. She wanted me to conceal the child in the raincoat. I nodded. The woman took a final look at her daughter, then rushed off to the SS doctor and her destiny. Within moments, she passed the selection successfully. She was saved—temporarily. But her three-year-old was now on my back wrapped in a blood-spattered raincoat, her shield against death. I did not want to risk my life, but how could I abandon the child?

I realized that if I remained where I was, I would inevitably be thrust forward to the doctor, to face selection, to be chosen for life or death. No, I thought, I won't take the risk. I'll walk back. Back from Srulek and the "emperor." As far back from the white-robed doctor as possible. I needed time to think, time to decide what to do next. I had to act, to do something.

I turned and twisted my body as the crowd was being shoved forward. The cruel German voices, the sporadic shooting, the barking dogs went on without pause. I stood on my toes, straining to see the Dutch mother, hoping that she might come back to retrieve her daughter.

In the crush of humanity, the raincoat and the child slipped from my shoulder. The child began crying. I became frantic. Should I abandon her and save myself, or should I pick her up and chain my fate to hers? I bent to comfort the child.

"You cursed Jewish parasite! What's in the bundle? Open up!" An ugly storm trooper with a whip was standing over me.

The three-year-old was frozen into silence. The storm trooper viciously kicked the bundle. The coat fell open, and the child, trembling and crying, was revealed.

"Is that yours?" the German yelled.

I stood up and remained silent.

The German unslung his machine gun and pointed it at the girl. "Who's the mother?"

Suddenly a middle-aged woman emerged from the crowd. "I'm the mother. I lost her. I lost her."

She fell over the child and began kissing her. Then, along with the raincoat, she gathered the small girl in her arms and stood up. The storm trooper believed the woman and shoved her back into line. Then he turned to me. "Get the hell over with the men!"

His whip hit my back and wrapped itself around my body. He kicked me loose and punched me toward the males. But I couldn't take my eyes off the brave woman who had sacrificed herself to lighten the anguish of a child she didn't even know. I stared at her, and I saw an angel holding a bundle of braids. She was also my savior, for though I didn't want to abandon that breathing bundle, I wasn't brave enough to risk the gas chamber.

My eyes followed the line. The woman and her newly adopted child were not only moments away from the decision of life or death. They climbed the wooden barracks steps. The SS doctor pulled away the raincoat. Silence for a moment, as he sized up the child and the woman.

"She can walk. Can't she?"

The woman nodded.

"Put her down then. *Los!*"

An SS aide stepped forward and pulled the girl from the woman. "Here. Here's where you go." The white-clad SS officer pointed to the barracks entrance only a few feet away.

The little girl began to cry loudly and sat down.

"You can either go with her or not," the SS officer barked at the woman. "But *schnell.* Make up your mind."

In an instant, the sadistic bastard had transferred the choice of life or death from himself to the woman. She could abandon the child and save herself, or she could accompany the child.

The woman's conflict was so apparent, it was heartbreaking. She moved slowly toward the girl, and death; then quickly away to the left, for life. She hesitated, then once again walked back to the girl. Her hair was in wild disarray. Her mouth was clenched. Her conscience was tearing her apart.

The SS doctor quickly tired of his sport. He ordered his aide to shove both the woman and the child into the barracks. The storm trooper grabbed the hesitating woman's arm and pushed her forward. She fell over the little girl's body.

"Move. *Los!*"

Suddenly a screaming young woman ran wildly up the steps. It was the child's real mother. She pushed the storm trooper aside and threw herself on the crying little girl. She kissed her face, arms, and head. She comforted her. She covered the child's body with her own.

Even the SS men stared in wonder for a moment. But not for long. In violent reaction, the storm trooper she had pushed leveled his machine gun and pulled the trigger, bringing the entire episode to an abrupt end. The mother, the child, and the middle-aged woman were grotesquely sprawled in their own blood only a few feet from the barracks entrance.

How efficient those Germans are, I thought. They create a dilemma. And they solve it. Decisively.

* * *

I now moved as far to the rear as possible. I edged toward the left and the wire fence that separated my area from the adjacent compound. Before the huge hangarlike structure beyond the fence, I noticed a number of men dressed in civilian clothes, walking about in relative peace and calm. No striped uniforms. I began moving in that direction. Near the fence, a Ukrainian soldier suddenly stopped me.

"Hey, you, what's wrong? Are you lost?"

"No. I just brought a gift over for one of your comrades." Though trembling inside, I tried to keep my voice sure and steady. I began pulling Mama's kerchief.

"Oh, so you're one of those diamond guys. Anything for me?" The Ukrainian's face split with a greedy smile.

"Yes, for you. What's your name?"

"Vania."

"Okay, Vania. Here." I handed him Mama's bundle. "I'll be here tomorrow. And if you're here, I'll have more."

Vania offered me a cigarette. *"Vy zakuryte?* Want a smoke? We're busy here today. Many transports. Why don't you get back where you belong?" He escorted me to the nearby fence.

I was through the fence! I walked quickly toward the closest barracks. I looked back and waved to Vania, who was still standing there, dreaming of diamonds. I had no idea at all what our conversation had been about. But I must have said the right things.

Some people in civilian clothes passed by, but I was afraid to stop and ask questions. So I moved on with a look of assurance. In the distance, I saw several SS men standing at ease, and on the towers, guards with mounted machine guns and searchlights. At the barrack, I opened a door marked *Lazarett.* I knew the word meant "sickroom." I was barely inside the room when I heard a voice. "Hey, Tosca, we have a patient. First one today."

I faced the attendant, not knowing what to say. It seemed he was Jewish. But what was this all about? The man noticed my confusion and called Tosca again. Tosca appeared. We faced each other, wide-eyed and speechless. At last, Tosca managed a word. "Jacek?"

"And you're Wolf. Aren't you?"

A silent nod.

"But why 'Tosca'?" I asked.

"That's my nickname. They like my arias from *Tosca.*"

We fell into each other's arms. Wolf "Tosca" had been my buddy in the Tlomackie Synagogue choir. He'd been one of the best alto soloists there.

"But, Wolf, what's going on? Out there, it's hell on earth, and here, it's all peace and quiet. And you guys look so great." I told him about Vania, the Ukrainian. "He really expects me to bring him diamonds."

Wolf laughed and led me to the back room, just in case an SS officer dropped in and asked questions. "Listen, Jacek," Tosca whispered, almost breathing into my face. "This is gold and diamond country; we call it Switzerland. Today we live and are loaded. Tomorrow we may be dead. You see, all the clothing taken from the Jews is brought to those two hangars." He pointed through the window. "There we search each piece for valuables. Then we pack the clothes in neat bundles and ship them off to Germany for poor Germans. *Winterhilfe,* they call it."

Tosca paused for a moment and looked at me. "You must be starving. Wait here a minute." He disappeared and a moment later returned with a pot of soup. "Here, dig in."

After almost thirty-six hours without food or water, I ate rapidly and stopped only to ask more questions.

"Tosca, can girls work here? My girl—she's out there somewhere. I want her here. But those fucking Germans will probably kill her. If I find her, can I bring her here?"

"Are you crazy? You were lucky the tower guards didn't see you. Or maybe they did see you, but you were lucky finding that Ukrainian. He was your cover. Besides, how could you ever find her? By now, she may be gone, or marched off to the camp where the real gas chambers, the concrete ones, are. They keep going day and night. And even if you're lucky enough to find her, how'll you get her back here?"

He looked at me sympathetically. "No, Jacek. It's a dream. And your getting over here was also a dream, pure luck. It could never be repeated. Even with you, it's not safe yet. To make you legal here will be a problem. We're counted twice a day. The SS must account for two hundred twenty of us. No more, no less."

I put the pot down and shook my head in despair. "My girl's out there, and my parents, too. And I can't do a damn thing to save them. What good am I?'' Tosca looked at me sadly. ''For that matter,'' I added, ''who knows if I can save myself?''

''Well, Jacek, you made it today. But who knows for how long? See, the Germans know that we hide gold and diamonds, that we eat and dress well. So they replace us every few weeks. I've been here about three weeks now. In another week or two, I may be up in smoke myself. Who knows? So you live for the moment and don't think about the future. You just try to survive for as long as you can.''

We walked back to the front room. After a while, Tosca turned to me with a smile. ''I've got an idea. I think something can be arranged. There's a guy here who's on his deathbed. He'll probably last a day or two. When he dies, I won't report him. You'll just take his place. Meanwhile, I'll show you where to hide.''

I realized that Tosca was in charge of the *Lazarett,* including the kitchen. I thanked him and went into hiding.

CHAPTER 28

That same evening, the critically ill patient died. The following morning, I took his place at the *Appelplatz,* the counting square. No one knew the difference.

The count took place by fives, at 6 A.M., and a short while later, I was working at the hangar, sorting clothing and examining each article for jewelry and money. The hangar was divided into two halves, each with a separate work force. Each item of clothing had to be thoroughly searched, and any valuables that we found had to be deposited into wooden barrels marked "Dollars," "Watches," "Diamonds," "Gold," "Swiss Francs," and so on. With the frequent arrival of transports, the work was overwhelming. We worked twelve hours a day, with only half an hour for lunch. Despite the strict supervision of SS guards, many of us managed to hide valuables, especially diamonds. At 6 P.M., another count took place at the *Appelplatz,* and dinner was distributed outdoors. Each inmate received a bowl of soup and 200 grams of bread daily. Enough to starve on.

Often, after hours, Tosca would assemble his friends to listen to his liturgical and operatic melodies. He helped the inmates forget their plight and introduced a spark of joy into their dismal lives. His alto had turned into a fine tenor, and he begged me to join him as a baritone.

"Come on, Jacek. Let's give these village hicks a taste of Warsaw's Tlomackie genius. How about *Ave Maria* or a *Rezei?*"

But I couldn't do it. Each time I opened my mouth to sing, I choked up. Everything was too fresh in my mind—Halina, my parents, my friends, everything.

Tosca didn't ask me to sing again.

As the days passed, I grew more and more restless. One evening, I cornered Tosca in the latrine. "Tosca, you are not stupid. What's going to happen with us? You know what we did in Warsaw, even though you weren't there. You know how we fought. How we made the bastards pay. How we defended ourselves to the end. What about escaping from here? There must be something we can do. A tunnel, or maybe bribing some guards. What about just breaking out?"

Tosca shrugged. "Do you think we haven't discussed it? We have, a million times. But the same question always comes up. Say you make good your escape. Then what? Where do you go from there? The woods around here are full of anti-Semitic partisans. They'd just as soon kill Jews as Germans. Besides, if one of us escapes, the *yekes* will shoot twenty-five in reprisal."

I listened and shook my head. "No, Tosca, I can't just sit around and wait. Something's going to happen before they get me in those gas barracks. Screw the Germans, screw the partisans. I have to get out of here."

"What do you mean?" Tosca asked.

"You'll see. When the time comes, you'll see."

But as time passed, I learned how much fear there was among the inmates. Many had other members of their families in the compound. Escape, and the SS would shoot them all. I understood their predicament. If I escaped, would the Germans execute twenty-five or fifty inmates who knew me? Would they include my friend Tosca, who had sheltered me?

But we were all in the claws of the Germans. All doomed. No one could be safe. My actions couldn't put the people I cared for in more danger than they were in already. So I decided to try to escape. Alone. But how?

The question plagued me day and night. I worked and thought of escape; ate and thought of escape; slept and dreamed of escape. Every day I searched for a loophole, an opening, a plan.

Sundays were work-free. Most of the workers relaxed on the grass outside their quarters, despite the death-camp setting. Some sewed. Some talked. Some simply dozed in the brilliant May sunshine.

On this Sunday, I was sitting alone about fifty feet from the camp fence, thinking about escape and about Halina. Suddenly I noticed two Polish peasant women slowly approach on the other side. I looked at them curiously. How brave, I thought. How daring. They were carrying two large loaves of peasant bread and seemed to be unafraid of the SS guard in the tower above them, who was just standing at his post, smiling.

As I sat there wondering about this, the women began to wave their arms. They seemed to be urging me to come to the fence. I stood up and took a few steps toward them. "Come closer. Bread for diamonds or gold."

I looked up at the guard. He smiled his approval and nodded. I ran to the fence and quickly traded several gold rings I had found in the clothes we packed for the bread and a chunk of cheese. The women disappeared, and I ran with my prize to the *Lazarett,* to Tosca.

"Calm down, Jacek. It's nothing new. It goes on all the time. But make sure you pay the guard off."

"How can I do that?" I asked.

"It's simple," Tosca said. "Just toss a package over the fence with some rings. Use a stone for weight. When the *yeke* goes off shift, he'll pick it up and be happy."

I ran back to the fence and followed Tosca's instructions. The package landed close to the tower, and the SS man smiled. Feeling quite satisfied with the turn of events, I dropped to the grass and dozed off. I awoke to the sound of nearby voices. The same two peasant women had returned. I looked at them, then up at the tower. The guard was looking the other way. The women waved to me, and I walked slowly toward them. At the same time, I tried to gain the guard's attention and approval. But he was staring across the field in the opposite direction.

I hesitated. The women urged me on. I went forward to make the exchange as before.

All hell broke loose. The tower's siren went off. Machine-gun bullets peppered the ground around me. I raised my hands up high.

"Don't move! Stand still!"

Within seconds, a jeepload of SS men and Ukrainians pulled up. They searched me, stripped me of the bread and my hidden jewelry, then cursed and beat me with their whips and fists.

Moments later, all the inmates were ordered to the *Appelplatz* to watch the execution of a Jew accused of smuggling and attempted escape. It was useless for me to explain that I hadn't tried to escape. The SS needed their Sunday show, their carnival. Across the square, among the other dispirited Jews, I could see Tosca, standing mute and helpless.

The square snapped to attention. Even the SS men and Ukrainians saluted as little Srulek rode up on his white pony. "What's all the fuss?" he asked me in Yiddish.

I wiped the blood from my face. "I was trying to trade for bread, that's true. But I wasn't trying to escape."

Srulek looked around, then ordered the Ukrainians to keep their hands off me. He rode to the tower and exchanged some words with the guard. Then he galloped back.

"*Los!* Everyone back to the barracks! There'll be no execution. Only whipping." He shouted his orders in a childish voice, speaking half in German and half in Yiddish. "Twenty-five *am Arsch!*"

Relieved, I stood bewildered at the power of this little monster. Not only did the SS obey his orders, they actually feared him. Two husky Ukrainians now seized me and bent me forward. A burly SS man approached. A moment later, as Srulek counted, I felt the whip.

"*Eins, zwei, drei . . .*"

The whip smashed down on my back, curled around my torso, and cut into my belly. I bit my lips and choked back my tears. I remembered—a lifetime ago—when Mama used to beat me for hanging around Grandma Masha's tough neighborhood and getting my good clothes dirty. Then I had refused to cry. Now I would not scream, I would not beg. The pain was brutal, but when the count was over, I straightened up and stood erect. Defiant.

Srulek smiled and tapped me with his little whip.

"A real Warsaw rebel! You're not easily scared. Here."

He handed me a chocolate bar, then galloped off on his pony.

Tosca was beside himself with wonder as he dressed my bleeding cuts in the *Lazarett.*

"You were born under the star of fortune. And what a way to be saved! Srulek usually buries people. It's the first time I've ever seen him save a Jew."

Smiling painfully, I asked what had actually happened at the fence.

Tosca laughed and shook his head. "What a question! The guards changed shifts, you fool. On Sundays, they're on two hours instead of four."

Even in my pain, I too started to laugh. "What stupidity! What ignorance!"

"You've got to *bench Gomel,*" Tosca said. "Give thanks to the Lord for saving you from certain death."

That was my first experience with flogging. I returned to my barrack and again thought back to my childhood in Warsaw. How I'd looked forward to the Saturday afternoon movies. I'd always arrived early, anxious for a good seat. I recalled the excitement, the awe I felt as I watched Errol Flynn or Clark Gable, cast as sixteenth-century slaves, being whipped and forced to row creaking old galleons across the seas. How could I have known then, how could I have dreamed, even in my worst nightmare, that I myself would one day be a captive slave, beaten and whipped?

I swore to escape. I swore to reach freedom. I swore to fight back.

CHAPTER 29

The days passed slowly. But I knew that time was running out. Any day, the SS would switch the present work force and bring in fresh manpower. At worst, that meant we would all be gassed. At best, they would dress us in striped uniforms and march us off to slave labor at the main Majdanek camp.

Yet each of us hoped for a miracle. We buried any thoughts of death. And we buried valuables—mostly gold and diamonds, wedding bands, engagement rings—three to four feet deep in the ground, just in case some of us survived. Even if we didn't make it, at least we had kept them from the Germans.

But my mind was immersed in escape. I searched constantly for any opening that might lead to my freedom. I sensed a possibility in the area where the inmates loaded clothing into the freight cars bound for Germany. I maneuvered for an assignment there. Tosca's influence might have helped me, but I wanted no one to know of my plans, no one to suspect me. Besides, even Tosca might not be sympathetic. He might be one of the twenty-five picked for execution in reprisal for my escape.

Instead, I would bribe one of the Ukrainian guards at the loading platform. About thirty men worked in the loading gang. Many traded with the railroad workers, exchanging jewelry for food and tobacco. I became friendly with a *Volksdeutscher* engineer named Jan, who often showed up with his puffing old locomotive. Already loaded with valuables, he had a passion for large stones—diamonds. "At least two or three carats," he whispered to me one day.

I listened and promised. I had no such large diamond. And neither did anyone else. Most diamonds we discovered were rather small. But Jan was just a country hick who wanted to get rich quick. I sensed his ignorance. I found a sizable semiprecious stone, shiny and bright yellow.

When we met again, he took me into his cabin and showed me a rucksack full of food. "You'd better have something big for this."

"You're lucky, Jan, very lucky," I said. "I was able to latch on to a magnificent diamond. But it wasn't easy. I had to steal it from an SS officer. You've got to get this train out of here before the six o'clock *Appelplatz* count. Otherwise, he might discover it's missing."

Jan trembled as I handed him the treasure, wrapped in paper and cloth. He moved his fingers over it. His eyes shone with greed. "It feels like five carats."

"It could be even more," I told him. "Who knows? But you better get these wagons moving. If the bastard finds out it's missing, he might stop the train and search the crew as well."

Jan was trembling with excitement. "Yes, I'll pull out right away."

Of course, I planned to be aboard, stuffed in among the bundles of clothing. I was ready for my trip to freedom. As Jan hooked up the wagons, I fought for breathing space in one of the tightly packed freight cars. The inmates continued loading the car, making it harder and harder for me to breathe or crawl.

It became darker, and only a faint ray of sunshine penetrated the window, several feet away. I struggled toward the light, pushing the bundles aside inch by inch. All I could think of was reaching that window. Soon I heard the workers slam and seal the door. It seemed that Jan was as eager to get the train out of there as I was.

As I got closer to the window, maybe two or three feet away now, I could smell the fresh air. The locomotive hissed, and the train lurched suddenly, back and forth, pushing the bundles together. Grabbing the barbed wire strung across the tiny window, I held on tightly despite the pain. My hands were cut and bleeding, yet I wouldn't let go of that breath of life, my opening, my chance for freedom.

Smoke from the chugging locomotive now began to stream past

my face. I loved it. I was filled with joy as the train picked up speed and left the SS compound.

As we passed the suburbs of Lublin and moved through an open landscape of trees, fields, and farms, I felt a resurgence of hope. I shuffled the bundles to make more room. I covered my bleeding hands with rags, then started, slowly but steadily, to rip the barbed wire away from the window. I bit my lips and closed my eyes to distract myself from the pain. Finally, the window was clear and open, ready for my next move, my leap to freedom. I was worn out but content. Soon I fell asleep. I dozed fitfully through the night as the train jolted on.

I woke early the next morning when we stopped to change locomotives. Train crews passed and exchanged greetings. I could hear farmhands, speaking in Polish, discussing the weather and crop conditions. The fresh air smelled good. The early morning sun shone on my face.

If only I knew where I was! I wanted to travel farther and farther from Majdanek. Instinctively, I felt there was greater safety in distance. Yet I was afraid the train might take me straight into the lion's mouth, into Germany. I decided to wait until sunset before trying to jump the train. By that time, I figured, we would have traveled about thirty hours and would be perhaps 200 kilometers west of Majdanek, but not too close to the German border.

When it was almost dark, I decided it was time to jump. The train had stopped on a siding near a wooded area to let a military transport pass. All was quiet. With my hands braced against the stacked bundles, I pushed myself feet first through the window. Satisfied that no one had followed me into the woods, I walked for several hours.

The forest was now pitch-dark, and I had no idea where I was. I lay down for a moment's rest and fell fast asleep, exhausted. When I woke up, the sun was shining, and I could smell the sweet aroma of grain. I was on the edge of a golden sea of wheat.

I'm really free, I thought. But for how long? My throat was dry, and my stomach ached. I needed food and water desperately. It had been more than two days since I'd had even the scanty rations of the camp.

In the distance, I saw a barn. Near it stood a lone house, bordering the wheat field. I started walking toward it. As I drew closer, I looked around warily. I saw no one, not a soul. Everyone must be working in the fields, I thought. I quenched my thirst from a well near the house. I found a large loaf of bread, which I stuffed greedily into my mouth. Then, rather than risk the unknown, I decided to wait in the barn and take my chances right there. I sat for hours, inhaling the sweet fresh air, luxuriating in my freedom. All kinds of memories and thoughts went through my mind, always beginning and ending with Halina.

At last, I heard footsteps approaching and a dog barking. Not wanting to give anyone cause to suspect me, I stretched out openly on the straw-covered floor and pretended to be asleep. Soon someone tapped me lightly on the leg.

I opened my eyes and looked up at a pretty, red-cheeked girl, accompanied by a small white dog. She was about my age, barefoot, and dressed in simple peasant clothes. I sat up and apologized for my intrusion.

"Please forgive me, but I was tired and hungry," I said. "In fact, I helped myself to your bread and water. I'd like to do some work to repay you."

"What a poor soul," she replied. "May Christ watch over you. Wait here. I'll bring you something to eat."

Moments later, we were sitting together on the barn floor, eating and talking. Her name was Manka, and she had two younger brothers. Her grandparents lived with her parents in the house, and together they all worked the farm.

"They'll soon return from the fields," she said. "I came home early to prepare supper."

I told her the story I had made up to explain my circumstances. "My parents were killed in the bombing of Warsaw. The Germans caught me while I was praying in church. They tried to ship me to Germany for forced labor. But I jumped the train."

She was sympathetic but explained that her folks were suspicious of "city slickers."

"Don't worry, though. I'll handle them. Just leave it to me." She smiled, and I knew I was in good hands.

I hadn't traveled as far as I thought. To my astonishment, I learned I'd jumped the train only sixty-five—not two hundred—kilometers from Majdanek. This meant I was still deep in the heart of Poland's Zamojski forest. But for now it seemed safest to stay where I was.

Thanks to Manka, I became a temporary part of the Boguslaw

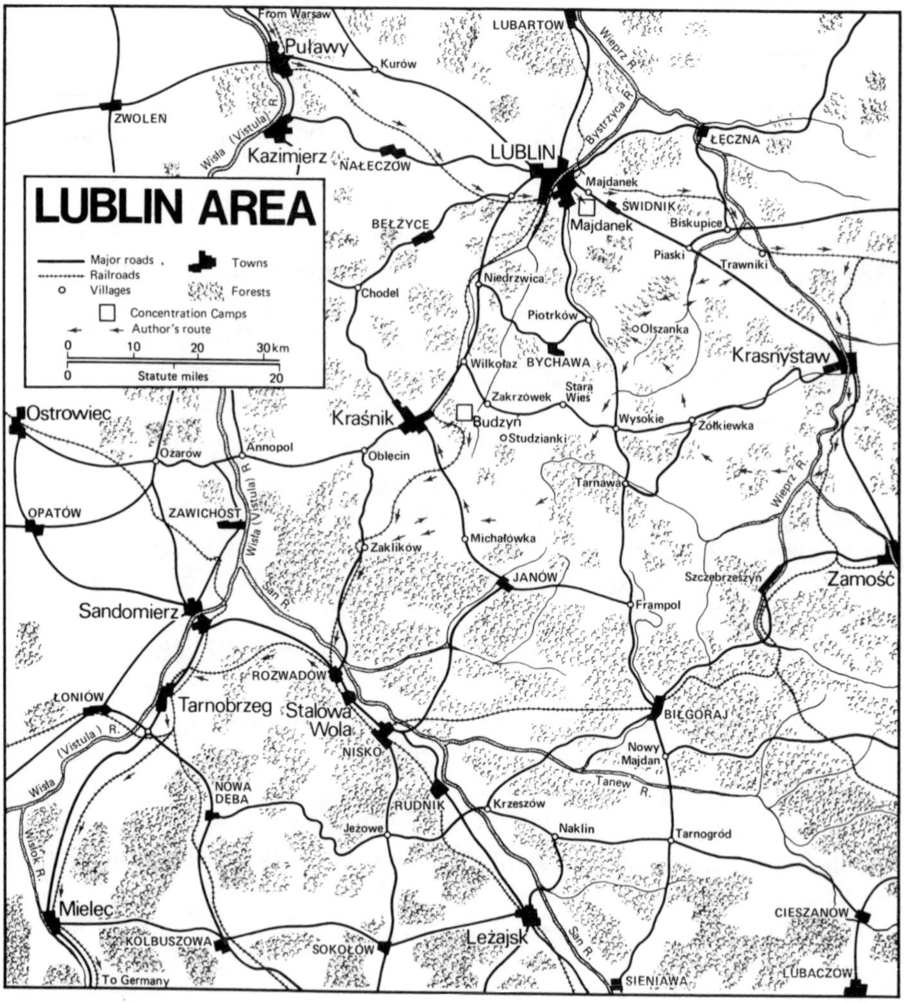
LUBLIN AREA
Major roads
Railroads
Villages
Towns
Forests
Concentration Camps
Author's route
0 10 20 30 km
0 Statute miles 20
From Warsaw
Puławy
Kurów
LUBARTÓW
Wieprz R.
Bystrzyca R.
ZWOLEŃ
Wisła (Vistula) R.
Kazimierz
NAŁECZÓW
LUBLIN
ŁĘCZNA
Majdanek
ŚWIDNIK
Majdanek
Biskupice
BEŁŻYCE
Piaski
Trawniki
Chodel
Niedrzwica
Piotrków
Olszanka
Krasnystaw
Wilkołaz
BYCHAWA
Stara Wieś
Zakrzówek
Ostrowiec
Kraśnik
Budzyń
Wysokie
Żółkiewka
Studzianki
Ożarów
Annopol
Oblecin
Tarnawa
OPATÓW
ZAWICHOST
Wisła (Vistula) R.
Wieprz R.
Zaklików
Michałówka
JANÓW
Szczebrzeszyn
Zamość
San R.
Frampol
Sandomierz
ROZWADÓW
ŁONIÓW
Tarnobrzeg
Stalowa Wola
BIŁGORAJ
Wisła (Vistula) R.
NISKO
Nowy Majdan
NOWA DĘBA
Tanew R.
RUDNIK
Krzeszów
Wisłok R.
Jeżowe
Naklin
Tarnogród
Mielec
CIESZANÓW
KOLBUSZOWA
SOKOŁÓW
Leżajsk
San R.
To Germany
SIENIAWA
LUBACZÓW

household. I differed from them in almost every way: speech, mannerisms, tastes, eating habits, clothes. They attributed this to my big-city background. The Boguslaws were true Polish peasants. They had never visited—or even met anyone from—their capital. and they had no idea I was Jewish.

I stayed away from the nearby village. I avoided face-to-face meetings with the neighbors. And I ate by myself in the barn to avoid old Boguslaw's embarrassing and probing questions. "Christ be my witness, Jacku, we won't make fun of you. Tell us about all those fancy things you city folks do in Warsaw."

Manka always came to my defense. We'd go to the barn together, and there, I would invent tales of wonder about the big city. I had to be very careful not to give away my Jewishness. Still, I enjoyed doing it, and she, naive girl that she was, swallowed every story I managed to concoct.

My boots, however, turned out to be a serious problem. Everyone envied them. There I was, claiming to need work to earn cash for my trip back to Warsaw; yet when Boguslaw offered me lots of money for the boots, I refused. Even though I needed the money to cover my fare and *Kennkarte,* I wouldn't part with them. I knew the boots would give me the proper appearance later, while I was traveling. The suspicions and needling increased daily, and I wondered how much longer I'd be able to stay at the farm. I was afraid if they knew I was a Jew, they would hand me over to the Germans.

Then, one evening, I was resting alone in the barn, contemplating my situation, when suddenly I heard strange voices outside. "Praised be Jesus Christ. In the name of the Father, and the Son, and the Holy Ghost. Amen."

I peered through a narrow crack in the barn wall as a young man came out of a trio and shook hands with old Boguslaw. The young man put his rifle down and waved to the others.

Partisans. Operating out of the nearby woods, they had come to their farmer friend for provisions. Grandpa Boguslaw offered them homemade vodka, and they traded gold and watches for more vodka and food.

I decided to join them. I was tired of my aimless, isolated existence on the farm. Fighting the Germans would be more to my liking. And I was aching for revenge. I quickly gathered my few belongings and waited for the partisans to leave. Then I followed them, trailing Manka, who was escorting them to the road with her dog.

Before Manka was ready to turn back, I asked her to introduce me. "I want to join them, Manka. You know I don't belong here. I'd much rather be fighting the Germans."

Manka understood. She told the partisans about me and suggested they take me along. The three young Poles eyed me with suspicion. But Manka kissed my cheek and bade us all goodbye. "May God be with you and Jesus Christ be praised."

When she was gone, the partisans searched me. I had no papers, no documents. Only my old German Luftwaffe switchblade, which I had managed to conceal all this time. They took it from me, tied my hands behind my back, and marched me silently into the woods. Well past midnight, we finally reached their camp. One of them untied me and took me to a small tent guarded by two armed peasants. The chief emerged and introduced himself as Mlot. He spoke in fine, eloquent Polish and addressed me politely.

"I hear you're from Warsaw."

"Yes. Born and raised there."

He shook my hand. "*Servus.* Come in and sit down. Hey, Stachu, bring some vodka for our friend."

In the tent, we talked for hours. Mlot stood from time to time, bending his tall frame to accommodate the tent's low ceiling. Pacing slowly back and forth, he fired dozens of questions at me, sizing me up with his steel-blue eyes.

I posed as a Christian, answered his questions directly, and tried not to arouse his suspicions. I passed the test. Mlot returned my knife, introduced me to several members of the group, and assigned me to a platoon.

CHAPTER 30

The forests of southern Poland at this time were filled with a murderous conglomeration of bloodthirsty gangs, all called partisans. They had one common objective: to fight and expel the German occupiers. Yet they fought each other as well. They bathed in each other's blood and used slogans to rationalize their killing. They fought in the name of Jesus Christ, socialism, Stalin, the Catholic Church, a free Poland, and an independent Ukraine.

The AK despised the Jews and Russians and fought for a free Catholic Poland. The NSZ abhorred the Jews, Communists, and liberals and fought for a fascist Poland. The Banderowcy hated the Jews, the Russians, and the Poles and fought for an independent fascist Ukraine. The Armia Ludowa were the only ones who tolerated Jews; they loathed the AK and NSZ and fought the Germans for a socialist Poland.

A few Jewish partisan groups had also been started. But since the outfit I'd met up with was an AK unit, I had to conceal my Jewish identity carefully. I feared them, despite my non-Jewish appearance and good Polish accent.

Although Mlot and a few others in the outfit were well armed, most of the thirty-five men lacked rifles, hand grenades, and ammunition. Poorly equipped, we slept out in the open, using empty sacks for sleeping bags. Sometimes we had plenty of food; sometimes we didn't. But we always had vodka.

Most of the men were between twenty and thirty years of age. I was the youngest. The majority came from small towns in the area. They were either escapees from forced labor, as I pretended to be, or peasants, anxious to vent their anger on the Germans who had stolen their livestock. Mlot had been sent from up north to guide and organize them. They feared and respected him.

Mlot put me through a series of training exercises. I had learned in the Warsaw ghetto how to handle a gun, grenades, and Molotov bottles, but I couldn't let them know that. So I pretended to be a novice.

The men generally took advantage of my youth. They delegated minor chores to me, and frequently assigned me to night duty. I kept mostly to myself, as I sensed they were beginning to suspect that I was a Jew. They didn't come out with open accusations, but their remarks were pointed and obvious enough to me. Their jokes and tales of "bedouins," "cats," and "*parchy*" (parasites) were all aimed at Jews. And they repeated them with particular gusto in my presence. I was lucky to have Mlot's protection. He liked me and often said I was the only one in the outfit with class.

The men went on missions almost daily, to trade, to obtain food, to blow up railroad tracks or German outposts. They terrorized the nearby peasants, warning them not to cooperate with the Germans. Those who did paid dearly with their lives and property.

But they didn't allow me to take part in these actions. They said I was too young and too delicate. According to them, I was good for trading, not fighting. Their words smacked of anti-Semitism. But I kept my mouth shut. I hoped that some day I would get the chance to prove myself in battle. Then they would respect me.

That day soon arrived. Mlot returned from a short overnight mission to the nearby village of Olszanka with Father Ziolkowski, the local priest. Mlot gathered us all together. Then Father Ziolkowski blessed us and prayed for the success of our upcoming action. I sensed this to be a very important mission. Only Mlot and a few of his lieutenants knew the details.

Father Ziolkowski sprinkled us with holy water. "Blessed be the Almighty, Jesus Christ, the Savior of us all. *Dominus Vobiscum.*"

On my knees with the others, I recited the prayers. I could feel their suspicious eyes on me and thanked God for what Ala and Franek had taught me on our numerous visits to Saint Alexander's church in Warsaw.

The vodka flowed later that night, and it loosened Mlot's tongue. He outlined the mission. It was nothing less than a frontal attack on the SS compound in Trawniki, some twenty-five kilometers away. I gasped. When Himmler ordered Warsaw to be made *Judenrein,* free of Jews, the German businessman Toebbens managed to obtain special permission to transfer his slave-labor shops to Trawniki, complete with several thousand Jewish slaves. "Who knows?" I thought to myself, "maybe we can liberate all those Jews!"

But Mlot said nothing about Jews. Neither did his right-hand man, Janek Pila. Mlot explained everything else in detail. "The Ukrainian bastards will be away, guarding the workshops. We'll attack the SS post and kill as many Germans as we can. Their rifles, machine guns, and hand grenades, that's what we're after."

Pila urged us not to forget the ammunition. "Remember, the guns are useless without the bullets."

No one asked any questions. Half-drunk, the men cheered loudly and yelled their favorite slogans: "Death to the Krauts!" "Long live Poland!" "Death to the Communists!"

It was almost midnight when Mlot stopped the drinking and urged everyone to get some rest.

"You have five hours to get some sleep. You'll be awakened at five A.M., and you'll have only fifteen minutes to get ready. I want everyone up at five." He paused and looked at us. "But not everyone will go on this mission. I'll make the final decision in the morning. I'll give you the details then. *Do jasnej cholery!* Now hit the sack, you bastards!"

I prayed to be among those chosen for the action. I pleaded with Mlot as he entered his tent. He pushed me aside. "We'll see in the morning."

I tossed and turned all night. I had to go on the mission. I had to prove to the others that I could fight. And I had to see Trawniki with my own eyes. But more than anything, I wanted to avenge the cruelties inflicted on Halina, my parents, and my Grandma Masha. I would never forgive the Germans for taking them away from me. The SS had to pay for it.

I was especially obsessed with thoughts of Halina. I dreaded to think of her fate. I assured myself that she was alive, that perhaps she was struggling somewhere but that she was still living. There's hope in life. And we'd both sworn to survive. I drove away thoughts of the gas chambers.

In the morning, Mlot, wearing his warrior's sash and with his automatic rifle slung over his shoulder, started choosing his men. He needed at least twenty-five, and many volunteered.

At first, he ignored my attempts to join. But later, he smiled and slapped me on the back. "You're my new assistant. Don't disappoint me." He handed me his gun and laughed sarcastically. "Now get going!"

Mlot gave us a short briefing. He emphasized our immediate goals. "We're good for nothing without long-range weapons. Look at us. Thirty-five fighters and only a handful of grenades. It's a shame. This mission is to kill SS troops. But even more important, we're after at least a dozen rifles and some automatics. That's our goal. And you—Jacek, Wojtek, Bystry, Malpa, Ziemian, all of you new guys—while we shoot it out, you'll attack their arms depot and load up with as much as you can carry. Each of you has a pistol and a grenade. Use the grenades only as a last resort."

We stopped for nothing, not even water. We marched steadily over side and dirt roads for over four hours, until we finally reached the outskirts of Trawniki shortly after nine. In the distance, we could see the church steeples and the village.

Mlot turned to us. "The camp's at the southwest end of the village. We rest here until the scout patrol returns."

In no time at all, the patrol was back. Everything was as we expected. Mlot picked a husky young peasant from the Wlodawa region to start the assault. Stryjek was short and plump, but fast and gutsy.

"You start a fire a few hundred feet from the post," Mlot instructed. "We want to draw as many SS as possible away from the guardhouse. Then we'll attack from the rear."

Crouched low, we made our way carefully across a big wheat field. We were strung out in a long column, heading single file toward a thick forest. Behind the forest lay Trawniki.

My pulse quickened as we maneuvered through the trees. Then suddenly I saw it. Dreadful and ugly, the Trawniki SS camp.

Mlot dispersed his men and ordered me to follow him. We moved slowly along the edge of the woods, then positioned ourselves about a hundred yards from the guardhouse. The camp lay to our left. It had a dozen or more wooden barracks encircled by a double barbed-wire fence and at least four guard towers. A morning fog hung over the site, but I could see the inmates inside and a number of SS troops and Ukrainian guards. In front of us stood a small guardhouse that was being used by several dozen soldiers as shelter for themselves and their weapons. Prisoners were working nearby on two new brick and wood structures. Some were speaking in Yiddish.

As we watched, the prisoners suddenly stopped working for a brief rest. The ten or more SS men on duty joined their comrades at the guardhouse for coffee. They put their rifles down and sat on wooden benches outside. Mlot looked back to see if everyone was ready.

For me, it was simple. Wait for the shooting to divert the SS men from the guardhouse. Then make a dash for all the weapons I could carry. As prearranged, the smoke now began to rise on our right.

An SS officer stood up and ordered several of his men to investigate. "It must be the goddamn peasants again," I could hear him say. "Chase them the hell outta here!"

Leaving their weapons at the guardhouse, the soldiers got up and walked toward the smoke. *"Kein Spur von Bauern.* No peasants. Just wind and dry weather."

Several more soldiers joined them with buckets and spades.

"Bring some of the Jews to help," the officer commanded.

"Richtig. All right."

At that moment, Mlot signaled Stryjek to open fire. Leading his group, Stryjek attacked with hand grenades and Molotov bottles. Bullets flew from all sides. The SS troops panicked. The *Oberscharführer* grabbed his automatic. The other guards seized their weapons. All of them ran straight into Stryjek's trap. Now the entire camp was on alert. Sirens screamed. Loudspeakers blared. SS men and Ukrainian soldiers fired.

Mlot ordered his men to attack from the rear. His automatic was causing havoc among the SS. They couldn't return to the guardhouse, nor could they move forward. They fell into position and fired blindly around them.

Mlot signaled, and I took off for the guardhouse. Wojtek, Bystry, Malpa, and Ziemian followed. I was thrilled when I saw the Jewish slaves running for freedom. I screamed to encourage them. "Run! Run! Run!"

They ran in all directions. Some fell, shot by the SS.

I entered the guardhouse. Not a soul was there. Only boots, rifles, and ammunition belts. I loaded the weapons on my shoulders. Passing a window on my way out, I saw a guard tower right in front of me. The guard was busy with his machine gun, shooting into the compound.

The alarm had brought many Jews out of the barracks. They ran wildly, not knowing what was happening. Some were trying to break out, but the machine gun in the tower was cutting them down. I jumped out of the open window, unhooked my grenade. Throwing it with deadly precision, I blew the tower to pieces. Smoke engulfed me as the wood planks collapsed, bringing the structure to the ground.

Only a moment ago my face had been filled with hate and anger; now I was laughing uncontrollably. I looked around for another grenade. I wanted to blow up the other towers. I didn't care what Mlot's orders had been. My feelings were totally with my fellow Jews as I saw them running for freedom into the forest. I would have liked to join them and lead them in a new partisan fighting group. But it was all happening too fast. There was no time to think. My mind jolted me back to reality. If I ran away now with the rifles and ammunition belts, it would be treason. No, I wouldn't desert.

I ran back for the rifles. My "buddies" were already leaving as I picked up my load. Choosing a shortcut, and with my body bent low under the weight, I reached our rendezvous ahead of the others. Still, it wasn't enough. They'd already begun calling me names: "Bedouin!" *"Parch!"* "Jew!" One threatened, "Wait till Mlot lays his hands on you!" They spat at me as we moved deeper into the safety of the woods.

Mlot and his men were still busy firing at the trapped Germans. Soon he began his withdrawal, retreating slowly behind the cover of the trees and bushes. Stryjek's men were taking the brunt of the battle. They were still fighting even as Mlot and his group retreated. To confuse and divide the enemy, each group was to take a separate route back through the forest.

Mlot caught up with us. He ordered his men to help us with the captured weapons. No fatalities so far, only several slight wounds. The other novices and I had emerged without a scratch. We took the long way back, avoiding the open fields. In a serious mood, Mlot counted our spoils. Sixteen rifles; twenty grenades; and one automatic, a Schmeisser.

I had captured the Schmeisser, four rifles, several ammunition belts, and three grenades. But my achievement only irked the others. They muttered loud enough for Mlot to hear, "The cat's lucky. You saw how he risked our lives—the entire operation—just to help the Jews."

The farther we got from the Germans, the safer they felt. And the bolder their statements against me became. Even Mlot found time to criticize my attack on the tower. "You're smart, fast, and lucky. But you used your only grenade to save Jews. And that was against my orders."

I lowered my eyes. I had no defense or reply. I could only wait for his anger to subside.

CHAPTER 31

That night, back at our camp, none of us went to sleep. We stayed awake with vodka and tobacco. Despite our excellent haul of weapons, no one celebrated. Stryjek and his men had not returned. Tension and anxiety engulfed us all as Mlot kept everyone on the alert. There would be no rest or sleep until we knew the fate of those twelve men.

The night was long, dark, and difficult. Isolated, I felt the anger and hatred around me. The men despised me. Their suspicion of me had now become a reality. I was the scapegoat, the *Zydek,* the Jew.

Just what was my crime? I wondered. That I was born Jewish? What's wrong with that? Besides, I never chose it. No one ever asked me. Fate and heredity had condemned me. I faced a tribunal and a jury made up of both the educated and the ignorant, the strong and the weak, the religious and the faithless, the rich and the poor, the young and the old. I faced civilization itself, a civilization that was battling fanatically over its future and its existence; a civilization that was splintered, yet curiously united against my survival. I was a criminal. I was a Jew.

I didn't have to wait long for the partisans' hatred to explode. The night was hardly over when Mlot came up behind me.

"Hey, *chlopcze,* pal, turn around and face me. Look at me and listen carefully. Obey, and nothing bad will happen to you."

He motioned for me to walk in front of him into the forest and away from the camp. I obeyed. With a gun in my hand and a grenade under my belt, I felt apprehensive, but safe. Still, I was trembling inside, uncertain of what would happen next.

"Those morons are all convinced you're a Jew, Jacku. Till now, they were only suspicious. Now, they're sure. When you first joined us, I was certain you were Jewish, but I didn't mind. In fact, I liked you and wanted you near me. But now, everything's different. They'll never accept you. Disappear before you're harmed. Disappear, and right now."

Mlot extended his hand. "Give me your gun and grenade. Your belt, too. Everything except your knife. That's yours. Keep it. It's a Luftwaffe, isn't it?"

I nodded, angry but obedient.

"Here's some bread and vodka. You'll be safe. I'll cover for you. Just follow me."

He blindfolded me, then led me farther through the forest. A while later, he tapped my shoulder. "*Servus,* Jacku. Sorry we must part. Walk as long as you can before you take the blindfold off."

His voice came to me from the distance. "*Servus, chlopcze.*"

Alone, I walked on in sorrow and frustration as the tears rolled down my cheeks. Finally, I tore the rag from my eyes and sat down. I ran my fingers lightly over the grass and embraced a young tree. I wanted to think, to stop crying, but I couldn't. It seemed so easy to cry, surrounded by the forest's soothing calm. There were no people around to spoil the tranquillity. Most of my sixteen years had been a steady chain of disappointments with people. All kinds of people. Young, old, males, females, Germans, Ukrainians, Latvians, Poles, Christians, even some Jews. Here and there a ray, a sprinkle of gentleness from a few. But by that point in my life, I had begun to predict that even they, that slim minority, would some day also explode with hatred and evil. At that moment, I felt completely abandoned by society. Condemned by people. Protected only by the forest.

"God, oh, God," I looked up at the sun, "You are up there in safety. You have chosen me to be Jewish, to be mankind's testing ground, a guinea pig for their hatreds. But I'm tired of the struggle. I'm going to stay here close to the trees and the leaves and the beautiful green blanket of grass."

I fell asleep.

* * *

When I awoke, it was hours later, and I felt rested. With no plans or ideas, I started to walk. If only Halina were with me, I thought. I tried to imagine the warmth of her body, her face, her presence. In her absence, I was grateful to the sun for its comfort.

I walked for two days—first west, then northwest, avoiding all villages and farms. I shied away from all living creatures. I walked, slept, ate little, and contemplated. I listened to the sounds of nature.

Finally, in the early morning of the third day, I found myself on the edge of a narrow paved road, bordered on both sides by steep embankments. Singing voices were drifting up from the distance. I stopped and looked down the road. A long column of people, led by a number of soldiers, some on horseback, were marching toward me. I ran for cover and hid in a thick clump of bushes a few yards from the road.

The singing was getting louder.

"Oh, Marianna, *moja slodka* Marianna." I knew the song from my school days, and the people were singing it beautifully. Their voices warmed my heart. As the column passed before me, I recognized the people as Jews. They were being escorted by SS guards and Ukrainians.

But they were wearing civilian clothing, not striped uniforms. They must be from some ghetto, I thought, not a concentration camp. Now, in mid-1943, the fourth year under Germany's yoke, could there be a ghetto left? They must be marching to work somewhere. Later, they'll be coming back. Anxious and afraid, I remained in hiding. I was happy, though, to discover that Jews still existed and that some ghettos still functioned.

The column continued to stream past me. An endless flow of people, five across, singing, marching. There were perhaps a thousand or more, most of them young. It must be a huge ghetto, I thought. At last, the column passed, and the strains of "Marianna" grew distant. But I still heard the echo in my ears, the sound of living Jews, of life and hope.

I made up my mind to wait all day in the same spot. I would join them on their march back to the ghetto. I wanted to be among my own people, among those who wouldn't reject or ridicule me. Among Jews, I could obtain the money and documents for my trip back to Warsaw, to Milanowek, to wait for Halina. I knew there was risk involved, that once in the ghetto, wherever it was, I might not get out again. But I felt I could handle it.

The day passed slowly. I talked to myself, debated the pros and cons, weighed the risks, and finally I heard the voices again. The column appeared in the distance, the same as before. My heart pounded as I lay near the road and waited. The sun had set, and the sound of insects was in the air. Now the Jews were marching past me, row after row, in the dim spring light.

I spotted a Ukrainian guard, then another. Then a long stretch with no guard in sight. I bolted to my feet, darted across the embankment, and broke into the column. *"Amhu! Amhu!* I'm one of you!"

The marchers recoiled in shock. I studied their faces for any sign of recognition or welcome. I wanted to ask questions. But I couldn't. They just kept singing and marching. Two of them pulled me to their side and kept me there. I understood. They had to sing. They didn't want to, but they had to. They, too, wanted to survive.

"Amhu," I repeated. "I'm one of yours. Trust me."

They looked at me in amazement. I had come from nowhere to join them. Why?

We walked on in silence. Then some of them began whispering in Yiddish.

Why had I risked my life to join them? They were prepared to risk their lives to escape. Some already had. My joining them was beyond reason, beyond their ability to understand.

Soon, to my bitter regret, I learned what they meant. There was no ghetto. And they weren't civilians. They were slaves, like the slaves in any other concentration camp. Their striped uniforms simply had not yet been distributed. And they were working among many civilian engineers and mechanics at a German aircraft plant.

Budzyn, a subdivision of Majdanek, now was visible in the distance. Its master, the feared and despised *Oberscharführer* Feiks, was waiting for us on his white horse. I saw the usual wooden barracks, the guard towers with machine guns, the double barbed-wire electrified fences. All in the middle of nowhere, deep in the heart of a dense forest. A group of buildings nearby, the *Siedlung,* housed the guards and the German civilians who ran the aircraft plant.

Enraged and bewildered, I bitterly cursed my fate. How could I have so mishandled my cherished freedom? I had risked my life to gain it; now I had lost it again in an instant. "My fucking luck," I kept repeating, disgusted with myself.

But I had no time for self-recrimination. The gates of the camp were now wide open. Together with all the others, I was being herded into the cage.

It was all too familiar. The guards, the vicious dogs, the long whips and machine guns. They were once again in control of my life.

At the Budzyn *Appelplatz,* Major Sztockman signaled his deputy, Lieutenant Szczepiacki, to start the count. Both men were Jews and former officers in the defeated Polish army. They were the chief kapos in Budzyn. The Germans were now using their talents for administrative purposes. And to give them the appearance of authority, the major and the lieutenant were allowed to wear their old green uniforms.

Lieutenant Szczepiacki ran down the assembled columns of inmates, quickly counting them by fives. When he came to me, he suddenly stopped. I was an extra, a sixth.

"What's going on here? Where's your group? Where the hell are you from?"

I didn't trust him. I stood mute. I had no answer.

Across the yard, Commandant Feiks, perched on his white horse, was waiting for the official count. One of his aides noticed the confusion and yelled out, *"Mach doch weiter! Mach dass du weiter kommst!* Keep moving!"

Major Sztockman approached and pulled me out of the column. Holding his whip high over my head, he walked me swiftly to the rear. I liked his face and hastily poured out my story.

"I'm Jewish," I said. "I escaped from Warsaw. I thought this would be a ghetto, so I joined the column from the woods."

The major kept walking. "From Warsaw? You fought in the uprising?" he finally said in Polish. "Stand there."

He pushed me into the rear line of inmates. Commandant Feiks galloped by. Sztockman saluted and reported. *"Alles in Ordnung, Herr Oberscharführer!"* All in order.

Later that evening, the major, a tall and well-mannered man, summoned me to his room in the barrack. Something about me had impressed him. My candor? My history? My youth?

"So you were part of the uprising in Warsaw," he said. "We heard about it here. It was a gallant and courageous battle. Even the SS men are still talking about the Warsaw rebels. Well, kid, screw them. But here, young man, I'm trying to save thousands of Jews from the gas chambers at Majdanek. And my chances are reasonable, as long as I get along with Commandant Feiks and as long as no one gives him an excuse for any pogroms. Even you, a Warsaw rebel, can manage to stay alive here. I'll cover and account for you, if you promise to behave. And if you promise not to attempt any escapes. Do you understand me?''

I nodded and promised. I had no choice.

''Tomorrow you'll start work at the aircraft plant. I'll give orders to place you with the others from Warsaw in Majzel's group. You'll like that better than starving here in the camp. Now go get some rest. You'll work hard tomorrow.''

CHAPTER 32

Labor camp Budzyn was a nightmare. No gas chambers, no crematoria, no striped uniforms. But agony, torture, and starvation. Every day.

Several thousand Jewish men and about one hundred women were imprisoned in the camp. They were housed in wooden barracks, marched to work every morning, and returned every night. All under the whips and guns of SS and Ukrainian guards.

Most frightening of all was the prospect of falling into the hands of the camp's youthful blue-eyed master. Commandant Feiks, still only in his late twenties, personified the worst of German hatred for Jews. He used men and women to satisfy his sadistic whims. He especially enjoyed catching his victims by surprise, then experimenting with new techniques of torture and death. He elevated cruelty to a science. No one could explain his inhuman behavior toward the inmates, or, for that matter, his attitude toward Major Sztockman, the only Jew he addressed by name and seemed to respect.

Sundays at Budzyn were days of dread. On those days, when no one left the camp to work at the aircraft plant, Feiks had us all to himself. One Sunday, he appeared during lunch. Everyone was sitting outdoors at long wooden tables, sipping the thin, watery soup that passed for food. Suddenly Feiks zoomed through the camp on a motorcycle. A machine gun was cradled under his arm. Before anyone could move, he sprayed the tables with bullets. The serving barrels were perforated. Little fountains of soup spouted out of the holes and poured over the inmates who fell to the ground. Not all of them got up again. Dozens lay dead or wounded.

On weekday evenings, Feiks amused himself in a different way. After the *Appelplatz* count, and a full day's work at the aircraft plant, he would suddenly decide to beautify the compound. This meant that dozens of guards would order everyone out of the barracks on what Feiks called an *Ausholzung*. While the guards hovered over us with whips and dogs, we would stoop and pull up weeds and wild shrubs with our bare hands. With no pattern of consistency, Feiks would then gallop up on his white horse and spray us with bullets. He would roar with laughter as we rushed for cover. Again, dozens would die or suffer.

And Feiks loved "culture." He treated us to special dramatic performances. Often he would applaud excessively and then line up the slave "actors" for execution. "You see, actors are parasites. Therefore, they have no right to live." His submachine gun would zigzag the stage, spraying death among the performers.

Not a day went by that Feiks didn't find several souls who displeased him for some reason or other. Those unfortunates would first be whipped, then turned over to Feiks, who would drag them to death as he galloped around the compound on his horse.

But I witnessed the climax of his bestiality one Saturday morning. Otto, the Ukrainian officer, rushed us out of our bunk beds early, long before roll call, with a volley of machine-gun fire. It was still dark and cold. In front of the gate stood Feiks, smiling, dressed in his best officer's uniform, looking neat and handsome, and apparently in a good mood. It seemed to me that he never slept.

I looked around me at the fifty or so young Jews, the slaves that Otto had chosen for this occasion. They all looked the way I felt; depressed, stunned, frightened. Why were we there? What was Feiks up to this time? Not a hint.

I had instant diarrhea. I was wet. I was afraid to betray my fear and my shit. Oh, God, if I could only change my pants. I got the chills.

Feiks screamed and snapped me to attention. I regained some strength. I began talking to myself, disciplining myself. He ordered us onto a truck. With a contingent of SS men and Ukrainians, we were off to a small town in the area known for its relatively large Jewish population.

In prewar days, it was a poor and peaceful town. Its Jewish residents were mostly shoemakers, carpenters, tailors, and shopkeepers. Also, the town had its righteous: the rabbi; the *shamos,* synagogue caretaker; the *shochet,* ritual slaughterer; and the *Yeshiva* students. They had dwelt in peace among their Polish Christian neighbors for centuries. Harmony was often lacking, yet they coexisted and Judaism flourished.

But on that Sabbath morning, Commandant Feiks decided to end those centuries of coexistence once and for all. When the trucks entered the town, they headed straight for the Jewish quarter. The SS announced their presence by firing machine guns at random into the clusters of small frame houses. No one was yet on the streets. In a few seconds, dozens of men, women, and children began to flee out of back doors and windows, heading for the nearby woods.

Feiks ordered his men to cut them down. They swiftly obliged. Soon bodies were lying about in small pools of blood. Now the SS blocked off the narrow dirt streets as the Ukrainians went from door to door to force the inhabitants out of their homes into the square next to the *shul,* the small village synagogue. Frightened families began to fill the square. Mothers and fathers. Weeping children. Elderly grandparents.

The families of small-town Polish Jews were so tightly knit that only brute force could separate parents from children, brothers from sisters. Family members often preferred to die, rather than be parted from one another. In this, Feiks's men once again obliged.

At last, perhaps seven or eight hundred souls were gathered in the square—weeping, clinging to one another, praying. Still in my truck, I watched the scene with growing dismay.

To allay their fears and avoid total panic, Feiks ordered a number of able-bodied adult males to go back to their homes for some belongings.

"Take just what you'll need for the trip," he commanded. "When the trucks arrive, you're all going to another ghetto. We have work for you there."

At gunpoint, he also separated about fifty young men from their families for work at Budzyn. These men were immediately loaded onto our trucks. The remaining Jews, the weeping women and children, the old and the sick, Feiks ordered into the *shul,* their house of prayer.

"Pray for a safe journey," he told them. "You're all going on a long trip."

The terrorized Jews slowly crammed into the small wooden structure until it was overflowing. They suspected his motives, but they had no choice. They prayed in fear. They waited for trucks that were never coming.

I could detect Feiks's glee as he ordered the doors and windows shut. He had them in their own house of God, on their own Sabbath, in the company of their own sacred scrolls. Then, as I watched in horror, I saw Feiks toss a can of gasoline on the porch. He was roaring with insane laughter as he picked up his submachine gun. He whirled around, as though in a peculiar state of ecstasy. Then he fired the gun at the can.

In an instant, the gas exploded. Wood and flesh fueled the flames. More gasoline cans were hurled. The entire structure, and everyone in it, was ablaze. The screams rose in deafening chorus with the flames. Some people tried to break out through the windows, but machine guns mounted on the trucks cut them down mercilessly.

Sick to my stomach, I watched the inferno from a distance. All my own fears, anguish, and self-pity vanished. I wanted to jump on Feiks's neck. To squeeze it. To wrench the last breath out of his body. But my mind told me I was helpless. All I could do was turn away my eyes to the forest.

And vow to survive. To escape.

To tell the world what I had seen.

CHAPTER 33

I had to get out. But the electrified double barbed-wire fences, combined with the guard towers fortified by mounted machine guns and searchlights, made escape from Budzyn almost impossible. I had to try elsewhere.

So I looked at the aircraft plant, where I spent most of each day and where several dozen Ukrainians and German *Werkschutz* guards handled the security, which was less stringent. Together with Yosl and Motek, eighteen-year-old twins from Warsaw, I devised a simple plan of escape. We would hide in a haystack near the north fence until quitting time. Then, during the hubbub that always accompanied the 6 P.M. roll call, we would make our break and head for the forest. At that hour, the Ukrainian fence guards were withdrawn to make the head count, and we would stand a better chance of getting through.

On the night before our planned break, I lay on my bunk and dreamed of freedom and of Halina. But already she'd become remote in my mind. Today's reality crowded out even my dreams.

In the morning, gray clouds covered the sky. Rain had fallen all night, and suddenly I was filled with misgivings. But I dared not think of failure. Then my morale sank even lower when Motek pulled me out of my bunk and into the latrine.

"We'll have to postpone it, Jacku," he said. "My brother's got a fever and diarrhea."

"Damn! It sounds like he's afraid."

"No. Just give him a few more days. He'll get over it."

I talked to Yosl. He insisted we go without him. "Just save yourselves. Don't wait for me. Go. Go."

I saw the confusion in their faces. Maybe their experiences in Budzyn had softened their stomachs, made them fear the risks of escape. But Feiks and what I had seen had hardened mine. I understood their predicament. But I couldn't wait. I was determined to try for freedom. No postponements. I would either succeed or perish.

When the hour finally arrived, I was alone. From the haystack, I watched the Ukrainians leave the fence for the roll call. The slaves were already coming out of the plant and lining up in fives.

A chill ran through me, but I shook it off. I dashed for the fence, squeezed under the barbed wire, and disappeared into the forest. I saw no one. I heard nothing. I knew it wouldn't be long before they discovered my absence. But I knew they wouldn't march off until they had thoroughly searched the plant for me. They would search outside, too. All the nearby farms and villages. But I counted on the forest. I planned to run as far as my strength and the trees would last. For days, if necessary.

I heard the sirens. But that was back at the plant, and I was outside, free. I ran deeper and deeper into the forest. But my ignorance of the terrain soon filled me with terror. The trees were thinning out. The forest was disappearing. And then, suddenly, ahead of me stretched a broad, flat pasture. I was totally exposed. In the distance, I heard the sound of dogs. The *Werkschutz* guards were coming closer. They were combing the forest, and they didn't have far to go. Almost out of breath, I re-entered the forest. The guards and dogs drew nearer. I'd always been afraid of dogs. Their fangs and sharp claws panicked me. But even more, I feared being captured again.

Someone must have seen me go under the fence. Someone must have followed me. How else could they converge around me so quickly? They must know where I am. And then again, maybe not. Maybe they're just looking. A faint trace of hope filtered into my thoughts. I reached the center of the small forest, climbed a tree, and decided to sit it out right there. The barking grew louder. I heard voices.

But I was still praying for a miracle. I couldn't fail. Not me. I was the survivor, the last of Grandma Masha's twenty grandchildren. She had made me swear, right there in her bedroom. Her last words before the SS men came for her had been: *Survive, Izaakl! Survive!* Her voice echoed in my ears. It was mixed with the barking of the dogs.

"I must survive. I will survive." I repeated it over and over, a litany.

But as the guards and dogs came closer, my resolve and determination slowly dissolved, gnawed away bit by bit by fear. The entire world of hate was closing in on me.

And then they were there, right beneath me, at the foot of the tree.

"Los, Jude! Runter, you parasite."

The dogs were barking wildly, trying to leap up the tree. I looked down in horror. It's a dream. Please let it be a dream. Let there be no terror, no Germans, no dogs. But they were there. And the guards were aiming their rifles at me.

"Runter! Eins, zwei . . ."

I suddenly remembered Yankele in the Warsaw cemetery, in the tree. They had gunned him down out of the tree where he had tried to hide. I dropped to the ground and began to run. In seconds, the dogs were on top of me. It was no contest. I heard a loud command, and the dogs backed off.

I looked up and saw a potbellied *Werkschutz,* the chief of guards at the aircraft plant. I recognized him, and he, me. I got to my feet, trembling. My clothes were in shreds, my hands and legs bleeding.

They tied my hands behind me, and we started back to the plant. The accompanying guards cursed me all the way. But "Fatso" protected me. For some reason, he liked me. I had no idea why.

By the time we returned, the sun had set, and darkness blanketed the plant. But the 2,000 slaves had not returned to Budzyn. They were still waiting in the yard. They were waiting for the capture and return of one escaped Jew.

The guards were sitting around a campfire, singing. First a solo voice, *"Tsygane-tchka."* Then the reply in unison, *"Tsygane-tchka Moloda."* Their song told the story of a beautiful young gypsy. They sang while the flames reached to the sky. The fire warmed their bodies and the song warmed their souls. The dark star-filled sky, the sounds of singing, and the sight of the Ukrainians huddled around the fire in their long black coats created a moment of beauty that pierced even my fear. But the beauty in that night clashed with the darkness of the guards' purpose and the even darker ordeal that I knew awaited me. So much beauty in this world, I thought. So much beauty. But even more evil and misery.

At the plant, I was handed over to the Ukrainians and SS men. They punched me repeatedly as they pushed me to the head of the column. I had delayed their evening meal, and they were furious. I was no longer feeling pain. I was waiting for death—the final peace. But it didn't come. I was being saved for Feiks.

As the column approached Budzyn, everything grew foggy. My life. My existence. My past. All of it dissolved into abstractions as the final minutes of my life ticked by.

I wanted to scream for Halina. For some miracle. For some super-giant to reach down and avenge us both.

Then, out of the night, I saw a great white horse galloping straight at me. It was no supercreature coming to avenge me. It was Satan's steed. It was carrying Commandant Feiks. Wild with anger, Feiks stopped in front of me. He jerked the reins, and the horse reared up and whinnied. Its legs missed my face by inches. I drew back in fright. Feiks's whip curled itself around my neck like a lasso. Then, with a mad howl, he galloped through the camp gates to the center of the *Appelplatz,* dragging me all the way. I was too stunned to know what was happening. I was choking. My eyes were bulging, my body aching.

Feiks uncurled the whip, rolling me on the ground. I lay gasping in front of a dozen SS officers, in front of the Ukrainians, in front of every inmate in the camp. The column had been marched straight to the *Appelplatz* to watch the carnival. I regained my composure and stood up. I saw Major Sztockman approach with his aide, Szczepiacki. I closed my eyes. I couldn't bear to face him. It no longer mattered. I had wanted to survive, so I had risked my life and my honor, but I had failed. I had failed not only myself, but also my Grandma Masha, my parents, my sister Hela, and Halina. I had failed all my people. Now who would survive to tell their story?

Feiks addressed the silent, hungry assemblage. "We will shoot this dog and hang him up for everyone to see! There'll be no dinner tonight. And this dog's group, the Warsaw rebels, will stand in the *Appelplatz* through the night!"

Major Sztockman stepped forward and saluted Feiks. He then

walked up to me and crashed his whip down on my head. *'Fünfund-zwanzig am Arsch!* Twenty-five lashes!"

To my astonishment, Feiks didn't object. Szczepiacki seized my head and bent me forward. Otto, the Ukrainian, raised his whip.

"Eins, zwei, drei, vier . . ."

As the pain tore through me, I wondered why a whipping before an execution? With every lash, the knot at the end of the whip cut into my flesh. Yet at the end of the twenty-five, I stood erect, without a tear.

Sztockman addressed Feiks.

"Herr Oberscharführer, noch inmer so stark und Arbeitsfähig. After all that beating, he's still strong and stands straight—a special kind of man. Let him work. You can always finish him off."

As Sztockman spoke, Szczepiacki slapped me around. I knew now they had teamed up to save me. They were beating me to pacify Feiks. The thousands of prisoners were watching in dazed silence.

An insane scream split the air. "No! That dog must be executed, finished! *Heute einer, Morgen zwanzig.* Today, we spare one. Tomorrow, twenty will escape."

Feiks leaped from his horse and strode up to me. He looked me squarely in the eye, expecting me to wince, to fall on my knees and beg. I just stood there motionless, inches from his whip. I refused to budge. Two sets of blue eyes met, master's and slave's.

Suddenly Feiks ordered Otto to hold me. Then he turned his whip around to the blunt end and started to beat me over the head with all his strength. It was obvious he wanted me on the ground, at his feet. As each blow fell, I swallowed the pain and called on every fiber in my body to keep me up. I had to remain conscious, on my feet. The blows continued to rain down on me. But I wouldn't close my eyes. I was afraid they would never open again.

At last, Feiks finished. Painfully I straightened back to attention. I felt the world was crushing me. The sky was falling like a shattered mirror on my face. But I stood.

Sztockman moved forward and addressed Feiks again. "You see, he's something special. Only a bullet will finish him. And you have time for that. Let him work. I'll keep an eye on him."

I couldn't understand Sztockman's persistence. He was actually trying to save me. An angel, I thought. But it won't work. I can't escape the German bastard.

Feiks howled again. I ground my teeth, bit my lips, clenched my fists, swallowed my pain. The commandant pulled up the reins, and this gigantic, beautiful white horse stood right in front of me, with his hind legs bent, his front legs high in the air. Feiks's red-cheeked doll face contorted while his white teeth flashed in anger and hatred.

He wrapped the rein around my neck, pulling me off the ground. My tongue was hanging powerless, my bulging eyes rose to the sky. I saw the death's-head insignia on his cap. I saw the star-filled sky. I wanted to be up there on another planet. Feiks screamed something about my boots and my looks.

"Help me, Mama!" I cried in pain. My dangling body came alive. I felt wires, needles, huge blades cutting through my legs.

Feiks suddenly relaxed the horse's reins. I fell to the ground. I saw blood. My legs were bleeding. My boots, my beautiful black shiny leather boots, were hanging in shreds.

"You beast, you German sadist, you destroyed my beautiful boots, you destroyed my pride!" I screamed inside. I had wanted never to part with them. I felt strong and powerful in them. Now all I felt was a hatred so great it went beyond my pain.

I saw an SS officer standing near me. In his hand, the shiny blade of the stiletto he had used to cut up my boots and my flesh was still dripping with my blood.

Feiks screamed, "Today one, tomorrow twenty!" I felt the rein on my neck once again. The horse stopped, and the rein relaxed again. I dropped to the ground, but this time I saw no boots—I had lost them on the way—only bleeding, burning legs. I scrambled to get up. Most of my physical strength was gone. All I had left was stubborn determination to stand up, to face him, to be as tall as he was.

He screamed again, pointing to the wooden platform nearby. He ordered me to climb the steps to the gallows. I could count my final seconds. I had watched Feiks hang many people in the past. It was now my turn. I faced the rope. Then, in a surge of strength, I stepped back from the platform and stood near Feiks. He raised his whip over my head again. "Up the platform!"

I shook my head, heard my own voice, quiet and clear. "No. Never on the rope!"

Feiks laughed. His laugh turned to a shriek. "Can you imagine, this dog, this Warsaw bandit, is disobeying me! This louse! No! I'll show that scum no mercy! Get that pig up on the platform!" He let out a maddened howl at Otto, the Ukrainian. Feiks dismounted and, waving his submachine gun, pointed to his aides and to the gallows. They understood and rushed toward me. Within seconds, a hail of punches landed on me from all sides. I closed my eyes as they dragged me to the platform.

Suddenly I was floating in the air. I became panicky and started to push my fist into my mouth. "Why can't I breathe?" flashed through my mind. All at once, the pressure eased, and I crashed to the ground. I heard screams, voices, heavy bootsteps. I had kept my eyes closed all this time.

Once again, I felt myself floating. That same pain in my neck and that same panicky feeling of choking. I wanted to scream, but I couldn't find my voice. Then another release, another crash. Again I landed on the platform.

The crowd at the *Appelplatz* gasped. Twice they had seen me up on the gallows, and twice the wooden contraption had pulled apart. Twice when I should have been dead, I survived.

"A miracle," the crowd murmured. Feiks and his aides were staring. Just staring.

"Herr Oberscharführer, why not another twenty-five lashes? Let's see if he can take that." Sztockman, out of nowhere, appeared again.

Feiks did not object. Perhaps he feared to see one more failure on the gallows.

In an instant, two Ukrainians freed my neck, grabbed my hands, and bent me forward again. *"Eins, zwei, drei, vier . . ."*

I intended to die with dignity and pride. To show Feiks that Jews were not afraid of death.

Halfway through the lashing, an SS man replaced the Ukrainian to complete the punishment. Otto had grown tired wielding the whip. To everyone's amazement, including my own, after the third twenty-five lashes, I was still on my feet. And to Feiks's disbelief and outrage, I retreated several steps farther from the gallows platform.

"Halt! Not another step!" he screamed.

Szczepiacki ran up and started beating me again. Blood was pouring from my head and body. I tore off my shirt and wiped the blood from my eyes. I had to see. Feiks mounted his horse and galloped around me. He cocked his submachine gun and ordered me to walk in front of him. I forced myself into an erect posture and started to move. I was prepared for the bullets to end everything, once and for all. I almost wished it. I glanced at Major Sztockman as I passed. I wanted to whisper, "Thank you, Major. Sorry it didn't work."

Suddenly a volley of machine-gun bullets tore up the dirt around my legs. I bent my head and covered my eyes. Another volley of bullets. I was sure I was hit. But where? I raised my head and turned to face Feiks and the world for a final time. I saw his face, a contortion of laughter and hatred.

And suddenly he cried out, *"Lauf zu den Waschraum!*

"Run to the washroom!"

I understood what he meant. He had conceded to Sztockman. He had given in to some mysterious whim to let me live. I walked slowly but surely to the wash barracks, several hundred feet away. Szczepiacki followed and continued to beat me, just in case Feiks should change his mind.

Some hours later, Feiks kicked open the door of my barrack. He wanted to see me. "Is he still alive?"

The inmates near me picked me up from my bunk, splashed me with buckets of cold water, and helped me stand at attention. Feiks approached, stopped, then looked me up and down. He struck me twice across the face and left, muttering to himself.

The next morning I was told about Feiks' visit. I remembered nothing; I must have been unconscious.

Major Sztockman sent an angel of mercy with some coffee, bread, and crude bandages. So I managed to walk out with the others for the count on the *Appelplatz.* My body was raw and sore, my face swollen, my stomach wounds were still bleeding. I had to lean on a stick to stay upright, and I had large lumps all over my head. But I had gained new hope and a further determination to survive.

That new hope vanished the moment I reached the *Appelplatz.* Feiks appeared on his white horse and promptly summoned me forward. A Ukrainian guard, using red dye, painted my clothes with three large crosses, marking me for "special treatment." Feiks then tossed his long reins around my neck and dragged me around the square. It was his way of showing the assembled prisoners that although I had survived, my life would no longer be worth living. I realized my ordeal was just beginning.

Feiks then instructed Sztockman that I was no longer to be taken to the aircraft plant. Instead, I was to circle the *Appelplatz* all day long, carrying a load of bricks on my back. Only half an hour's rest and soup once a day. No bread or any other food. Should I collapse or try to rest, the guards had orders to shoot.

Sztockman listened and saluted. *"Jawohl, Herr Oberscharführer!"*

My pace around the square slowed a bit more each day. And each day lasted an eternity. Summer had come, and the sun beat down on me relentlessly. The bricks on my back seemed to grow heavier. The machine guns in the towers seemed like cannons. The guards seemed like vultures . . . waiting . . . waiting for me to fall, to faint, to die. I felt my body rebel against my brain, against my conscious will to survive. My legs became swollen from hunger, despite Sztockman's compassionate supplements of bread. Messengers would appear in the secrecy of night and leave potatoes and bread on my bunk. I knew the food came from Sztockman. The others had nothing to share. They were fighting their own losing battle against hunger, torture, and disease.

Feiks often added to my torture. He would roar by on his motorcycle or ride over on his horse. "You pig, you filthy Jew. You wanted to escape. Up there, that's the only escape." He pointed to the sky. I ignored him and continued to circle with my burden of bricks. But always I would feel his whip before he left.

Bit by bit, I felt the strength disappear from my legs. I knew it was only a matter of hours, or days at the most, before they would buckle completely. And then the bullets would fly. My only pleasure came from my dreams of Halina, floating through my mind like a beautiful golden ship sailing across a sea of pain. But it was all I could do to close my eyes and think of her. Was she alive? Would we meet again? How could I survive?

I knew the answers to my questions, but I dreamed anyway. Papa and Mama must surely have died in the gas chambers of Majdanek. My Grandma Masha, my sister Hela, my cousins, aunts, uncles, friends—all gone. So why should I be different? No. The Germans, the Third Reich, won't spare a single Jew. Not one.

Then early one morning, one of Sztockman's aides rushed up to my bunk. He took my clothes and gave me others, marked with only one cross. "From now on, no more bricks! During roll call, stand in the back. Not in front."

He disappeared and left me in a state of confusion. But soon it began to make sense. Feiks didn't appear that morning for the count. "They transferred him to the Russian front," Szczepiacki explained. "You're no longer a three-cross special. You're going back to the aircraft plant. Don't hesitate or you're lost. It's a miracle!"

I was reborn that morning. When I joined the others on the long road to the plant, a huge roar greeted me. "Jacek, with the iron *tuches,* iron behind," they laughed. They offered sticks, canes, and all kinds of contraptions they called "crutches." I hopped, I limped, I struggled. But with each step I took, I gained a renewed will and a fresh hope for the future.

CHAPTER 34

With Feiks gone, the degree of daily torture and brutality lessened. But the pattern of life in Budzyn remained the same. The Jews still worked as slaves. The morning and evening counts continued. And hunger and disease were rampant, just as before. My life centered on survival. I had to regain my physical strength.

One evening at the *Appelplatz*, Major Sztockman approached me with a smile. "You're looking a little better these days, Jacku. Eh?"

Not knowing what to expect, I remained silent.

"You're not planning any more escapes, I hope," he said. "I think you've had enough. Remember, even though Feiks is no longer with us, they'll still kill twenty-five of us for everyone who escapes. Do you understand?"

I lowered my eyes and again promised I would not try, at least not from Budzyn. Sztockman, still my guardian angel, then assigned me to an outfit called the *Umschulung*. This consisted of a group of teenagers who were being trained by the Germans to build and repair the wings and fuselages of their JU-88 bombers. This helped speed my recovery, because during the training period, we performed no physical labor. Instead, we had twelve hours of daily instruction.

As my health improved, I grew increasingly aggressive. I decided to put my old smuggling and trading experience to good use. A German engineer, Meister Jovanic, was in charge of the stockroom. He stole countless pieces of equipment and fine tools every day. I, in turn, traded them to the civilian Polish laborers and truck drivers for food. I then traded the food to my fellow inmates for the money, watches, and jewels they had managed to hide. I no longer felt hunger.

By stuffing Meister Jovanic's pockets with valuables, I became his darling—his smart, blond, blue-eyed *Jude.* With typical German mentality, he often praised me. "A kid like you, I'd gladly adopt. You're a good Jewish boy. I'll see to it that they kill you last." It seemed to be an almost religious conviction with Germans—all *Juden* must perish. Jovanic's mind never strayed from this ultimate goal.

At last, the *Umschulung* course ended. The young slave-students were ready for the Budzyn assembly line. But that didn't happen. The new specialists were ordered, instead, to the more sophisticated aircraft plant at Mielec, some 200 kilometers southwest.

I sought out Major Sztockman and thanked him for everything he had done for me. He remained characteristically silent. His face betrayed no emotion at all. He just shook my hand and wished me luck. A short while later, I once again found myself aboard a cattle car.

At Camp Mielec, we were welcomed with striped uniforms, the ones I had despised and feared for so long. We had to surrender our civilian cross-marked clothing for the blue and white prison garments. In addition, we were each branded like animals with a tattoo on the right wrist, a "KL" for *Konzentrationslager,* concentration camp.

I was appointed group leader of the night shift. Our crew worked twelve hours every night. We were supposed to sleep during the day, but the SS commander of Mielec had his own brand of torture. He ordered the guards to assign kitchen chores, cleaning jobs, and other manual labor to anyone they found asleep.

One morning, after we had completed our nightly twelve-hour shift, the SS detained me and my crew for several more hours. They were expecting a very important personage, and they wanted to show him that there was no shortage of qualified slave labor at Mielec.

The plant suddenly snapped to attention. A host of SS officers and top-ranking Nazi officials were escorting down the assembly line the most prominent man in the German munitions industry, Baron Alfred Krupp. Trimly dressed in a dark pin-striped suit, Krupp was pausing on his tour to speak to various workers. Now, as the group stopped in front of me and Meister Schultz, the chief engineer, I grew apprehensive.

"Is this one Jewish, too?" Krupp inquired.

Schultz nodded.

"Is his work satisfactory?"

"That's why I'm here, Herr Baron," Meister Schultz smiled proudly, "to make sure that the scum does the work properly."

Standing straight and stiff, Krupp tapped me on the shoulder with his elegant leather gloves. "Well, he doesn't look Jewish at all. I can depend on your patriotism to make him serve the Reich well. *Heil Hitler!*"

Instinctively, I despised him. I wanted to leap at him, wrap my fingers around his throat, see for myself whether he was the superman he pretended to be. But he moved on, his entourage followed, and I watched him walk away.

As the spring of 1944 unfolded, new hope was born among the Jewish slaves. News of Germany's military disasters was slowly seeping through to us. As the Allies advanced, the Germans retreated closer and closer to their own soil. But on every occasion, the Jewish slaves were the first to be sent away from the front lines. God forbid that the Allied armies should set any of us free.

Finally, orders came to evacuate Mielec. The Russians were approaching, and the plant was to be mined and abandoned. Hastily, the Germans carried out these orders. They stuffed all the Jewish slaves, about a thousand of us, into cattle cars that headed west. For several days, they held us in an open field at Wieliczka, a small mining town, while Berlin decided where to send us next.

Sheer panic possessed Wieliczka. Hundreds of German civilians and wounded soldiers wandered through the rail station. They were searching desperately for any open spot on any train that would take them west, away from the approaching Russians. In terror, they climbed onto the roofs and platforms of the cars. Yet nearby, several dozen cattle cars stood empty. They were reserved for us, the valuable Jewish slaves. Soon the frantic Germans began screaming for places aboard the cattle cars. But the SS had orders to make certain that no Jews went free. The cars were to remain empty at all costs, ready to transport the Jews to the next gas chamber or concentration camp. At gunpoint, the SS chased their own brothers away. Killing Jews was still more important than saving Germans. I found the entire scene difficult to comprehend. I laughed and cried at the same time. The survival of even a single Jew seemed only a remote possibility.

Finally, at night, they packed us back into the cattle cars, this time at least a hundred people per car. There was no room to move. We took turns sitting. And they gave us no food for this ride to the unknown. My friends and I formed a ring, sitting back to back, leaning against each other to avoid being crushed. The weaker souls fainted within the first few hours. By the following morning, a quarter of the people in the car had died. To make more room for the survivors, we stacked the dead one on top of the other. At sundown, we reached a huge rail intersection. This, I knew, indicated a sizable city nearby. The long cattle train full of Jews—dead and living—pulled onto a siding and stopped.

Soon I heard the SS guards outside. They were complaining bitterly, cursing us, the slaves, for their inconveniences and hardships. The huge steel door of my car was pulled open. A wave of putrid air instantly rushed out. The SS guards fell back from the stench. They returned and tossed several buckets of cold water over the mass of stinking human flesh inside.

I made my way to the open door and sat down, gasping for air. Some German railworkers were standing there, talking to the guards. They wanted to know where the slaves were coming from.

"Where are we?" I suddenly heard myself ask.

To my surprise, while the SS remained silent, one of the workers answered. "You're in Dresden, you parasite! You think you've got it bad? Well, we're suffering, too, and all because of you Jews!"

I looked at them all with disbelief. They were blaming me and the rest of the people in the cattle cars for their defeats on the battlefield. They were blaming me for their casualties and shortages. Me and the other slaves. Almost dead, yet guilty.

Stone-faced, I stared back at them.

The following morning, the doors were sealed again, and the train proceeded on its endless journey to nowhere. No one had escaped. No one jumped. No one even tried. How could we? We were emaciated and demoralized, famished and thirsty. Our uniforms stank. Our arms were tattooed. Our heads had a stripe shaved down the center, the *Lausestrasse,* the lice boulevard. We hardly had the

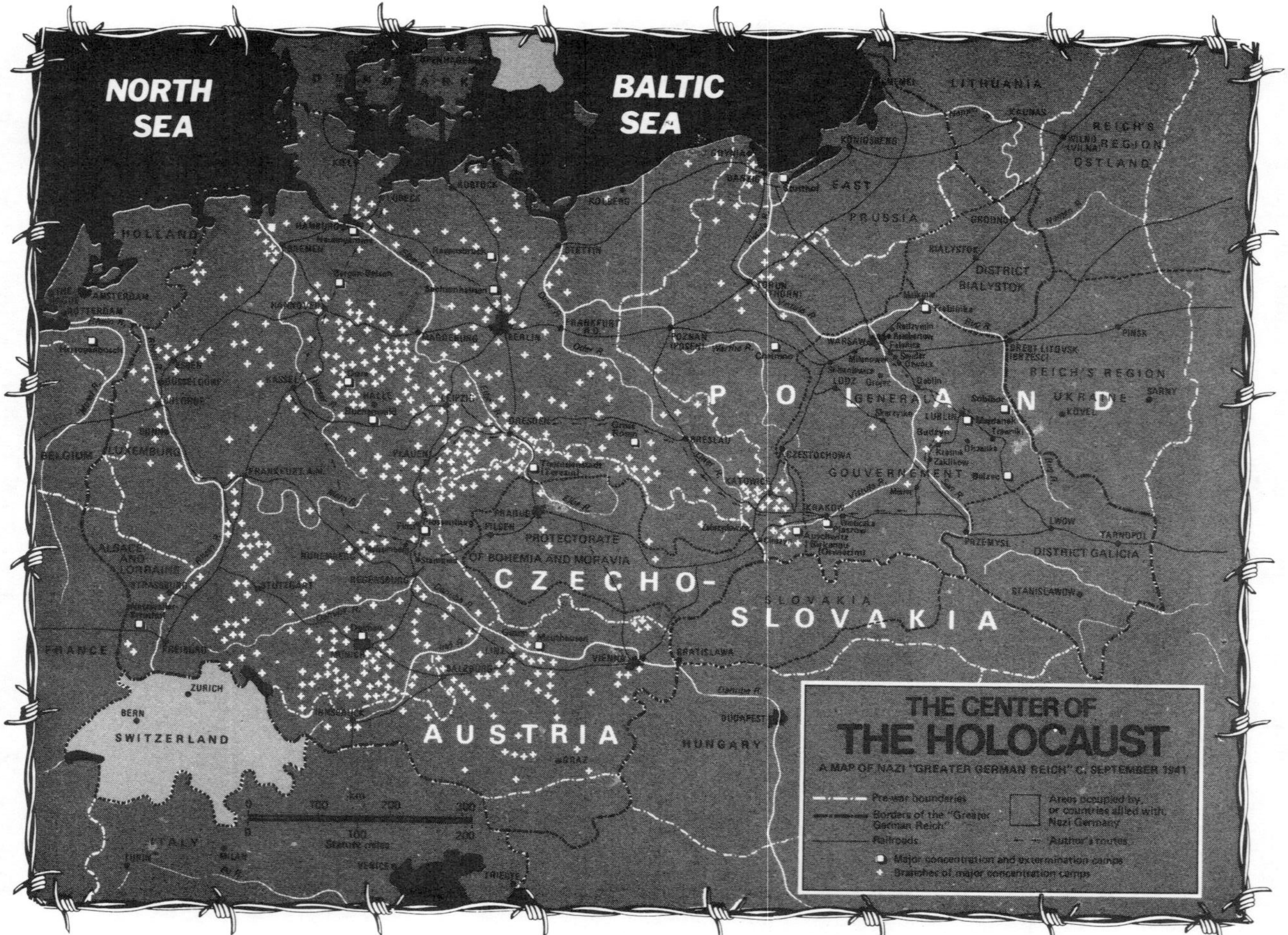
THE CENTER OF
THE HOLOCAUST
A MAP OF NAZI "GREATER GERMAN REICH" C. SEPTEMBER 1941
Pre-war boundaries
Borders of the "Greater German Reich"
Railroads
Areas occupied by, or countries allied with, Nazi Germany
Author's routes
Major concentration and extermination camps
Branches of major concentration camps
NORTH SEA
BALTIC SEA
HOLLAND
BELGIUM
LUXEMBURG
FRANCE
ALSACE AND LORRAINE
SWITZERLAND
ZURICH
BERN
ITALY
AUSTRIA
CZECHO-SLOVAKIA
PROTECTORATE OF BOHEMIA AND MORAVIA
SLOVAKIA
HUNGARY
POLAND
GENERAL GOUVERNEMENT
EAST PRUSSIA
LITHUANIA
REICH'S REGION OSTLAND
REICH'S REGION UKRAINE
DISTRICT BIALYSTOK
DISTRICT GALICIA
BERLIN
VIENNA
BUDAPEST
BRATISLAVA
KRAKOW
CZESTOCHOWA
BRESLAU
DRESDEN
PRAGUE
PILSEN
STETTIN
KOLBERG
HAMBURG
BREMEN
AMSTERDAM
ROTTERDAM
STUTTGART
REGENSBURG
FRANKFURT A.M.
LEIPZIG
HALLE
KASSEL
MAGDEBURG
HANNOVER
KOENIGSBERG
KAUNAS
GRODNO
BIALYSTOK
WARSAW
LODZ
LUBLIN
BREST LITOVSK (BRZESC)
PINSK
SARNY
KOVEL
LWOW
TARNOPOL
PRZEMYSL
STANISLAWOW
GRAZ
TRIESTE
TURIN
MILAN
VENICE
0 100 200 300 km
0 100 200 Statute miles

strength to walk, let alone evade the enemy. Besides, where could we go? We were now in Germany, where every human being was anxious to exterminate us.

As the train rolled on, I noticed through the barbed-wire-covered window that we had started to climb through a mountainous region. We were winding through small forests and passing through dark tunnels. We were moving higher and higher into the mountains.

The next day, the train finally came to a complete halt at a small station. According to the neat black and white sign, we were in the village of Floss. I had never heard of the place and had no idea where it was. No more than half the slaves managed to crawl out of the cars. Those still capable of walking were lined up by fives. Then they marched us for some two hours still farther up the mountain to a place called Flossenburg.

It was a huge and remote concentration camp. As we approached the massive gates, I realized for the first time the immensity of Germany's sophisticated mass murder system. I stared at the enormous sign over the entrance:

"*Jedem Das Seine. Arbeit Macht Frei.* To each what he deserves. Work liberates."

The message was totally ironic. The type of work the Germans were extracting from us was liberating indeed. It liberated us from life.

CHAPTER 35

Flossenburg was indeed a huge camp, accommodating at least 25,000 inmates. It was considered a *Straflager,* or special punishment camp for enemies of the Third Reich. Located on top of a mountain, it overlooked lovely valleys below. The view was breathtaking but of no consequence to us slaves. We had no capacity left to admire nature's beauty.

The slave colony consisted mainly of German political prisoners, criminals, homosexuals, Czechs, Russians, Frenchmen, and Poles—all Christians. My transport brought the first Jews to Flossenburg. Most inmates worked at a nearby underground installation, called 2004, assembling Messerschmitt fighter planes. They worked in two twelve-hour shifts, which were often held up because of delays in counting the slaves at the *Appelplatz.* If one prisoner was missing, 20,000 would be kept waiting hours at a time while he was located. One Jew, it seemed, was more important to the Nazis than a fighter plane. He had to be accounted for, dead or alive.

The remaining inmates, several thousand slaves belonging to the *Straf* detail, were condemned to the daily physical exhaustion of stone cutting at the *Steinbruch* quarry, high in the mountains. It was a dreaded assignment.

A few hundred elite prisoners, mostly German, worked at the camp's service facilities—the kitchen, supply rooms, disinfection chambers—and other less taxing jobs right on the camp premises.

Flossenburg was staffed solely with German SS officers and guards. There were no black-uniformed Ukrainian troops to be seen. The inner administration consisted almost entirely of German kapos. They served as foremen, record keepers, barracks chiefs, and such. They were often as cruel as the SS themselves. In keeping with the German policy of camouflaging the true nature of their camps, an orchestra played Wagner and Beethoven every Sunday afternoon, right in the middle of the *Appelplatz.* The musicians, of course, were inmates.

Flossenburg also boasted its own bordello. To use it, one had to obtain a special permit. But these were distributed only to those who cooperated with the system—namely, the kapos. The privileged few were the only ones who were physically well enough to have sexual desires, anyway. The kapos also enjoyed special canteen privileges that enabled them to buy cigarettes, tobacco, beer, and other small "luxuries."

Despite its classification as a concentration camp and not an extermination facility, Flossenburg still had a gassing barrack and a crematorium. Though small in size in comparison to Auschwitz or Majdanek, they were just as efficient. They operated around the clock and disposed of hundreds of corpses daily.

On our arrival at the camp, we were forced to go through an *Entlausung,* or disinfection. This meant that we had to stand all night long in the nude in cold and wet asphalt chambers, where we were brutalized by the SS and kapos.

In the morning, still in the nude, we were lined up in rows of five for "selection." I knew well what the word meant. The selections in the Warsaw ghetto and in Majdanek were still vivid in my mind.

Hauptsturmführer Gruber, the camp's chief medical officer, now appeared, trailing several SS aides. He had an intelligent bearing, emphasized by gold-rimmed glasses. But there was a hard, cold glint in his eyes. He was to determine who would live and who would die.

In terror, I followed his every move. He was fast, efficient, and businesslike. He passed down the line of prisoners, sizing them up and pointing with his whip. Those he pointed out had a red cross painted on their foreheads. But what did the cross mean? Life or death? I suspected the worst.

As Major Gruber approached, I straightened my nude body, pulled in my stomach, and forced a smile to my lips. The major looked at me sternly. He turned my head to the side to observe my profile. Then he walked on.

"He passed me," I wanted to scream. I wasn't marked.

With the selection over, those smeared with red crosses, almost a third of us, were ordered to don their old clothes. They were marched off to a place called "Pig's Corner." There was no reason to waste new striped uniforms on them. Pig's Corner, a block of four barracks set aside from the rest of the camp, was located just above the crematorium. Those the SS hierarchy thought were unfit to work, or unable to be further exploited, were dumped there. They would be kept for a few days before they went up in smoke at the nearby crematorium.

I was assigned to Block Four, situated high in the mountains. With my remaining strength, I started to climb the crude stone steps to my barrack. My new striped trousers were too big, my jacket too small, and my wooden shoes clumsy and uncomfortable. I could hardly wait to reach my bunk and collapse.

A giant figure loomed before us at the entrance to the block. He was standing there in a neatly pressed prisoner's uniform, holding a whip and wearing a bitingly cruel smile. His head was not shaved like ours. His long hair was swept back smoothly. The green triangle and the number sewn on the left side of his uniform identified him as a criminal inmate. The "D" insignia stood for *Deutscher,* German. All of us came to a dead stop even before he uttered his first word. *"Halt!"*

He shifted the whip to his other hand and surveyed us. "My name is Alois. They call me 'The Bloody.' I'm your new kapo. Before you enter this barrack I want to tell you the rules.

"There will be no shitting or pissing in the bunks. No diarrhea. No stealing. No black marketing. And no disobedience! The first time you break any of these rules—twenty-five lashes. The second time—" He left the punishment unspoken.

One by one, we passed this monstrosity as we entered the barrack. Suddenly I felt his whip. I wanted to scream in pain, but I stifled my cry. I already knew why he was called "The Bloody," and I didn't want to provoke him further. Of all the hellish quarters in Flossenburg, Block Four was the worst. I was angry and bitter that I had to end up there.

At dawn, Alois assigned us to work detachments. He escorted fifty of us down the long row of steps, across the *Appelplatz,* and over to Pig's Corner at the edge of the mountain. I looked down and recoiled in horror. The entire valley was clouded with smoke. But through fleeting breaks in the cloud, I could see piles of naked bodies. They were all lined up for the crematorium, which was burning full blast.

Suddenly I heard a shout. "Pigs! Filthy Jewish scum! Why are you standing there? Bring out the *Musulmänner!*"

It was an SS man ordering us to empty the Pig's Corner barracks of their dying or dead.

"Right here!" He pointed to Block Twenty-three. "Empty this shit house. Criss-cross them in layers of six."

Inside Block Twenty-three, dozens of human cadavers awaited me. Many of the fifty- or sixty-pound bodies were still breathing. Their lips were sealed, but their bulging, begging eyes were pleading with me.

Alois's whip slashed through the air. *"Los! Schnell!* Move them out!"

We began to cart the bodies out. I could feel their bones and joints. Not a spot of fat. Their skins felt like plastic gloves that could easily slip off their skeletons. They were a nameless mass. I hated their bodies. I hated their foaming thin lips. I looked into their eyes and their eyes stared back at me as I carried each one to his final disintegration into ashes. I stared into their eyes fully expecting to see fear but saw only apathy and innocence. They looked at me instead of at the red, violent flames of the fire that devoured them. They were alive, yet they had no fear of the flames. Are apathy and innocence stronger than hate, fear, and anger?

The storm trooper's whip suddenly stung my back and interrupted my thoughts. I staggered and dropped the body I was carrying. I felt the searing pain of the whip and rejoiced in the knowledge that I could still feel pain and fear. I still wanted to survive. More than ever.

That night, I couldn't sleep at all. Those big brown eyes. Those big blue eyes. Those big wide-open green eyes. Millions of eyes stared at me all night long. I hated all those eyes. I hated Pig's Corner. I hated the world. I felt like screaming a loud, powerful scream with my eyes wide open. I was afraid of myself. I feared for my sanity. I couldn't look at those eyes much longer.

I had to find another place to work before all those eyes drove me mad.

Weeks passed, and I continued to cart corpses. I was searching frantically for an alternative. I used every spare moment during meals, on breaks, at work, at the *Appelplatz,* during the Sunday concerts. I spoke to prisoners and kapos alike. I even tried to talk to some SS men, but that was risky.

At last, I became friendly with Karl the Stuttgarter. Karl was a German criminal who worked at the disinfection chambers. He was a rough sort who screamed steadily at the new arrivals. But I noticed he seldom laid a hand on them.

My friendly overtures to him finally paid off. "Get me a transfer to work with you, Karl, and I'll make you rich. I'll load you with gold and silver."

The absurdity of my suggestion, considering my status as a slave, amused Karl. He would laugh and call me a *Scheisskopf,* a shithead. But he was flattered that I was so eager to work with him. And he thought maybe I could help him get his hands on the few valuables some of the prisoners had managed to hide, which would give him more power and prestige. After weeks of wooing, Karl finally succumbed and arranged for my transfer to the *Entlausung* halls, the disinfecting area, as one of his assistants.

Some twenty other inmates, mostly German and Czech Christians, also worked there. I was the only Jew. The work wasn't hard, the food was more plentiful, and I worked indoors. This last advantage was important, because as the months slipped by, I was shielded against the winter frost and snow that arrived early in that mountainous region. And I received extra clothing, including underwear, socks, and even a sweater.

I soon became a part of the elite, an inmate with connections.

As a rule, Jews who arrived at Flossenburg were without any visible belongings. They had long before been stripped by the Nazis of all their earthly possessions. There were some, however, who managed to hide gold coins or other valuables. But getting these valuables through the disinfection process was almost impossible. When prisoners entered the *Entlausung* chambers, they were nude. And when they emerged, the SS searched their bodies before handing them their new prison garments. The valuables found in discarded clothing and on a prisoner's body were collected and registered by a special SS *Schreiber,* or bookkeeper. They were then sent to the Reich's treasury in Berlin.

Because I could speak Yiddish, Karl placed me in charge of receiving the new arrivals before the *Entlausung.* I would try to convince them to turn over their valuables to me before entering the shower halls. In return, I would promise them additional bread or soup for a certain period. Gain some privileges, or lose all you have and risk a beating. I gave the valuables to Karl, and he, in turn, supplied me with all the food I needed to make good on my promises.

To further enhance my security and prestige, Karl arranged to replace my yellow triangle bearing the letter "J," Jew, with a red triangle and the letter "P," Polish Christian. My prison number was P-14461. The insignia were neatly sewn on the left side of my coat and above the knee of my right trouser leg. From then on, I was recognized officially as an Aryan Christian in the eyes of the camp's SS administration.

CHAPTER 36

The bordello at Flossenburg was an exclusive establishment located behind the *Lazarett,* the hospital, somewhat outside the camp premises. To reach it, you had to go through the first layer of fences, past the private vegetable gardens of the SS officers.

The bordello was divided into two sections, one for SS use, the other for the camp's elite inmates, the kapos. Through Karl's contacts, I gained access to the establishment. But I seldom used my permits to satisfy my scanty sexual appetites. The permits were too valuable. Each one was worth ten bread portions or fifteen cigarettes.

My access to the bordello also allowed me to speak to and trade with the girls, who were all inmates selected from special women's camps, such as Ravensbrück and Stutthof. Most of them were beautiful girls in their early twenties, all Christians. The SS code strictly forbade sexual intercourse with Jewesses. So Flossenburg's bordello was staffed solely with Aryan beauties. Their presence was not voluntary. All were compelled to be prostitutes, even though some enjoyed their situation because of the special status it gave them. Extra food and gifts were showered on them by the visiting SS officers and kapos. Since the girls weren't permitted to leave the premises, I often helped them trade their gifts for more needed objects.

Fräulein Wilhelmine, a fat, ugly SS officer, was the madam who ran the house. She was strict, brusque, and contemptuous of the girls and would often confiscate the gifts she found. Therefore I had to trade them away quickly, before Wilhelmine could lay her hands on them.

One of the youngest girls in the bordello was Yvonne, a nineteen-year-old from Nancy, in eastern France. She liked me and told me about herself. When she was seventeen, Yvonne had helped her brother escape from the Gestapo. Eventually they were both seized. Her brother was shot, and she was sent to Ravensbrück. After almost two years in Nazi hands, she had been recently removed from Ravensbrück by Wilhelmine and brought to Flossenburg. Yvonne had had no inkling of her new profession until she was installed in the bordello with ten other girls. But now she accepted it as her means of survival. She was assigned exclusively to SS officers.

Magda was a Polish girl from Warsaw. She, too, had suffered almost two years in the camps. Magda had been caught on the streets of Warsaw and sent for forced labor to Germany. While working as a maid for a local Nazi official, she became friendly with a German soldier who was on leave. Her "employer" discovered her affair and dispatched her to a concentration camp. Her lover, who had violated the Nazi race code by having a personal relationship with an inferior Slav female, was sent to the Russian front.

Like Yvonne, Magda had also been recruited at Ravensbrück. She came from an intellectual family and often lamented her fate on my shoulder. She frequently talked of suicide.

She and I had a special bond; we both came from Warsaw. She understood my serious attitude toward life and was fascinated by my stories of the ghetto uprising. I told her about my family and about my love affair with Halina. She was free of anti-Semitic prejudice and always listened sympathetically and patiently. We found comfort in each other. There were several other girls I often spoke to, but Yvonne and Magda were the ones I got to know best. We trusted and confided in each other.

The girls and I often bribed Wilhelmine. Sometimes she would let me visit the bordello without using the valuable permits.

Malicious and resentful, Wilhelmine envied the friendly and close relationships some of the girls had with the SS officers. One day, she picked a dozen of these girls and escorted them back to Ravensbrück. She was gone for several days, and Yvonne, Magda, and I enjoyed her absence. We knew, however, that she would soon be back with another batch of innocent young flesh to pander to the lusts of the SS beasts and kapos. As expected, Wilhelmine arrived one Sunday morning with a fresh load of terrified girls. They knew nothing of what lay in store for them. They were soon shocked into reality.

"Jacku, where've you been all week?" Magda asked when I showed up one evening, several days later. She led me into her small room, seated me on her bed, and breathlessly began to tell me about one of the new arrivals. "She's from Warsaw. She's blond and beautiful. She's only eighteen. And her name's Halina!"

A shudder went through me. At last I managed a word. "Halina?"

Magda nodded.

"Where is she?" I jumped up and headed for the door.

Magda pulled me back. "No, stay here. Don't go. There's someone with her now." Her voice turned bitter. "Wilhelmine assigned her to feed the SS. In fact, she's with *Obersturmführer* Krauze. He likes her. This is his second visit in three days."

I could barely breathe. Or speak.

Magda seemed to read my thoughts. She gripped my arms. "She can't be your Halina, Jacku. It's impossible."

"I . . . I . . . I can't . . ."

"For Christ's sake! Your Halina's Jewish. This one's not. She couldn't be. They wouldn't have brought her here. Besides, she doesn't look Jewish. I'm sure she's Catholic."

"But Magda, Halina's been passing all along. She could act as Catholic as you."

"Holy Father! Then it might be her. When I told her about you, she suddenly got jittery." Magda crossed herself and sat down. "Wait here, Jacku. She'll be coming to my room in a little while."

I sat beside her, frightened and silent. My mind was in a turmoil. What if it was Halina? How would I behave? "I'll go crazy if it's her," I whispered. "I'll go absolutely crazy."

Magda tried to comfort me. "It'll be all right, it'll be all right. You'll see. I'll pray for you both. But in the meantime, we have another problem. That's why I wanted to see you. She's sick. She needs medicine. Her stomach's bad. She cries all night long."

"What's wrong?" I asked.

"Bleeding ulcers. But we're afraid to tell Wilhelmine. She'd send her to the hospital."

"No, that's too risky," I said. "They make selections there. They'd just send her to the gas chambers. Don't ever let her go to the *Lazarett.*"

Suddenly the door opened.

Magda and I stopped talking.

I looked up and held my breath. A beautiful blond girl was framed in the doorway. She was standing on the threshold, looking inside. She started to enter the room, then stopped abruptly. She was tall and slim. Her face was pale, with prominent cheekbones. Her hair was cut short. Her eyes were blue and sad.

I rose from the bed and moved closer. I couldn't believe my eyes. The girl was Halina. My Halina. My darling, darling Halina. We both stood rooted. Immobilized. Unable to speak. My eyes clouded with tears. They began to flow uncontrollably, as if a spigot had suddenly been turned on.

Halina, too, began to cry. Through the mist in my eyes, I could see the tears flowing down her cheeks.

An instant later, we closed the distance between us. We wound our arms about each other. I pressed her to me. She held me tightly. Her arms groped around my back. She was trying to find the exact way to hold me. To make me a part of her. I buried my head on her shoulder. In her hair. She was sobbing. We stood like that for some time.

At last I caught my breath. I moved my hands to her beautiful face, cradling it in my palms.

"Halina . . . Halina."

"Jacku . . ."

Magda rose from the bed and tiptoed from the room. She was weeping softly as she closed the door behind her.

"Halina. Thank God you're alive!" I said.

"*Kochanie.* Yes, I'm alive. But I want to die. What have they done to me? How can I live like this? Tell me how!"

"Please, please, Halina. Don't talk now. Don't say another word. You're alive. That's all that matters. I love you."

"But I can't go on like this. Even to survive. I won't make it. I know I won't."

Suddenly the door swung open with a bang. There stood Wilhelmine. "I knew you were hiding someplace, *du Drecksack,* you bag of garbage," she shouted at me. "You're becoming a regular pest!" She grabbed me and shoved me toward the door. "Get out, and don't show up for the next three days!"

For a moment, I gazed beyond Wilhelmine's fat, ugly face and saw my precious Halina, who looked so frail standing next to the beast beside her. So lost. So frightened. So very beautiful.

I felt as though my heart was slowly being squeezed in a vise.

"Raus! Los!"

I turned and disappeared down the hall.

CHAPTER 37

"What's wrong?" Karl the Stuttgarter asked the following day. I hadn't slept all night, and now I was walking around in a daze.

"Nothing," I lied. "I need sleep. I need a *Schnaps.*"

"If you ask me, what you need is some ass! That's what's wrong with you."

I refused to reveal what was bothering me. Instead, I disappeared into one of the storage rooms, where I'd hidden a bottle of homemade vodka. I finished off the bottle, then fell into a drunken stupor. When I awoke hours later, my head was splitting, and I felt like vomiting. I had slept almost the entire day.

In complete misery, I walked across the disinfecting halls.

"Hey, *du lieber,* buddy," Karl kidded me. "Stop acting like a prima donna. Everybody's talking about you." He grabbed my shirt and shook me up a bit. "I don't care what's on your mind. But you'd better pull yourself together before the *Oberscharführer* gets wind of it. He doesn't give a shit about your problems. And don't get me into any trouble."

"Karl, I have a big problem," I finally admitted. "Meet me in Block Number Two after the count tonight. I gotta talk to you."

Karl hesitated. He wanted to go to the bordello, but something about my behavior made him change his mind. Later that evening, I explained my predicament to Karl. I was afraid of what his reaction might be, but I needed his help. Karl listened to me for a while, then started with his usual underworld curses.

"Du Speckjäger, du mistiger! Your girl friend's right here under your nose. You can see her and fuck her. And you're complaining!" He laughed. "If she's really so beautiful, give me her name, and I'll fuck her, too."

He dismissed the entire matter, slapped me on the back, and walked away. I felt angrier and more confused than ever.

To my surprise, a few minutes later he returned.

"I know, you devil, you're in love," Karl said. "And that's a headache. I was in love once, and it almost ruined me. In fact, that's why I'm here in this camp—because of that bitch." He leaned forward sympathetically and promised to help, if it was possible.

The next day, I got some medication for Halina's ulcers. The kapo at the *Lazarett* gave me several jars of a milky fluid in exchange for an extra pass to the bordello. Then, on the camp's secret black market, I bought some silk stockings to soften the bitchy Wilhelmine. I needed her cooperation now more than ever. She had to let me spend time with Halina. Yet she couldn't know of our relationship.

The next evening, loaded with a salami and three pairs of silk stockings, I headed for the bordello. I walked straight through the SS entrance, the forbidden one, and right into Wilhelmine's office. I dumped my black market gifts on her desk. Pleasantly surprised, Wilhelmine cracked a slight smile and softly ordered me out. *"Mach dass du raus kommst.* Get over to the other side. That's where you belong."

The other side. Exactly what I wanted to hear. Within minutes, I was back in Halina's arms. Magda locked the door and kept watch outside.

For so many months, survival had taken all my strength. I hadn't even thought about making love. But now I was in Halina's arms, after dreaming of her for so long. It wasn't sex. It was an urgent, almost suicidal yearning to consume each other. To unite and disappear into another world. We hardly talked. We just made love and cried and stared into each other's eyes.

Magda knocked on the door. I knew my time was up. We dressed quickly. I promised to return soon, with new plans. Halina kissed me a final time as I urged her to be brave, to hold on, no matter what.

"Jacku, you know what your mother told me when we parted in

Majdanek? She said to me, 'Halina, Jacek will survive. So take care of yourself if you don't want him to have another woman.' So you see, I've got no choice. I have to survive."

I kissed her, gave her the medicine, and ran.

I had to find a way to send Halina back to Ravensbrück. In Flossenburg, she would waste away. Her distress would aggravate her ulcers. And her ulcers would kill her. Not even the medicine would help. Halina would never be able to keep serving the SS with her body. The fact that I was nearby only made it worse.

Besides, I'd worry myself sick as well.

Again, I asked Karl for help. He shook his head in disbelief. *"Du lieber, du hast richtige jüdische Chutzpe!* You've got balls even to ask!" He looked at me curiously. "Well, I'll have to discuss it with the *Oberscharführer.* I'll tell him she's your sister. Let's see what he says."

I couldn't sleep, and I hardly ate. I was waiting for Karl's answer. Mechanically, I went through the usual daily routines.

Every morning we assembled in the *Appelplatz.* It began with the voice of the chief *Lager* kapo screaming and whistling for all to assemble. Within minutes, more than 20,000 slaves were lined up in rows of fives and groups of hundreds. Even the dead corpses of those who died during the night were carried down to be counted. The SS guards sealed off the square. Latecomers were punished or simply shot. Soon the camp commandant arrived and received the report from the senior counting officer. So many ready for work. So many sick. So many dead. So many in Pig's Corner due to be liquidated. SS Colonel Stawitzky always made a speech in reply.

"We, the SS," he thundered, "demand cleanliness, and you pigs resist the showers and disinfection *Kammer.* We, the SS, observe comrade loyalty, and you steal from one another. We, the SS, appreciate culture and the arts. You pigs hide in the barracks or are busy stealing potato skins, instead of listening to the Sunday symphonic concerts!"

I was in a rage. It took every ounce of my strength to stop myself from screaming out: "You beast, how dare you preach ethics and morality! What have you done to Halina? What have you done to us? Which one of us is the pig?"

Several days had passed before Karl approached me again. He cursed in a jovial manner and slapped me on the back. *"Heute Abend* in Block Twenty-three. That's where Hans is, *das Arschloch,* that asshole. We'll meet there tonight, *verstanden?*"

I saluted with a smile. *"Jawohl!"* I sensed something special.

That evening, Karl talked and drank for hours. He poured himself cup after cup of homemade vodka *"Bimber."* He talked of everything under the sun and finally pulled me aside into the small room that belonged to the block kapo, Hans.

"It's all set, *du mistiger.* The *Ober* will arrange things with Wilhelmine. He thinks you can afford ten gold coins."

"But, Karl, that's a—"

"Yes, that is a fortune. But that's the price. Don't look at me. I just do it as a favor. Don't be so *schlau,* stingy, *du Rebecca,* Jewish shrewdie." He seemed annoyed.

The price was high, but at last I had some sort of definite arrangement, something I could start to work on. I poured more *Schnaps,* and toasted "Karl, the humanitarian." He liked that, so we continued drinking until curfew.

I slept well that night. Even though I didn't have the ten piggys, I had a deal. I would search and borrow. I knew that my black market credit was good and that my friends would help.

On Sunday morning, I raced to the bordello. It was an unusual time to visit there, but I needed to talk. Besides, Wilhelmine was generally more lenient on Sundays. I had seen Halina several times already, but now I had a plan. Fate would handle the rest.

I found Halina and Magda still on their bunks. Magda wanted to leave us alone, but I stopped her. "Lock the door and stay put. I want to talk to you both. Right now."

Halina had weakened and lost weight. It frightened me. "I've got a plan to get you out of here. My contacts are working on it. Wilhelmine'll be sending you back to Ravensbrück as unfit for the job. You'll return as a *Häftling,* an inmate." I turned to Magda. "Would you like to go, too?"

"Oh, yes, Jacku. Yes. If you can do it, yes! We'll stay together, Halina and I. And I'll help her. I'll look after her."

"They must send back at least four or five girls at a time," I continued. "You can be part of the group."

Magda was delirious with joy, but Halina suddenly took my hand and looked into my eyes.

"Jacku, *kochanie,* darling, I didn't come from Ravensbrück. I wasn't an inmate there."

"What do you mean? You came with the last transport. Wilhelmine brought you all from Ravensbrück. Didn't she?"

"Kochanie, it's such a long story. Try to understand."

Fear clouded her eyes when she saw how upset I was.

"You see, I was only in quarantine in Ravensbrück. I didn't have a number. I didn't work there. I just happened to be there when Wilhelmine arrived. Had I known she'd bring me here, I would have killed myself. He told me to trust him, to believe in him. He said he'd arrange everything. He sounded so sincere. A real gentleman bastard!"

"Halina, please, slow down!" I said. "I don't know what you're saying. Who are you talking about?"

"It's such a long story, Jacku. So many things happened. How can I make you understand?"

"Please try, Halina. I'm listening. I want to know everything that happened to you; I have to know, so I can help get you out of here. Okay? But go slowly, and don't get yourself too excited."

"Oh, Jacku, all this time you were the only one that kept me going, I kept seeing your face in front of me, saying what you said a hundred times: 'Survive, Halina. Survive. We'll meet in Milanowek.' That's what kept me going, week after week." She kissed me lightly on the forehead.

"You remember when we parted at Majdanek's reception center? I never forgot that moment. I never forgot you, *kochanie.* I dreamed day and night of seeing you and touching you once again." She put her arms around me. Magda sobbed softly.

"We were pushed into a crowd of women," Halina continued. "I looked for Mama and Mala, but the crowd was huge—hundreds, maybe thousands. I couldn't find them anywhere. Then came the disinfection. That little monster, Srulek, promised no gas in the showers. But some of the other girls from Warsaw and I urged everyone not to go. All of a sudden, machine-gun bullets were flying all around us. People fell dead right next to me. It was awful.

"So we had no choice. Either we went to the showers or we got shot. Slowly, slowly, we started to walk up the steps.

"God, I remember how I just closed my eyes and saw your face before me, saying, 'Survive, Halina. Survive. We'll meet in Milanowek.' And there I was, in front of those showers, a minute away from my death." Her eyes widened. "But a miracle happened to us! We heard a rumbling in the pipes, and then the faucets blazed powerful sprays of cold water. No gas! No gas! We screamed and embraced each other. Complete strangers. We danced with each other in the nude. Those Dutch girls from Holland. I couldn't understand a word they were saying, but we laughed and cried and danced like little children playing in the water.

"They took away all my civilian clothing and my beautiful leather boots, the ones you got me, remember? And some mean SS woman handed out these ugly striped uniforms. I cried and carried on so. It's a good thing there was no mirror around. But what happened next was even worse. They shaved my head! Cut my hair off completely like a soldier! It's still so short, I hate it.

"They marched us in fives until we reached Majdanek. It took hours. They put the women to work in a special field. The work was hard, but nothing out of the ordinary. Just cleaning, gardening, digging ditches, but everything with our bare hands. And the food was very bad and very scarce. The SS women were spiteful and sadistic. They beat and molested us constantly. Days and weeks passed, so slowly. My only support came from my thoughts of you. I used to close my eyes and lie on my filthy bunk bed and just dream of seeing you again some day."

Halina paused for a moment as Magda handed her a handkerchief and some cold *Ersatz* coffee. We both encouraged her to continue.

"One morning, some SS officers and SS women appeared at the *Appelplatz* for a selection. You never knew what was going to happen, who would be chosen and for what. A better place or the gas chamber? This time I didn't even try to guess. A tall blond SS man stretched his hand out and sort of brushed me with his whip. He winked, 'Get out, *raus!*' I stepped out and stayed there for maybe an hour, together with a group of other women, until we numbered about two or three hundred. Then they marched us all the way back to the reception center, to the place where we parted, Jacku. I was so scared, I thought they were taking us back to be gassed. But when they gave each of us a bread ration with jam, we were all completely confused. So we just walked and held hands and prayed.

"I thought of escaping. The road was empty and foggy, with forest on both sides. I thought maybe I could make a run for it and disappear. But those ugly guard dogs really scared me. And anyway, I was in a striped uniform with a shaved head, so where could I run? When we reached the reception center, they loaded us into waiting cattle cars, the same kind that took us from Warsaw to Majdanek. You remember the jumping, Jacku? We still had so much guts and energy then. And there I sat with all those other women. We were like a flock of passive, resigned sheep."

We were all quiet for a moment. Then Halina quickly resumed.

"The next morning, we reached the *Arbeitslager,* Skarzysko. It was a labor camp, a munitions works. We had to fill canisters with chemicals and gunpowder. That's where I got sick, breathing in those poisons all day long. And that's where I met him, the bastard!"

"Who, Halina?"

"Krupp. Alfred Krupp. The baron. He came to inspect the plant."

"Krupp, that beast? I don't believe it!"

"Yes, Jacku. Krupp himself. He came with a lot of SS officers and engineers. Everyone was so excited. The day before, they made us scrub the place until it sparkled. They even gave us soap to shower with. Anyhow, when Krupp passed by my position, he suddenly stopped and looked at me. And for some reason, I smiled. I really don't know why. 'Are you Jewish?' he asked. 'No!' I shouted. 'No, I'm not Jewish. I'm here by mistake!'

"To this minute, I don't know what made me say that. It just came out of my mouth. And it sounded so stupid, because all the girls there were Jewish.

"Krupp just kept looking at me. Then he asked me who I was and where I came from. 'Halina Litewska,' I said. 'I'm Catholic—from Warsaw.' One of his aides wrote it down in a notebook. Krupp smiled and continued his inspection. I thought they'd shoot me for lying.

"But instead, that same afternoon they summoned me to the camp's administration office and gave me civilian clothes. Everyone was stunned. Nobody knew whether to envy me or pray for me. I didn't know, either. I sat in the back of a military vehicle, watched by two gendarmes, the ones with the helmets. We drove to Katowice that same evening."

Halina went on, "They brought me to a really luxurious hotel with a huge lobby. Like the city, it was full of soldiers, gendarmes, and SS officers. They took me to a big room on the third floor and turned me over to a neatly dressed woman, a secretary type, Fräulein Margo.

I was scared to death. I was expecting an interrogation, some kind of torture. I thought I was in Gestapo headquarters. But then she led me into a small bedroom with a bath. She told me to undress and bathe to my heart's delight. At that moment, I didn't care what came next. I stayed in that tub for what seemed like hours. It was two years since I'd had a real bath. I'd forgotten how good they felt.

"Well, anyway, I went to sleep on a soft couch wrapped up in a beautiful silk robe. Everything was so mysterious and magical—from rags to riches. I couldn't believe it. I slept for hours. Fräulein Margo finally woke me. She gave me a skirt and a blouse and a pair of shoes. Can you imagine, high-heeled shoes! I didn't know how to walk in them anymore. I kept falling. I had to practice how to walk! Suddenly I became suspicious. Why was she dressing me up so late in the evening?

" 'It's not so late,' Margo told me. 'It's only ten P.M., and the baron likes to dine late.'

"I thought I'd die. Krupp had not only arranged to bring me there, he was going to dine with me in person. But what would happen afterward? He thought I wasn't Jewish. I was really confused. I didn't know what to do.

"What if he made love to me and then shot me like a dog, just like the SS gangsters did in the ghetto? I started thinking about running away. I was in civilian clothing, and my hair had grown back a little. I looked pretty good.

"Fräulein Margo sensed my fear. 'Halina, be a good girl,' she said. 'Behave and cooperate. The baron's a very nice man. But don't forget, this is Gestapo headquarters.'

"Krupp finally came. He was polite and elegant, and the food was fantastic. The only thing was, I couldn't eat. I'd been eating shit for so long, my stomach couldn't take it. I nibbled and drank a little wine, but it was still too much, and my ulcers started acting up. I remember asking him what would happen to me, where I would go from there. He didn't answer me. He just said, 'Trust in me. I will arrange for you. All will be well.' He said that over and over.

"When I woke up the next morning, Krupp was gone. Fräulein Margo was gone. And my room was locked. The street below was full of army trucks and soldiers. Soon the SS kicked open the door and took me into the basement with some other girls. They were evacuating the hotel, loading files and cabinets into trucks.

"They were in such a hurry, I was scared to death. But then one of the girls said, 'The Russians are coming. You can hear the guns. We'll soon be free!'

"I couldn't believe it. Germans on the run? Were the Russians so close?

"Then some drunken woman yelled out, 'Hey, *kurwy*, you whores!' She was pointing at me. 'Yes, you. All of you! What's the difference—Germans, Russians? We'll fuck 'em all. All of 'em!'

" 'Don't be so sure, you bitch!' one of the girls shouted back. 'The Russians'll cut your guts out when they find out about your collaboration with the Krauts!'

"I was dazed. I had no idea what was going on.

"An SS man appeared and took us all to the railroad station. He put us on a train with two gendarmes, and in the morning, we were at Ravensbrück. They put us in quarantine there, and before long, Fräulein Wilhelmine arrived. She looked me up and down and said, 'We need a blond one. You'll do.' I had no idea what she meant."

Halina started to cough, then paused to sip the cold coffee. For a moment, she just looked at Magda and me.

"Neither did any of the other girls. We had no idea where we were going or why. But it didn't stay a secret for long. When we got here and the fat one gave a long speech of do's and don't's, we figured it out pretty fast. Some cried, some fainted, and others . . ."

Magda stopped her. "Yes, dear, we know what it meant and what happened. Rest a little now. You're too excited."

Halina rested her head on the pillow and relaxed. I sat near her, caressing her gently.

"I don't think there will be any problem, Halina. You're going back to Ravensbrück, and Magda, so are you."

Magda clutched my hand. "But when, Jacku? When do we go? I want to get out of here so badly. Can we go today, tomorrow? Oh, Halina, can you believe it?"

Halina nodded her agreement. "Yes, yes. Out of here. I won't last long here."

She closed her eyes with weariness. The long story she had just told us had sapped her strength.

I kissed her tenderly, and she opened her eyes again. She took my face in her hands. "I love you, Jacku. I love you more than ever." Then she fell asleep.

By Monday evening, I had the ten piggys. I had begged, borrowed, and traded all day Sunday to accumulate the gold coins. And now I had them.

"Mein lieber, du Speckjäger!" Karl exclaimed when he saw the money. "I knew you'd get it, *du Kapitalist.* Now you need an armored car to transport it."

The arrangements from that moment on went like clockwork. The *Oberscharführer* got his gold. He paid off Wilhelmine. And she set up the transfer. By the end of the week, Halina, Magda, and three other girls were ready to leave for Ravensbrück. Wilhelmine never suspected my involvement.

I spent my last hour with Halina in privacy; Magda kept watch outside their room. We made passionate love. We clung to each other as if there would be no tomorrow. We swore to fight for our lives, to survive, and to meet in Milanowek. I ran out of the room. I didn't want to exhaust her anymore. And I didn't want to say goodbye.

CHAPTER 38

Early one morning in the spring of 1945, I was about to get off my bunk for the usual 6 A.M. roll call, when suddenly I felt my blanket being pulled away.

"They're gone! They're gone!" my friend Sasha was screaming. "None of them are here anymore!"

All at once, everyone in the barracks was buzzing with excitement. I sat up and hollered. "What in hell are you talking about, Sasha? Have you gone berserk?"

I quickly put on my pants and wooden shoes and ran out to the *Appelplatz*. Sasha was right. The guards, the SS storm troopers, the new Luftwaffe guards; they were all gone! The sight of the empty guard tower was incredible. Not a soul. No machine guns. No lights. Just a barren structure.

Thousands of inmates began wandering around in wild excitement. It had all happened so suddenly, so strangely. Not a hint of anything the night before. Everything had been perfectly routine. And now, overnight, all the Germans had abandoned the camp. Unbelievable! I couldn't imagine that the Nazis had deserted us, left us free, just like that. All thirty thousand of us. It was too miraculous. Something was wrong. There had to be some catch. There had to be.

None of us could accept what we saw. Hundreds of prisoners were standing near the triple-wire fences. They were testing for electric current. Nothing. No juice. The wires were dead. We could have walked right out the gates or crawled through the fences. But no one did. No one dared. We suddenly felt united. Yesterday's enemies, the kapos, suddenly became our friends, seemed to care for us, for our safety.

The *Lagerältester,* the chief kapo, now climbed onto a table in the *Appelplatz.* "No one will leave the camp or break through the fences!" he shouted. "Believe me, I tell you this is a trap! The SS are hiding out there in the woods with machine guns. They're waiting to destroy us. They're looking for an excuse to kill us all. But we won't give them one. All of us will stay right here. Let's call their bluff. Let's wait for the Allies. Right here!"

It made sense. The Germans had tricked us so often. Why not now, as well? We all listened and obeyed.

It was my sixth spring as a slave. I was afraid to hope that this would be the last, that I would soon be free. Each succeeding spring had only gotten progressively worse. Why should this one be different?

For three days, we remained in the camp. We sunbathed on the *Appelplatz.* We ate whatever food we found. We waited tensely and listened to the constant speeches by the kapos and block leaders.

Then, almost at midnight on the third day of their disappearance, the Germans reappeared. In trucks, in jeeps, and on foot. They were angry and violent. They returned to the towers with their machine guns and searchlights. The high-voltage electricity was turned on again. And curfew was strictly enforced. Even the elite kapos were no longer favored. The Germans locked them up with the rest of us. And the barracks filled with sorrow and dejection. I turned to Sasha. "We gave them no excuse. So now they've returned to finish us off without one."

At about 8 A.M. the next morning, much later than normal, all the inmates were rushed out to the *Appelplatz.* But there was no counting. Squads of SS, with German shepherd dogs and machine guns, were roaming the camp. They were searching all the barracks and executing on the spot any Jew they found in hiding.

"Juden, raus! Alle Juden, sofort raus! All Jews out! Immediately! Out to the square!"

The Jewish prisoners became panicky. It was obvious they were being separated from the Gentile prisoners for special treatment. And that could only mean torture or death. Slowly, hundreds began to assemble in the middle of the square. They couldn't hide. All of them were wearing the yellow triangles and the letter "J" on their uniforms. To further intimidate them, the SS picked some Jews at random, those who were hesitating, and machine-gunned them in cold blood. Soon more than 3,000 terrified Jews were standing in the *Appelplatz.*

I was "safe." My insignia was clearly marked "P," in a red triangle. Still, I had the chills. Out there were so many Jews I knew. My friend Sasha, who was also passing as a Christian, was standing beside me. We were both pretending not to be concerned about the slaughter. But there were enough anti-Semitic bastards around us who, if they knew, would be only too happy to point us out and scream, *"Jude! Jude!"* That, perhaps, would satisfy the SS, and then they themselves would be safe.

But nobody pointed at us, even though some Gentile prisoners suspected me of being Jewish. Karl the Stuttgarter, who knew and was standing there among the kapos, just winked at me. *"Rebecca,"* his eyes said, "stay put. Don't move an inch."

Soon all the Gentiles were dismissed. And the Jews were marched out of the camp. The *Appelplatz* was empty, except for two or three dozen Jewish corpses. These were dumped on a cart and wheeled to the crematorium, which had again begun to function. Flossenburg was back to normal.

CHAPTER 39

As soon as the condemned Jews had passed through the gates, the remainder of us began to worry about what would happen next. There was no work. The Messerschmitt plant had been abandoned and blown up. The girls at the bordello had disappeared. Hunger became extreme. We, the slaves, subsisted on only a watery soup and some grain. Even the "elite" began to run out of food.

Then, suddenly, after about a week, instructions came from the beleaguered SS chiefs in Berlin. Flossenburg's remaining inmates were to be marched some 250 kilometers south to Dachau, deep in the Bavarian hinterland, a new enclave.

Pandemonium broke loose as the hungry masses heard of evacuation. They did not want to follow the path of the Jews. Suddenly, in midmorning, hundreds of desperate inmates began an assault on the kitchen and its storage rooms. They blasted open all the doors, barrels, chests, and sacks, grabbing with both hands all they could manage. They stuffed their mouths, their pockets, and their shirts with potatoes, carrots, grain, and bread.

The entire episode lasted only minutes. The SS with their dogs rolled in on half-tracks, machine-gunning right and left. The dogs went wild.

The desperados did not care. They did not give up. Despite the hail of bullets and rivers of blood around them, they continued scrounging blindly, frantically, for food. When it was over, several hundred dead and wounded lay unattended. Several hours later, all the remaining prisoners were ordered to the *Appelplatz*.

I was in a huge column of some 5,000 *Häftlinge*, the previously privileged prisoners. A few of the other hidden Jews—Sasha; and Romek and Leon, the musicians—were nearby. We were all marched to the gate in rows of five. Several SS guards with sacks of grain were stationed there on either side. They were passing out one handful to each inmate. This was to be the total provision for the march to Dachau. This was to sustain us while covering sixty to seventy kilometers a day—or night, since after that day, we were to march only at night.

Our pace was steady and uninterrupted—at least twelve hours of marching with no rest, additional food, or water. That torture soon began taking its toll. Prisoners by the hundreds began to slow down. Those unable to continue marching were shot by the SS, who were riding behind the column on motorcycles with machine guns mounted on sidecars.

I heard the gunfire clearly. It now became an almost continuous chain of staccato bursts. Anyone who fell, or attempted to sit down or rest, faced the same fate. Guards marching on both sides were constantly shooting. Pulling Sasha along with me, I pushed myself up ahead, as far from the executions as possible.

After the first night, we were herded together high on a hill, while the SS surrounded us from below. They were still concerned that no one escape. No one did. Everyone was too exhausted to move. A few were crawling around, looking for a cigarette butt or tobacco. They were offering their last remnants of grain for one puff. For three consecutive nights, our long column was driven through the dark side roads of Bavaria. Not a soul was to be seen. Even the villages we passed seemed deserted.

After the second night of marching, I developed blisters on my feet. I removed my heavy wooden shoes and carried them on my back. Then I threw them away altogether. I also discarded my ragged blanket. On the third night, I disposed of my jacket and sweater, as well. I was walking in my bare feet, with a torn shirt and wet pants. I was even ready to shed them, too.

My sense of reality was fading. I was beginning to see rings around the moon and the stars. I was using all my will power not to faint. The last few weeks of skimpy food rations had radically reduced my weight. My body was no more than a bundle of bones held together by a sack of skin.

Suddenly I felt a chill run through me as a vision of Pig's Corner flashed through my mind. No! I hadn't reached that stage yet. I wasn't a *Musulman* yet, a skeleton with a huge shaved head and big bulging eyes. A *Musulman* is apathetic and pain-free. His brain can no longer communicate with his body. It can no longer accept messages of fear or passion. His mind can only contemplate his own end. No! This is not me. Not yet. I can still feel pain and anger. I can still yearn for revenge. I can still survive.

Yes! I still wanted to survive. I felt this had to be my last great effort. That it would somehow be rewarded. I didn't know how. I couldn't predict anything. I just wanted to be the last Jew on earth. I wanted to march down on my final journey to the great exhibition hall of the World's Museum. Humanity would marvel at me, the survivor, who had managed the impossible. They would marvel at me, the last living specimen of 5,000 years of Jewish civilization. The Allies would bathe in the glory of their victory. The Third Reich would wallow in its ruins. But I, the survivor, would be condemned forever, neither able to rejoice nor to forget.

Machine-gun fire roused me from my reverie. The SS were shooting again. The column had to keep marching. I could see the SS in action. They were right behind me on their motorcycles. I urged myself onward. But the column continued to shrink. No longer caring, many inmates just sat down or tried to run. None made it. The SS gunned them down.

Karl the Stuttgarter, my ally for so long, tried to flee into the woods. But the SS shot him in front of me.

"This march will finish us all before we get to Dachau," I whispered to Sasha. "Only the SS will make it on their motorcycles. We'll go straight to heaven via a shortcut."

On the morning of the fourth day, April 23, Henry, the violinist, passed me, then slowed down again. He reached into his pockets and took out some leftover grain, a small knife, and a few other mementos. He handed them to his fellow musicians—Shlamek, Itzek, Yosek, and Heniek—and to me.

"Here, take this," he said. "Don't forget me if you make it. I can't go on. Let them finish me. How much can a human take?"

He started to slump to the side, but we all grabbed him and shouted, "Walk! Walk! Walk! You can't do this. We won't let you!"

We struggled with him, urging him to keep fighting. Finally, he was persuaded and continued to walk on his own. I returned his knife. "That's yours. Show it to me after it's all over."

The column was stopped for a rest on a small hill. The clear sky gave way to dark clouds; soon a heavy rain started to fall. But it didn't seem to bother the weary marchers. Exhausted, they fell to the ground and slept.

I climbed to the top of the hill to get as far away as possible from the trigger-happy guards below. On the way, I fell into a ditch of stagnant water. I crawled out, picked some grass and leaves for a pillow—enough to keep my head out of the mud—and fell asleep. I awoke to the sound of gunfire.

"*Du Sau!* You pig! Get back up there!" An SS man was kicking me. In my sleep, I had rolled all the way down the hill.

I got to my feet and started back up the hill. I could not see anything but steam. It was rising in thick clouds from the ground and the soaked inmates, who were lying there asleep. The rain poured down on us, but no one cared. Hundreds of inmates had rolled down the hill in their sleep. They felt nothing. Most of them lay wounded or dead, face down, shot in their sleep. They never knew what hit them. I managed to climb back up the hill, but I didn't fall asleep any more that morning.

At midday, the rain stopped, and the SS started to collect their gear and scream orders. "*Alles runter! Weiter marschieren!* Everyone march!" They fired their guns in the air to hurry us along.

The rain, which had trickled down my throat, had satisfied my thirst, but my hunger was indescribable. I had twisted my ankle as I rolled down the hill, so now I was walking with a limp. Soaked and barefoot, I was wearing only a pair of striped pants and the torn remnants of my shirt.

But I was still alive. Still alive, at two minutes to twelve. Still alive after six long years of horror and struggle. Would I make it? Would I ever know freedom again? I looked up at the sky as the sun's rays pushed past the clouds. I thanked nature for the sunshine. It warmed and soothed me, a mass of bone and will power.

We entered the town of Stamsried. Civilians and German soldiers were milling about the main square. The SS steered us away from the center of town, away from the civilians. But the civilians saw us, anyway. It made no difference. No one offered us food or hope in any form, even though we shouted and begged, "Bread! Water! Please!"

The SS squeezed us onto a side road. They shot anyone who moved too slowly. The sun was shining full force. The death march had cut the column to less than half its original length.

I dragged my body along. My strength was almost gone. Only my mind was urging me on. Only my will to survive. To see Halina. To watch the Third Reich collapse. My most cherished desires. Only they moved me forward. I lost sight of Sasha and the others. I didn't know whether they had fallen behind me, or I behind them.

Suddenly I heard a loud rumbling sound behind me. I watched in astonishment as the SS troops began to run for the woods. They were in absolute panic. They were riding their motorcycles across the open fields. They were abandoning guns and equipment.

Now a huge green monster of a tank came rumbling toward me. I jumped off the road into a ditch.

The tank passed me. Then another. And another. I could see stars painted on their sides. Soldiers in the turrets were firing their guns at the fleeing SS. Other soldiers were tossing packages on the road.

Frightened and bewildered, I just looked at the packages. Maybe they were bombs of some sort. Maybe they would explode. Then I heard someone shout. "Russians! *Zdrastvuytie tovarishche!*" That would account for the stars.

More tanks rumbled by. More packages rained down on us. I picked one up. I held it gingerly, turning it carefully in my hands. Then I read the lettering on the side: "U.S. Army—Ration C."

"America! American tanks!" I shouted at the top of my lungs.

The jubilant cry went up on all sides. "America! America! America!"

I opened my package and gulped its contents.

The tanks thundered by in an endless stream. I counted fifty, a hundred, even more. They passed for hours. Then artillery trucks appeared. Some of the trucks stopped, and the soldiers urged us in sign language to move back behind the lines. Other soldiers jumped from the trucks and ran into the woods after the SS men.

The rations had satisfied my hunger for the moment, so I started to walk in the direction the soldiers had indicated. Then it hit me: I was free! Liberated!

I suddenly became alarmed. Was it true? Was it real? Or was I dreaming? I didn't want to risk losing my precious freedom again. I wouldn't look for food and clothing now. I would walk and walk until I was sure I was safe.

The road was filled with an endless stream of American troops. "On to Berlin!" they were shouting. "On to Berlin!"

Their words floated to my ears like sweet music. I loved these troops, these brave American soldiers. They were so beautiful to me. Germany was collapsing. The SS were on the run. And I was watching the whole fabulous show. I never believed I would live to see it. But now I was free and walking farther and farther away from the front lines. The other liberated slaves, hundreds of them, were searching for food in every farmhouse and barn along the way. I urged them to move back with me, but they wouldn't listen. All they wanted was food.

Finally, alone, I dragged myself back to the village of Stamsried. Gum-chewing American MPs were standing guard over groups of German POWs. Now and then, a trickle of slaves showed up in their striped uniforms. The GIs talked to us, offered us food, and tried to make us smile. They didn't know what to do to help us.

They led me to a house occupied by U.S. soldiers. I understood no English. In sign language, they urged me to take some clothing left behind by the Nazi owner.

The GIs threw a party with wine, Coca-Cola, and spaghetti. I had never tasted Coca-Cola. I was afraid to try it. My fear triggered some well-meaning laughs. Johnny, an Italian-American, offered me some spaghetti that I wolfed down from my cupped hands.

I felt tired and weak. I needed sleep. The Americans promptly obliged. They prepared a bedroom for me, a whole room all to myself. White sheets, pillows, blankets, pajamas. But I was afraid to sleep on such a clean, soft bed. I stared at it for a long time, then climbed out the window and sneaked down to the basement, where I stretched out comfortably on the floor.

I fell asleep with my hand in my pocket. A few grains were still there.

CHAPTER 40

When I woke up, the sun was shining. It was a new world. The feeling of liberation was so strange, so different. More than anything else, it was my future that had been set free.

For the first time, I dared to let myself wonder about the people I cared about. Was there any chance that my parents had survived two years of torture and selections at Majdanek? And my beautiful Halina—could she have been found by the Americans, by the Allies, as I had been? Was she waiting for me somewhere? Would she have the strength to make her way to Milanowek, where we had promised to meet? The bitter taste of fear rose in my mouth when I remembered how frail she looked when she left Flossenburg. How far could the will to survive take her?

I must and would find her. But first I had to regain my own health. I was emaciated. An eighty-pound skeleton living on will instead of strength. I would eat, rest, grow strong again. Then I would find Halina—and my future.

I must have fallen asleep again, for the next thing I knew, someone was tugging at my sleeve and laughing. Several GIs were looking down at me, amused that I had actually chosen the hard basement floor instead of the comfortable bed they had prepared for me!

I got up and bathed for the first time in more than two years. I dressed in a shirt and a pair of blue pants and looked at myself in a mirror as the GIs applauded. In their celebration of that moment, they grabbed my old striped pants and were about to set fire to them. Instinctively, I stopped them. I ripped off the number: P-14461. I knew I would never part with it, never forget.

Then I began to eat. Spaghetti again—with eggs, salami, and real white bread! I ate ravenously, pausing only to smile at the soldiers and communicate with them in sign language. My appetite was insatiable; I was feeding myself and my plans.

Soon more Americans showed up, a Jew, a lieutenant, among them. Someone called to him, "Phil, there's a Jewish kid here from the camps."

Phil came closer. Tears formed in his eyes when he saw me. My newly acquired clothing was literally hanging on me and only emphasized my emaciation.

Phil forced a smile to his lips. He searched for the right Yiddish words. *"Ech Phil—Efraim fun* Pittsburgh. *Ech hob shon geharget* thirty-three SS."

He struggled in his broken Yiddish, but I understood him. He'd marked a stripe on his jacket for every SS man he'd shot or captured. And he had thirty-three so far. His goal was fifty, to avenge his uncles, aunts, his whole murdered family in Europe.

Our embrace was spontaneous and genuine. I was thrilled that not only were there still Jews around, but that some were in uniform and even aboard tanks. The Third Reich hadn't succeeded, after all.

But only a few hundred yards away, tragedy struck once again. In a nearby barn, some forty slaves, liberated only twenty-four hours earlier, were machine-gunned in their sleep by sadistic SS troopers. Only one of them survived to tell about it. Moniek, a boy of nineteen, was hit in the hand, which was bleeding profusely and later that day had to be amputated; he had escaped by pretending to be dead.

What fanaticism these Germans displayed. They hid in the woods and crept out at night to continue the all-important extermination of the Jews.

Without words, I thanked all the GIs again for everything they'd done for me. Then I resumed my march to the rear, as far away as possible from the front lines.

On my way out of Stamsried, I ran into the musicians again. They were all alive: Shlamek, Heniek, Itzek, Yosek, and, of course, Henry, who had come so close to giving up the day before. We greeted each other joyfully, then fell into step along the road that was now filled with U.S. troops and liberated slaves. We saw no Germans. They all seemed to have vanished.

When I regained my energy, I spent the next few days making inquiries about what had happened to the girls at Ravensbrück, planning my search for Halina. One of the biggest problems was the traveling situation. It was very difficult to go anywhere without permits and without money. I was marking time, hoping that conditions would ease up.

And then, on May 8, 1945, passing U.S. troops informed us of Germany's surrender. The war in Europe was officially over. Six terrible years were ending. But the devastation caused by the war was only now, in the relative calm of liberation, becoming clear. Examples of this were everywhere. Hundreds of emaciated people were extremely ill and even dying from overeating. Their hungry eyes misled them. Their stomachs could no longer accept the food they craved, the food that was now available.

One day, I approached a farmhouse to look for food. It was full of former slaves. Some of them had found a barrel of sour cream. They screamed for joy. One on top of the other, they attacked the barrel. They dug in, scooping up the sour cream and stuffing it into their mouths.

I watched them. They were wild. Their hands, faces, and clothes were covered with white. Sour cream was a delicacy they hadn't tasted in years. One of the men suddenly staggered from the barrel. He doubled up and screamed in pain. Another man grabbed his belly. Then still another fell to the floor. The men were writhing and twisting in agony. I tried to chase the others away from the barrel, but they wouldn't listen. They fought like animals to stay where they were, near the sour cream. With urgent shouts and sign language, I called the GIs from the road. They didn't understand, but they quickly followed me, guns ready.

In an instant, they were pushing the hungry men away from the barrel.

"No sour cream! No sour cream! Dough for baking. White dough for bread. For rolls."

As an ambulance arrived to aid the stricken, the GIs emptied the barrel into a ditch. It seemed as if the ordeal of the Jews would never end. Our long suffering was a darkness that cast a shadow far into the future. We had been starving to death for so long that even food itself was a danger to us. How I longed for revenge!

With a renewed energy that we didn't know we had, my friends and I settled in a farmhouse in the village of Meisenberg and set up a roadblock nearby. The roads were full of thousands of German refugees. We searched them, looking for the SS soldiers and other Nazi big shots who had escaped capture. They had discarded their uniforms and were trying to pass as civilians.

Once again a leader, I got hold of a gun and a switchblade. With only these weapons, we stopped all the Germans and made them strip; they meekly obliged. We were looking for the SS tattoo under their left arms. We marveled at our sudden power. Just a handful of liberated slaves, with few arms, could control hundreds of ablebodied "supermen." What defeat can do to a people! These Germans would walk straight into the gas chambers with far less resistance than the Jews.

Every day at dusk, we delivered our catch, dozens of Nazi big shots and SS men, to a special van that the Americans sent down from their headquarters in Regensburg. One young lieutenant was especially cooperative. But he cautioned me daily, "Jackie, these bastards will get theirs. They deserve the worst and more. But remember, you have got to hand them over to me alive. The sons of bitches have to be breathing."

"Hey, what the hell do you want?" I replied. "Just look at them. They're nothing but a bunch of beggars. Begging for life. Begging for mercy. Begging for cigarettes. Don't you see a defeated pack of sheep, ready for the slaughter!

"And always pleading innocence." I mimicked a groveling German. "Please, just a *Stumpf*, a cigarette butt. I'm innocent. I was only following orders. My best friends were Jews."

And then one day, right in front of me was a former *Hauptsturmführer*. I just could not part with that son of a bitch. I argued with my friend the lieutenant, urging him to leave the bastard with me.

"Pretend you didn't see him. He's not here. Don't you understand?"

The lieutenant answered by screaming at some other German prisoners as he handcuffed them and marched them away. He acted like he didn't see or hear me.

I saw in the German's round babylike face the typical "Herr Doktor" in charge of selections. The master of life and death. The dreaded robotlike murderer of my thirty cousins. The man to whom Hela and Halina were lights to be extinguished without dirtying his immaculate white gloves.

"You son of a bitch! You gangster! Now, when you're caught with your goddamn tattoo, you finally admit you're an SS man. But only a *Hauptsturmführer!* Only an officer guard at Buchenwald!" I spat in his face.

He hardly moved. His eyelids quivered as he knelt at my feet, begging for his life.

"You disgust me!" I shouted. "Look at you! The big hero, groveling on your knees! Look at all of you! The war ended only a few days ago. Only a few days of defeat, and already you're on your knees. For years you beat and starved us. Tortured and humiliated us. And then you forced us at gunpoint into the gas chambers. You make me sick! You coward!" I spat in his face again.

"For God's sake!" I screamed. "If I had a gas van I could gas you right now—and thousands like you—with no trouble at all. None!

"You murderer, do you feel any guilt? Well, let me tell you how I feel. I feel like tearing you apart. I feel like carving off your arms and legs—each part of your body—and feeding them to you on a silver platter."

I could not stop. "My God, do I want revenge! I will have revenge! For six long years, I promised myself to pay you back. To gouge the eyes out of your head and march through the streets of Germany, screaming, 'This eye is for murdering my Grandma Masha! And this eye is for sweet, innocent, six-year-old Davidek! And the rest of you is for my sister Hela and all my aunts, uncles, and cousins. For my friends. And for the suffering of my parents. And for my poor Halina. You starved them, humiliated them, tortured them, murdered them. Almost a hundred souls!"

"I promised myself a hundred times, a thousand times, more times than I can remember, to avenge their deaths and my own tortures. To whip your body the way you whipped mine. To make you bald and grotesque, with a lice boulevard down your skull. To kick out your front teeth. To make you swollen and emaciated. To dehumanize you. To throw you into Pig's Corner, ready for the ovens. All as you did to me. My God! I promised myself to do all that and more. And now? Now I'm choking, I'm drowning in my own tears.

"I can't go through with it, damn you, I can't be like you!" I screamed in anguish and rage.

Only the day before, I had an entire German village, hundreds of men, women, and children, assembled in the village square. I was ready to burn their houses, their possessions, their church. To do to them what I saw them do many times to us. Then I saw them crying, frightened little children, hanging onto their mothers' skirts. I saw the old ones kneeling, crossing themselves in silent prayer. I screamed and pushed them. I pretended to be tough and cruel. But I knew I couldn't go through with it. I knew I was only acting, that I didn't have the heart.

"God, oh, God! Why do you punish me so? First as an innocent victim, now as a clumsy executioner."

Suddenly, out of nowhere, Branko, the Gypsy, appeared. He pushed me aside and, with violent fury, grabbed the German by the neck. He dragged him down the road, then tied his arms and legs with heavy rope. Shrieking with hatred, he mounted a horse, attached the rope to his reins, and whipped the animal into a gallop.

I watched the miserable German's body bump along the rough dirt road. A trail of dust rose behind his torso. In the distance, I saw Branko turn and disappear behind the stable.

I tore across the road shouting. "Branko, come back! Don't kill him! Don't torture him! Don't be like them! Don't be like them!"

Branko galloped back now, sweeping the limp body before my eyes. He wanted me to observe and enjoy the spectacle, to share in the glory of revenge.

"Branko!"

I tried to grab the reins, but he pushed me away. He circled around me, and again I lunged for the reins. I felt Branko's boot strike my ribs. He galloped away as I screamed in pain, "Branko, don't be another Feiks!"

I dropped to the grass near the road. I lay there sobbing, when I should have jumped for joy. My body trembled as I listened to the last of Branko's mad cries. I was struggling with shame and embarrassment. I was disgusted with myself. Branko will make fun of me, I thought. He'll call me a softie. I could hear him saying it: "No guts in that Jew; he can't do what he's dreamed of doing all his life!"

Slowly I sat up. The beautiful Bavarian hills and the quiet village that stretched before me turned suddenly into a dark maze of streets and walls. I saw the ghetto. The Warsaw ghetto. The sweet aroma of spring turned into the smell of smoke. Our houses and streets were burning. Everything was in flames. The houses in the ghetto. The flesh in the crematoria. Ashes.

And where was my youth? What had happened to my youth? Was it all misery? All agony?

No. No, I'd been happy once a long time ago—as a kid, as a normal child playing soccer, laughing and teasing my sister. Disobeying my mother. A child full of mischief. A dreamer.

And what were my dreams now? Dreams of more torture? More murder? More horror? Could I ever force myself to do those things? Would revenge ever erase the smell of smoke that had destroyed my youth? Would revenge help me fulfill my promise to my Grandma Masha?

How much revenge could ever be enough? If I spent every day of my life for the rest of my life getting back at the Germans, would that be enough to repay the suffering I had seen and endured?

I knew I could never forget the past. But now I must have a future. And that meant finding Halina.

CHAPTER 41

I left Meisenberg with my new friends, Leon, Romek, and Joe, all in the American Army uniforms we had acquired. We were heading for Bergen-Belsen, a huge concentration camp for women a thousand kilometers away in northern Germany. We were hopeful. There had finally been a response to our inquiries: Romek and Leon had heard from other survivors that their sisters had been seen there not long before the end of the war. They might be alive. Like hundreds of others, we hiked and hitched rides. We had no permits and no money, so we relied on our wits and our luck. And we made it.

But our optimism faded soon after we entered the camp. There were thousands of desperately ill girls everywhere. Their condition was deplorable. The majority were beyond recovery, beyond help. The British Army's generous gifts of food had only made matters worse. Thousands died from diarrhea and other intestinal disorders. Their bodies couldn't adjust to all the food given to them by the British medical teams. None of the doctors had ever dealt with such chronic cases of utter starvation.

Still, I was thrilled to see Jewish girls. Except for Halina, I hadn't seen any for years. A few even displayed astonishing vigor. They were anxious to start living. Dorka was one of them—already searching for clothes and romance.

Most of the girls who had survived were too young to have been mothers. Nevertheless I looked for young Jewish children. I found none. The Nazi death factories had murdered them on arrival, hundreds of thousands of them, perhaps a million.

I could find no trace of Halina. But Leon and Romek learned that their sisters were still alive. They had been sent only the day before to the port of Lübeck on the North Sea, where a Red Cross ship was waiting to transport them and hundreds of other sick survivors to Sweden. The hour was late, past curfew, but we decided not to wait until morning. We traveled anxiously through the night, heading for Lübeck. Arrest or any other delay could cause us to miss the ship. We had to reach the port before its departure.

We finally arrived in Lübeck early the next morning. But the British authorities refused to let us board the vessel. "You need permits and inoculations. Sorry, it's regulations."

"But the ship's leaving at noon!" I said. "It'll be too late!"

"Awfully sorry. But too late's too late."

We refused to be discouraged. We still had our survivors' instincts. And we wouldn't take no for an answer. Within the hour, we were in a rowboat, circling the hospital ship. Soon we were climbing aboard on a dangling rope ladder. Hundreds of girls were lying on the main deck on canvas stretchers. They were all so pale, so emaciated, so pitiful.

Leon and Romek found their sisters. Renia, the older one, was the only patient on her feet. She was still in relatively good health and was caring for her sister, Dora, who was very ill. Their reunion was tearful and heartwarming. The fact that they'd all survived overwhelmed them.

But I was alone and desolate. There was no reunion for me. I felt like crying. I wanted to embrace someone. Anyone. I didn't want to live alone. I wasn't prepared for it. I had fought alone. Struggled alone. I didn't want to live in peace alone. It didn't seem fair.

I walked around the deck and spoke to the girls. They were from many different countries. I spoke in Yiddish, because it was the one language most could understand. They asked dozens of questions.

"Are you really Jewish? Where from? Have you seen my brother, Avrum, from Lublin? Have you met, maybe, my father? Have you heard of my husband? Did anyone survive from Dachau? Majdanek? Stutthof?"

They wanted to know. They wanted to hope. They gave me little notes—just in case I should meet anyone from their town, their *shtetl.*

I sat near them when there was room, stood when there wasn't. I made my way from stretcher to stretcher. I gave information, took messages, encouraged them to hope. More than ever, I was longing for Halina.

Suddenly, like an apparition, like a ghost from my past, I saw her: the face, the big blue eyes, the high cheekbones, the blond hair—short now, so short, like a boy's. Several stretchers away. She was lying on the deck. Alone. Sick. Halina. My Halina.

My entire being trembled. I shook with excitement. I didn't know what to do. I was afraid the shock of seeing me might harm her. But Halina had heard my voice. Without turning, she began to scream.

"Jacku, Jacku! It's you! It's you! I know it's you!"

I leaped across the stretchers as the other girls looked on in wonder. I bent over her.

Several nurses came running. They brought juice and pills. I ignored their warnings and gathered Halina in my arms. I felt her bones through her skin. Touching her, I knew how terribly sick she was. I put her down gently.

She fainted. A nurse quickly revived her and gave her some water. Halina couldn't contain her excitement. She tried to sit up. She was so ill, yet still so beautiful, so graceful. Her face was drawn, but her cheeks were rosy and her eyes full of light.

I touched her lips with my fingers. "Shhh . . . Don't. Don't strain yourself."

She wanted to talk.

"Don't. It's not important. So long as I've found you. Just rest and get well." I bent and whispered into her ear. "I need you, Halina. I love you."

But she had to talk and move and sit up. She even wanted to leave the ship. She clung to me like a frightened child. Her face paled, and her eyes grew wide with fear as she clutched me. She was gasping for breath. I felt her desperation. It frightened me.

Now a doctor was there. He took her pulse and looked into her eyes. "Get her to the emergency room at once."

I helped carry the stretcher. Tense and trembling, I waited outside, pacing the corridor. Memories raced through my mind. How we had met. How we had fought the Germans. How we had suffered.

I started talking to myself. I wanted her to get well. I wanted nothing else now. Nothing.

The door opened, and I hurried down the corridor to talk to the doctor.

"She's a very sick girl. Her lungs are bad—tubercular. And the ulcerized stomach won't hold any food. There's not much we can do."

My panic mounted.

"Go in to her. She keeps asking for you. Comfort her. She may not last much longer. We're very sorry, there's nothing more we can do."

Pale and trembling, I went into her room.

I stood and looked down at her, holding her hand. She made me sit beside her on the bed. She looked more peaceful than before, less agitated. But she seemed so much weaker. She could hardly talk, only whisper. Her face floated beautifully on the pillow. Her cheeks bloomed with color. Her fingers touched my eyes, my cheeks, my nose. She held a finger to my lips.

"You're all I have, all I want," she cried. "Please, God, don't take me away from him."

Her eyes began to glisten. She didn't have the strength to weep. Her tears just slipped down her cheeks, a final silent cry. In utter despair, I watched as my dream faded, my most cherished love drifted away. I couldn't sit still. Restlessly, I kept walking around and around her bed.

She stopped me and whispered, "Darling, hold me. Don't leave me alone. Save me. With you near me, I want to live. I don't want to go where Magda went, to die like she did, alone. I want to live with you, to love you, to take care of you. Please, please . . ." She fell back, exhausted.

I broke down. My tears mixed with hers. I sobbed and gasped for air. I licked her face, her eyes, her neck. I held her head close to me. I said nothing. I didn't know what to say. Suddenly I felt her body relax, her muscles give way like a released spring.

Her heart stopped. She lay motionless, her mouth open, as though she'd left something unsaid. Her eyes were staring at me, questioning: "What's happening to me? I want to live."

I looked down in disbelief at this most beautiful woman. Her hand lay motionless in mine. Halina, my dream, was gone.

"She's dead! She's dead! She's dead!" I screamed.

The doctor and nurses came running. They crowded into the

room. But I didn't need their confirmation. I had seen people die countless times before. I was an expert in death.

I stopped crying and stopped trembling. I felt suddenly as strong as steel. I circled Halina countless times, not wanting to believe that she was dead. Finally I sat down beside her. I touched her hands, her forehead, her cheeks. I closed her eyes and mouth and kissed her goodbye. I covered her face with the bedsheet, then turned to look into the nurse's frightened eyes.

"Halina, age nineteen, was once a ghetto girl, a slave. But she fought bravely and she died free."

CHAPTER 42

I was alone.

I pretended to myself that I had never found Halina. I pretended she was still alive, that I was still searching for her. To accept that she was dead, that she had died in my arms, that now I was totally and irrevocably alone, was impossible.

And then one day, some years later, when I was standing on a crowded railway platform, traveling from Prague to Warsaw, I heard a shriek.

"Izaakl! Izaakl! My Izaakl!"

"Mama! Mama!" I screamed, without turning around. I didn't have to. I knew it was my mother.

And she knew I was her son, her Izaakl, without even seeing my face. Just the back of my head.

Frantically, I pushed my way through the crowd. I screamed, "Mama! Mama! Mama!"

I saw her holding out her hands, reaching for me. The crowd realized what was happening. They made way for mother and son to meet. I broke through and enveloped her. She collapsed in my arms, unconscious. She was in total shock. I was bewildered and ecstatic. The impossible had taken place. My mother had survived! and by sheer accident, I'd found her in this crowded place.

We were in the small town of Zebrzydowice, on Poland's southern border, waiting for a train along with a thousand other refugees returning all over Europe. It was a hardened war crowd. Still, they all stood there, men and women, with tears in their eyes, wanting to help, watching this scene of a mother and son reunited.

An ambulance took us to a hospital. Mama was unconscious for a long time. But she came out of it.

"Izaakl . . . Izaakl . . . Izaakl . . ."

And so I was no longer completely alone.

I survived! I did it. Because . . .

You, Halina, gave me the reasons to go on. Because I desired so eagerly, so passionately, to touch you, inhale you, to embrace you and make you my own. I lay there on those bunks hungry and in pain, but I smiled because I saw your eyes instead of the crematoria. Your alabaster skin instead of the corpses in Pig's Corner.

And because of you, Mama. You hastily stuffed your jewelry into my shirt. You made me swear to save myself. I used your wedding rings to bribe the guards. Hiding in one of the trains that left the camp with the clothing of those they murdered, I made my escape.

And because of you, Rudy. Like you, I wanted revenge. So I joined the partisans, to go on fighting the barbarians. And when I threw my last grenade to destroy the tower with the SS troopers, I laughed and cried in ecstasy. Just like you, Rudy, I wanted to blow them into bits and pieces, and I did not care if I went with them.

And because of you, Yankele. In the cemetery, you jumped from tree to tree like a monkey, trying to evade their dogs and bullets. So did I, Yankele. When I escaped from Budzyn, they were chasing me in the woods with dogs and bullets and I was climbing the trees just like you did, Yankele.

And because of you, Papa. I remember at the huge *Appelplatz* when they tortured and whipped me. It was there, Papa, when I faced death that I did not beg or cry, did not plead or kneel. I wanted to die with pride and dignity. Like you, Papa.

And most of all, because of Grandma's miracles. The ones Grandma Masha and her friend, the Messiah, arranged for me. How else can I explain it? When storm troopers dragged me up to the gallows and pulled away the bench, I crashed to the floor. The nails fell apart. They dragged me up and pulled the rope again. This time the whole wooden contraption came crashing down. And Commandant Feiks gave up. A miracle. Grandma, I knew you made him stop.

And then when they made me drag myself around the *Appelplatz,* my hands chained and bricks on my back, I no longer had any strength left. I needed another miracle and you did not let me down. At the last moment, Feiks was transferred to the Russian front. I knew it was you, Grandma.

And finally I was marched from Flossenburg deep into the Alps. Right and left, people were dying. A real death march, Grandma. And when I was ready to collapse, you came again to my rescue. You sent the Americans and their tanks to save me.

I was liberated, I was free, I had survived.

Thank you, thank you, Grandma. And Mama, Papa, Halina, Hela, and Yankele, and Lutek, and Rudy and Sevek and Shmulek and all of you. You will not have died in vain, nor ever be forgotten. Despite them and because of them, our children and grandchildren and great-grandchildren will continue with even greater vigor and strength for another five thousand years. Despite them and because of them, we shall go on.

With books like Papa.

With courage like Rudy.

With love like Halina.

With innocence and kindness like Hela.

With faith and God like you, Grandma.

That I pledge to you.

I, the survivor.

EPILOGUE

For me, as for many survivors, the war did not end just because the shooting was over. In my own way, I fought on. I assisted the American Army's Counter Intelligence Corps in their search for the Nazis and SS men who had run the death camps. I remained in Germany for several years and testified against some of my former tormentors at various trials of Nazi war criminals. During the same period, I also assisted the Bricha, an underground organization that smuggled Holocaust survivors into Palestine before the birth of the state of Israel. In these and other ways, I tried to help the living and commemorate the dead.

Still, I yearned to be able to forget. I wanted a normal life, the ordinary concerns of work and home and family, the quiet happiness Halina had dreamed of, the kind of life the Germans had snatched away from me when I was only thirteen.

Finally, in 1949, I came to America to make a new start. I had sent my mother over the year before, and she had already found relatives. Strong-minded as ever, she insisted that I join her. I moved to Atlanta, where I founded a foreign trade company. Six years later, I moved the company headquarters to New York. For a time, my thriving business and my growing family pushed aside the shadows of the past.

But a survivor cannot forget. Every time my business took me to Warsaw, I went back to the past. I tried to learn the fate of old friends, and I rejoiced when on some rare occasion I found them alive—as I did my father's cherished friend Franek and his daughter Ala. I looked for people who could tell me the painful reality of the deaths, such as my father's, that I had imagined over and over. Most of all, I spent time with other survivors. We understood one another's silences.

Then in 1962 I founded the Warsaw Ghetto Resistance Organization (WAGRO), where we gathered about 500 survivors of the Warsaw ghetto—out of the 500,000 who once lived there. The rest of the world, the generation of the forties and fifties, did not want to hear our stories. Of course, people were shocked by the horrors of the extermination camps, stunned by the reports of the carefully, coldly, calculated genocide. But hearing about it once was enough; the whole subject was too morbid, too depressing, to bear repeating. My past came to seem like a guilty secret. Only now does a new generation seem interested in listening to the truth.

But I knew I had an obligation to my friends, my family, all the people I cared for. It is too late to save their lives but not too late to rescue their memories. So I kept my promise to tell their story and I wrote this book. The cost was five painful years spent in reliving the suffering of the past. I revisited many of the scenes mentioned here. I walked once again in the Jewish cemetery in Warsaw where Yankele was gunned down, even found the very tree we had used as a meeting point. I went back to the barracks of Majdanek, where uneasy visitors rarely break the silence of so many ghosts. I talked to fellow survivors from Budzyn, from Flossenburg. I looked up old friends and got them to help me remember. I found pictures of scenes from ghetto life in museums. I reread captured German documents, such as the report General Stroop made of the destruction of the ghetto; he was so proud of it that he made a second copy of the official report and sent it home in a leather-bound scrapbook to grace the bookshelves of his villa in Bavaria.

The story, as you have just read it, I have told to the best of my recollection. It is not complete. These pages tell no more than 40 or 50 percent of what I went through. Everyone who had a chance to read the manuscript in progress expressed disbelief that all these experiences could have happened to one person and yet he survived.

So I refrained from enumerating many more events: other escapes, another rescue from the firing squad or the gas chambers, a drowning child saved in the sewer, other whippings of twenty-five lashes, the slaughter of another entire community. As Grandma Masha said, "Enough is enough."

I have taken the liberty of changing some of the names to protect the privacy of relatives and friends.

As soon as the war was over, I began to gather information about the people who are frequently mentioned in this book. In some cases, the search took me years, but this is what I finally learned:

MAMA ZLATKA outlived the Third Reich by thirty-two years. A proud grandmother of three, she died in New York of natural causes in 1977 at the age of seventy-six.

MY FATHER passed the initial selection at Majdanek and managed to survive several months of slavery there. He was among the thousands of inmates killed by the Germans when they decided to liquidate that camp in November 1943.

FRANEK MALCZEWSKI continued his underground activities until he was captured during the fighting in Warsaw's general uprising of September 1944. He spent a brief period in SS camps, but he survived, and resided in Poland until his death in 1986. He is survived by his daughter ALA.

Lutek was captured in the Warsaw ghetto during the period of the big deportations that began in the summer of 1942. He was sent to Treblinka, where he almost certainly perished. The same fate befell AUNT EDZIA, AUNT PESA, and SHMERL, the cemetery guard.

MACIEK and his daughter JADZIA, after extensive torture at the hands of the Gestapo, were deported to Auschwitz, where they both perished.

RUDY, after jumping from the cattle car, made his way to a group of partisans. He was later killed fighting the Germans.

MIETEK, after escaping from the Rembertow labor camp, fought the Germans as a partisan and subsequently joined the Russian Army. As a young lieutenant, he participated in the capture of Berlin. He presently resides in the South of France.

SALA, the young girl I found in the sewer in Warsaw, survived two more years of struggle and hardship. Today she lives in southern Florida.

SS GENERAL STROOP was captured by American forces, then tried and sentenced to death for killing American prisoners. He was subsequently handed over to the Polish government, which conducted another trial that ended in a second death sentence. Stroop was hanged in Warsaw on March 6, 1952.

SS GENERAL GLOBOCNICK, commander of the camps in eastern Poland, including Majdanek and its subsidiaries, among them Budzyn and Trawniki, was captured by the British. He committed suicide in May 1945.

In 1987 I finally verified that the barbarian SS OBERSCHARFÜHRER FEIKS committed suicide in 1959 while a prisoner in a Russian P.O.W. camp.

ALOIS THE BLOODY, along with several other kapos from Flossenburg, was captured in 1945 and sentenced to prison by an American military tribunal.

The noble MAJOR SZTOCKMAN ended up in Auschwitz, where he was tortured to death by SS men. His assistant at Budzyn, LIEUTENANT SZCZEPIACKI, did survive, and is presently living in the United States.

SS OBERSTURMFÜHRER KONRAD, the head of the *Werterfassung*, was captured and tried for war crimes, of which he was convicted. He was hanged in Warsaw in 1952.

ALFRED KRUPP was also tried and convicted for war crimes. An American military tribunal sentenced him to a prison term of twelve years.

ARTEK, WOLF (TOSCA), SHMULEK, YOSEK, MRS. GRINBERG, and her daughter MALA disappeared without a trace. It seems inevitable that they all perished.

AFTERWORD

When *Survivor of the Holocaust* was first published in 1980, some reviewers questioned the authenticity of some events described by the author. They asked, "How could one individual survive so many dangers, unusual experiences and horrible tortures, including twice being hanged?" Since then, the following witnesses have contacted the author and confirmed the authenticity of the events he described.

HARRY ZANDSBERG has confirmed the torture ordeal and hanging described in Chapter 33. Mr. Zandsberg is the individual who poured buckets of water on the semiconsconcious author when SS Officer Feiks entered the barracks to see whether he was still alive. Mr. Zandsberg today resides in New Jersey.

GEORGE TOPAZ appeared with the author on the television program "Good Morning America" to confirm the hanging miracle. Mr. Topaz also described the author's torture in his own book, published in 1993. He resides in New Jersey.

SARA ACKERMAN was the girl the author saved in the sewer during the Warsaw uprising. In 1984 she prepared a special Thanksgiving reception for the author. Today she resides in Florida.

ALA (ALICJA) MALCZEWSKI DRZAL today resides in Warsaw. The author attended her father Franek Malczewski's funeral there in 1986.

DAVID JANEK LANDAU, who resides in Melbourne, Australia, met the author in Warsaw in April 1993, during the observation of the 50th anniversary of the uprising in the Warsaw Ghetto. Both men attended a special reception where Mr. Landau publicly confirmed the events on Warsaw's Muranowski Square and the author's role in the fighting and flag hanging on the roof as a symbol of Jewish resistance. David Landau was one of the leaders of the Muranowski Square ZZW fighting group.

ALICJA KACZYNSKA and her husband observed the daily battles of the Warsaw uprising from their house on the Aryan side of Muranowski Square. When this book was published in Poland in 1986 she recognized the author as one of the boys who had fought on the roofs. A non-Jew, she describes his role in her book *Obok Piekla (Near Hell)*, which was published in Poland in 1993. She and the author have met several times in Krakow, where she now resides.